There Is Another Way!

Also available from ASQ Quality Press:

The Principal's Leadership Counts!: Launch a Baldrige-Based Quality School
Margaret A. Byrnes and Jeanne C. Baxter

Running All the Red Lights: A Journey of System-Wide Educational Reform
Terry Holliday and Brenda Clark

ASQ Education School Self-Assessment Guide to Performance Excellence: Aligning Your School and School District with the Malcolm Baldrige Education Criteria for Performance Excellence
Peter G. LaBonte, ASQ

Process Management in Education: How to Design, Measure, Deploy, and Improve Organizational Processes
Robert W. Ewy and Henry A. Gmitro

Continuous Improvement in the Mathematics Classroom
Melody J. Russell

Continuous Improvement in the English Classroom
Janelle R. Coady

Continuous Improvement in the Science Classroom, Second Edition
Jeffrey J. Burgard

Continuous Improvement in the Language Arts Classroom
Vickie Hedrick

Continuous Improvement in the History and Social Studies Classroom
Daniel R. McCaulley

Permission to Forget: And Nine Other Root Causes of America's Frustration with Education
Lee Jenkins

Improving Student Learning: Applying Deming's Quality Principles in the Classroom, Second Edition
Lee Jenkins

Stakeholder-Driven Strategic Planning in Education: A Practical Guide for Developing and Deploying Successful Long-Range Plans
Robert W. Ewy

Charting Your Course: Lessons Learned During the Journey toward Performance Excellence
Robert W. Ewy and John G. Conyers

Claire Anne and the Talking Hat
Barbara A. Cleary

Living on the Edge of Chaos: Leading Schools into the Global Age, Second Edition
Karolyn J. Snyder, Michele Acker-Hocevar, and Kristen M. Snyder

Thinking Tools for Kids: An Activity Book for Classroom Learning, Revised Edition
Sally J. Duncan and Barbara A. Cleary

To request a complimentary catalog of ASQ Quality Press publications, call 800-248-1946, or visit our website at http://www.asq.org/quality-press.

There Is Another Way!

Launch a Baldrige-Based Quality Classroom

Second Edition

Margaret A. Byrnes
with Jeanne C. Baxter

ASQ Quality Press
Milwaukee, Wisconsin

American Society for Quality, Quality Press, Milwaukee 53203
© 2012 by ASQ
All rights reserved. Published 2012
Printed in the United States of America
18 17 16 15 14 13 12   5 4 3 2 1

Library of Congress Cataloging-in-Publication Data

Byrnes, Margaret A.
    There is another way! : launch a Baldrige-based quality classroom / Margaret A. Byrnes with Jeanne
C. Baxter.—2nd ed.
        p. cm.
    Includes bibliographical references and index.
    ISBN 978-0-87389-843-0 (soft cover : alk. paper)
    1. Educational leadership—United States. 2. School management and organization—United States.
    3. Total quality management—United States. 4. Education—Aims and objectives—United States.
    I. Baxter, Jeanne, 1934– II. Title.

    LB2805.B97 2012
    371.2—dc23   2012025178

ISBN: 978-0-87389-843-0

Publisher: William A. Tony
Acquisitions Editor: Matt T. Meinholz
Project Editor: Paul Daniel O'Mara
Production Administrator: Randall Benson

ASQ Mission: The American Society for Quality advances individual, organizational, and community excellence worldwide through learning, quality improvement, and knowledge exchange.

Attention Bookstores, Wholesalers, Schools, and Corporations: ASQ Quality Press books, video, audio, and software are available at quantity discounts with bulk purchases for business, educational, or instructional use. For information, please contact ASQ Quality Press at 800-248-1946, or write to ASQ Quality Press, P.O. Box 3005, Milwaukee, WI 53201-3005.

To place orders or to request ASQ membership information, call 800-248-1946. Visit our website at http://www.asq.org/quality-press.

∞ Printed on acid-free paper

Quality Press
600 N. Plankinton Ave.
Milwaukee, WI 53203-2914
E-mail: authors@asq.org
ASQ The Global Voice of Quality™

To Reese, Madeline, Kaitlin, and Brett
You are the light of our lives and the reason we are committed to improving K–12 education.

Here is Edward Bear, coming downstairs now, bump, bump, bump, on the back of his head, behind Christopher Robin. It is, as far as he knows, the only way of coming downstairs, but sometimes he feels that there really is another way, if only he could stop bumping for a moment and think of it.

—A. A. Milne, *Winnie-the-Pooh*

Table of Contents

List of Figures and Tables

Preface

CONVERSATION WITH THE TEACHER

We are all shaped by our life's experiences, and I am no exception. When I began my teaching career in physical education (PE) years ago, the principal way I was evaluated was (1) how many girls dressed for gym class, and (2) of those, how many took showers. Teaching in a high school with 5000 students in suburban Chicago, with a teaching load of seven 45-minute classes each day and 90 students per class, I asked myself, "Is this my sole purpose?" That question began my quality journey long before it was introduced in education.

The questions continued as I moved from that school district to another in Michigan, where the curricula had not changed in 30 years (the same number of years the department chair had been in the district). Students were disinterested and bored, and frankly, so was I. I asked myself, "Why aren't the students interested in learning this stuff?" I wrote a training manual for the students, explaining body types and specific exercises to address problem areas. Next, I changed the way we started class to make students responsible for setting personal physical goals. It helped, but wasn't a cure.

When my husband went back to graduate school, I changed districts again, and after a year became the department chair. Faced with a change in state legislation (PE as a requirement for graduation was cut from four years to one), a building project that took away all physical education facilities except one gym and the pool, and the real possibility that the district would dismiss at least half of all physical education teachers, I knew we had to take dramatic action.

First, this was a wake-up call because though I was the department chair, I was also the most recently hired, which according to our bargaining agreement meant that I would be the first to go. I also realized that *students were our customers*, and unless we met their needs, few would sign up for physical education as an elective. Second, I realized that the traditional approach to physical education, with a heavy emphasis on team sports, simply wasn't meeting the needs of many girls. Third, while I felt swimming was an important life survival skill, many girls stayed out of the pool more days than they were in. They simply didn't want to get their hair wet. Finally, I had the opportunity to make changes that heretofore were not possible. It was the urgency of the moment that led to the changes we were able to implement, and thus not only "save the day" and save everyone's job, but also change the future of physical education programs around the country. We had the first co-ed physical education program in the state, and possibly in the nation.

The first step was to define my purpose—to help all students learn the mind/body connections and gain the skills that would serve them over a lifetime to remain healthy adults.

This led to a scrutiny of the current curriculum and a decision about what are the most important things girls and young women needed to learn. This meant changing the ninth-grade curriculum to something we called "All About You," which required the girls to set individual weight and fitness goals, keep track of personal wellness data, create their own exercise/fitness program, and work it. We required everyone to take swimming, creative dance movement, which included balancing activities, and self-defense.

We spent a lot of time asking the girls what they wanted to learn about their bodies, and found as many experts (on hairstyles, make-up, clothing) as we could to give demonstrations and offer commonsense advice. (The demonstrations were provided during the time the class(es) were assigned to the cafeteria and, yes, we prescreened these folks and were careful about the message they brought to our students.) Other than that, we set a curriculum with one team and one individual sport choice every three weeks. For those who preferred team sports, they could make that choice. Students were not tracked and had the freedom to choose three times each semester. Sophomore girls were able to make similar choices. We also eliminated grading on the athletic model of winners and losers and began grading on individual achievement against personally set goals. This helped immensely, as the overweight girls and those nonathletically inclined had hope that they could succeed.

During that school year, we would have to share one gym, a pool, a wrestling closet, the cafeteria, and hallways around the gym area. This provided us with leverage to convince the male physical education teachers to institute a co-ed class for junior/senior students that would be based entirely on lifelong activities. We were able to teach golf, bowling, skiing, bridge, fly casting, and tennis. We instituted a policy of "appropriate clothes for physical activity" and defined that for the kids, but didn't require any specific clothing. Fortunately, we were able to use community facilities and actually taught golf at a local course; it was the same with bowling and skiing. We team-taught all these classes. While the men still offered football, baseball, and basketball to junior and senior guys, we no longer offered any team options. As it turned out, nearly every student in the school signed up for physical education, learned important skills, and had fun.

It was the most amazing experience of my teaching career because it taught me a lot about purpose, the need to identify the customer, planning for success, students' need for freedom and choice, and the importance of goal setting and collecting data. I also learned how to engage students in making improvements, and how much fun it is when everyone is working together to achieve a common purpose. Perhaps most amazing of all was the change in the attitudes of our students. No longer was it a hassle to get the girls to class on time or to have everyone in the pool nearly every day. I witnessed how rewarding it is for students who act as facilitators of learning as well as those who are the recipients of their work. It was amazing! It was the start of my quality journey.

I have learned that it's all about leadership and not at all about "boss management" or coercion. It is psychology; it is a different way of looking at the world—the glass is half full, not half empty. It is about optimism and hope and making decisions based on the data, not on intuition as I did in the beginning. Remember, in those early days I was going on "gut instinct" based on thoughtful reflection, but nonetheless, there were no training manuals or guides available to me. Dr. Deming? Who ever heard of him? There was no Malcolm Baldrige National Quality Award Program—or criteria for performance excellence. After the Michigan experience, however, my purpose has never wavered.

Through the years it became important to learn as much as possible to help more people be successful. I went back to school for advanced degrees in educational psychology, with an emphasis on learning theory and early childhood learning, and guidance and counseling. After that, as my work experiences changed, I founded a vocational school for disadvantaged adults. I began to learn from Drs. Deming, Juran, and the other quality gurus, and became a Stephen Covey (*The 7 Habits of Highly Effective People*) trainer. I was appointed to the board of examiners for the Baldrige Program, becoming a senior examiner in 2001. Every one of these experiences gave me a perspective that I have honed through providing training to thousands of teachers and administrators around the nation.

—Margaret A. Byrnes

HOW TO USE THIS BOOK

This training guide represents one way to look at the Baldrige criteria and use them to improve classroom systems. It is designed for classroom teachers at all levels as well as teachers in training. The approach described here has proven helpful to teachers all across the nation. Yet, true systemic change and, therefore, the ability to predict sustained, better learning results only comes when school administrators apply the Baldrige framework to the entire system. When teachers understand the Baldrige framework and how it applies to their work in the classroom, and systemic changes are made based on the criteria, everyone wins. We encourage administrators and other school leaders to use this training guide to learn about Baldrige-based quality classrooms so that they may lead and support teachers in their efforts to change.

We have organized this training guide with an introduction to quality theory and the Baldrige framework in the belief *that this knowledge will help you better understand* what we think is a logical approach to a complex subject: system re-creation. At times we were challenged because a Baldrige-based quality (BBQ) approach is not linear; it is one where all processes are aligned and integrated. *One problem in classroom systems is that many teachers are linear thinkers; linear thinking often fails to embrace integration of processes.* So, if that is your normal cognitive approach, you may have to reread and make adjustments. Included are examples from different regions of the country, different educational levels, and a variety of classes in the hope that you will be able to relate your own situation to the one we have described. We have included a tools selection chart in Chapter One, on page 13, and thereafter those tools used in the chapters are described in detail in the Toolbox section at the end of each chapter. This placement is to help you refer immediately to the tools instructions for each activity.

Our approach is very practical; the many activities have been tested and improved in our training sessions with "real" teachers. We urge you to make this training guide your resource while you become an active learner. *It is not a book that you should read and put on a shelf; it is a book intended for "doers." Depending on your learning style, however, you may need a first read-through to give you an overview before you begin.* Practice the activities, the approaches, PDSA, and the tools until you feel comfortable enough to go before a class of students. That is the best way to learn.

Imagine we are sitting together while you read this training guide. Each chapter begins with a personal conversation. These conversations are similar to how we would be conversing if you were right beside us, and it is our hope that they stimulate your thinking as well as set the stage for learning. It will help if you have the opportunity to learn with peers or colleagues in your school or district. If, however, a partner is not available, don't let that keep you from launching the approach.

Is a BBQ classroom for you? You need only ask the following questions to decide whether the use of the Baldrige framework and quality improvement approach would help. Are you satisfied with current and past learning results? Are you convinced that *all* students are learning to their maximum potential? Is the atmosphere in the classroom one of enthusiasm for learning? Are your students challenged appropriately? Who's working harder—you or the students? Are your students taking responsibility for their own learning, keeping track of their results, and setting personal improvement goals? Are you losing valuable instructional time due to disruptions or to the need to re-teach? Are you, their leader, enjoying the process of guiding students to greater learning? Are parents satisfied that their children are safe and engaged and learning what they need to learn? Is the next teacher in line satisfied that the students who come to him/her have the requisite skills needed on which to build future success? If your answer to any of these questions is "No" or "I'm not sure," then *There Is Another Way!: Launch a Baldrige-Based Quality Classroom* is meant for you!

Author's note to the second edition: A significant and not-to-be-discounted mantra of organizations seeking performance excellence is repeated cycles of improvement that require personal learning by the leader. Over the past six years, we have learned much from the many teachers and administrators who have come to learn the way forward. Their trust and openness has allowed us to grow (sometimes painfully) through listening and working tirelessly to make improvements to training activities so each could be successful. In rewriting this book, many of the changes have been inspired by these hardworking, well-meaning educators. One thing is clear, the notion of continuous improvement and personal learning means just that—the job is never done; there is always room for improvement, and listening is a key to learning. Thanks to them, I hope this edition brings light where there were clouds.

Acknowledgments

There are many people to thank who have helped make this revision a reality. Our heartfelt thanks go to the many teachers who unselfishly shared their materials for inclusion in this book. Your generosity is amazing, and we're certain your examples will inspire other educators to take the plunge.

Our personal journey of continuous improvement has been inspired by the feedback from teachers with whom we have worked. You've made us think, which has led to clarifications, and for this we are grateful. This book is a testament to you. We've been very touched by the enthusiastic support and joy of learning among teachers and administrators as they've embraced the BBQ approach. Thank you.

We also want to thank Paul O'Mara, our editor, for his expertise, insights, patience, and guidance. You are amazing, and we are very grateful for your support. To our copy editor and typesetter, Paul and Leayn Tabili, thanks so much for your attention to detail, expertise, and commitment to the final product.

Finally, we want to recognize and thank some special people who, over the years, have continued to provide us with valuable feedback and wisdom. Their imprint is "between the lines" of this book, and we remain grateful to each: Larry, Donna, Rita, and Sherry. We hope you know how deeply indebted we are to you.

Introduction

As our world continues the trend toward globalization and the need to develop twenty-first century skills, teachers face many new and changing challenges. We believe that every day teachers step into their classrooms determined to facilitate learning for every child. At the end of every day, teachers experience the joys, and frustrations, of their work. There is also the daunting truth that our current system, modeled to serve our industrial nation as it was over a hundred years ago, is not working for all children, partly, though not exclusively, because of the changing face of America and the influence of various technologies. This is a book for teachers (as well as a tutorial for principals, central office, and board members) meant to guide you in learning and honing new skills to change your classroom system from the traditional to a student-centered/ learning-focused one.

While writing this new revision of *There Is Another Way!* the drumbeat for educational change in the twenty-first century has grown louder and louder. Federal and state governmental leaders, the business community, and taxpayers each makes the case for change, and some espouse programs or cite data as evidence of why this or that program did not work. Teachers and other education leaders who have been in the classroom before the dawn of the new century can recall having experienced one after another program designed to effect major improvement in student learning, yet each has failed to bring about the improvement or expected change.

You've heard it before: "We know what works in education. We don't need any more research. We just have to do it." If those statements are true, then how do we explain the achievement gap? That pinpoints one of the problems. Teachers haven't embraced the concept (or haven't been taught the skills) of action research that embraces research-based "best practice" approaches as the starting point—not the end-all, be-all. Beyond that, there is ample evidence of the need for innovation and agility, engaging students as copartners with an emphasis on rigor and relevance, using technology tools and a critical thinking framework.

Many schools today are involved in *professional learning communities* (PLCs). This is an excellent way to engage teachers with a common bond (for example, same grade level, course, or team) in meaningful dialogue about student progress—using data and bringing together an understanding of the most effective instructional strategies. PLCs are having an impact (and we advocate their use) but they do not address all aspects of the school or classroom system. In short, a PLC is an *effective process* for engaging the workforce, developing/motivating high-performance teamwork, and promoting organizational learning.

Considering past "waves of change" and currently low national graduation rates, mostly in our urban areas, the reader might reasonably ask, why does Baldrige have staying power? Why is it not disappearing like so many of the rest of the "new ideas"? Let us explain: Baldrige is a framework of research-based system elements. *It is not a prescription for how to teach.* Be aware that this approach is *not an add-on program* that has a starting and ending point. It is a systems approach to organizational excellence. It is a management approach to reducing waste and rework while creating a *system* that is more effective and efficient.

During this journey you'll learn some quality tools that are useful when planning, analyzing data, or trying to understand the gaps between results and process. These tools are time-savers; they have been used in most, if not all, successful organizations for at least 40 years, though not necessarily hooked directly to the Baldrige framework. Be aware that the use of tools in isolation does not equate to a *Baldrige-based quality* (BBQ as we refer to it) classroom and will not yield the desired results. In a BBQ classroom you will discover the power of the framework and how to use the tools for continuous quality improvement to create a classroom where *all* children find ownership, joy, and success in learning.

Since this book was first published we've received some feedback from teachers asking for a more streamlined, easy-to-follow approach. With that in mind, we've organized this book to provide increasingly greater understanding of the BBQ approach and deeper levels of implementation: level one—beginning of alignment, level two—beginning a systematic approach to improvement, level three—the system is an fully aligned; process improvement is a routine way of life. Look carefully at the *classroom observables* (Chapter 8), as they clearly state the journey and offer signposts of progress along the way. Taken together, the observables build cumulatively toward changing the system from a traditional top-down "boss management" approach to a shared partnership where key processes are designed, aligned, and integrated, recognizing students as key customers and workers.

We believe that the observables rubric is a significant tool for teachers and principals, and we encourage you to check off each observable as you read about it, then go back then review it again as you implement the skills in your classroom and advance in your understanding of each.

Caution: you will quickly discover that the observables are not presented in a linear fashion within the book. This is because the chapters are organized more along the lines of the Baldrige framework categories, and some explanations/details may be found in another level of the observables. Even though we know many of you are linear thinkers, we're hoping you can get beyond that and go with the flow. Most of all, don't get discouraged by the number of observables in any level. They are all quite doable, and once you get started you'll be amazed at your progress.

1

The Baldrige Framework
and Quality Systems

CONVERSATION WITH THE TEACHER

What are the reasons why some students learn faster than others? And some never quite "get it"? How concerned are you about your students achieving on the state standardized or other required tests? Adding new programs (textbooks, software, kits, and so on) may provide some improvement, but unless you understand your classroom system and the root cause(s) of why some students don't learn, you can never be certain that you have optimized learning and the educational experience for all students. Have you ever experienced a situation where you feel compelled to add more rules, become more structured in response to a problem, only to discover that after a short while the problem returns and sometimes is even worse than before? Help is on the way, as you will learn a better way to address classroom issues.

Teachers who have created Baldrige-based quality classrooms routinely have students who learn more and enjoy learning. Teachers who have created Baldrige-based quality classrooms report they are less stressed, are having more fun watching students get excited about learning, and have a greater sense of efficacy. While we don't purport to have the answer to every problem, and realize that learning the approach might at times be overwhelming and may cause cognitive dissonance for a time, the end result will prove worthwhile. You don't have to take our word for this, just have faith and enjoy the journey. You'll be amazed at how students blossom in an environment where the teachers trust them and engage them as true partners in changing the classroom system.

In this chapter you will learn:

- What you need to know about Baldrige

- How it works in the classroom

1

- Classroom systems thinking

- A bare-bones introduction to the plan–do–study–act (PDSA) cycle

- What Baldrige-based quality isn't

- Compelling reasons to use a BBQ approach

- Overview of quality tools and their use

WHAT YOU NEED TO KNOW ABOUT BALDRIGE

History

In the late 1980s America was faced with an economic recession largely fueled by a loss of manufacturing to the Japanese, whose products were more reliable and of higher quality than those manufactured in the United States. (Following the end of World War II, Dr. W. Edwards Deming, the father of modern quality, had successfully predicted this would happen if Japan's leading corporations were to adopt his philosophy of total quality management.) U.S. business and governmental leaders met and shared the need for a program to recognize and learn from "best practice" among corporations in this country. There was a rather urgent need to turn the tide so American businesses could regain market share and the country could improve its economic situation.

Dr. Deming's theory was the basis on which the Baldrige business criteria were established. In 1987 President Ronald Reagan signed a public/private partnership into law that created the National Quality Award Program named after the late secretary of commerce, Malcolm Baldrige. Since then, criteria for healthcare, education, small business, nonprofit, and government have been added until now all sectors of the economy are represented by a set of criteria (sharing most of the same language). The Baldrige criteria have become the world's gold standard for organizational performance excellence. Today, there are quality award programs fashioned after the Baldrige in many states and countries around the world.

While there is a lengthy and very rigorous award process, the real value of participating in the Baldrige comes from using the criteria as a framework for improvement. Thousands of organizations use the criteria to improve their bottom line, especially during difficult fiscal situations. The need to do more with less, to reach ever higher standards of excellence, to innovate and to stay competitive for the future all play a significant role in *what motivates* any organization to embark on a Baldrige journey. Baldrige winners have an obligation to mentor others and to share their best practices openly. As of this date, the following K–12 districts have been honored by the Baldrige Performance Excellence Program Award: Pearl River, New York; Chugach, Alaska; Community Consolidated 15, Illinois; Jenks, Oklahoma; Iredell-Statesville, North Carolina; and Montgomery County, Maryland. In the Recommended Resources section we have included their websites so you can access information about each of these school districts.

Figure 1.1   Baldrige performance excellence framework for education.

The Baldrige Framework

As shown in Figure 1.1, the Baldrige Education Criteria for Performance Excellence is a systemic framework that, if followed, *will* lead to improved results across the organization: learning, student satisfaction, budgetary, workforce well-being, professional development, social responsibility, and ethics. Depicted in Figure 1.1 are the categories and their titles that would be used by schools or school districts.

That being said, the framework can also be applied to individual classrooms if we alter the names of just one category. Category 5 becomes Student as Worker Focus since your students are the primary customer and also the worker. We can apply the Baldrige because classrooms are subsystems of a school, which are subsystems of a school district.

Mark Blazey, in his 2011 book *Insights to Performance Excellence: Understanding the Integrated Management System and Baldrige*, deemed that the categories of Leadership (1), Strategic Planning (2), and Customer Focus (3) comprise the *Driver Triad*. Measurement, Analysis and Knowledge Management (4) is the *Brain Center* because data informs every aspect of the system. Category 5 (Student as Worker Focus) and 6 (Operations Focus) represent the *Work Core* since this is where and how the fundamental work of the organization takes place. Results (7) are the outcome of your system. We will use Blazey's model throughout this book since we believe it helps teachers clarify the ways in which categories are linked together.

Baldrige at the Classroom Level

To launch your Baldrige-based quality classroom, you're going to need to develop into a high-performing team with your students. To achieve good results you must understand systems (Figure 1.2). Here, in a nutshell, are the elements of a system "from 30,000 feet":

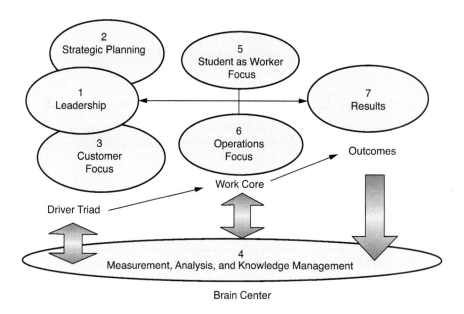

Figure 1.2   Classroom system framework.

- *Leadership.* The leader sets the tone, vision, passion, and expertise of the subject, demonstrates care/concern for all stakeholders and seeks information about each group, and leads strategic planning with students. A primary function is to seek information from the workers about barriers to success and then remove them.

- *Strategic Planning.* While it is crucial for teachers to align their classroom systems with other grade-level classrooms and/or courses along a continuum, each must also align with the school's vision, mission, and goals. It is because the classroom is where the "rubber meets the road" in education that there is a dramatic need for system overhaul at this level in addition to the district or building levels.

- *Customer Focus.* Perform a needs assessment. What do the students need and expect? Who are your other key stakeholders, and what do they need and expect? This information becomes essential prior to developing a strategic plan.

- *Measurement, Analysis, and Knowledge Management.* This relates to what is measured and analyzed and how the organization (classroom, schools, or a district) *knows* how well individuals and groups (subgroups and grade levels) are progressing toward the goals. Transparency is essential.

- *Student as Worker Focus.* This has to do with how safe and supportive the classroom environment is, how students are organized to get their work done, and how students are engaged/motivated to achieve class and individual goals.

- *Operations Focus.* This addresses the work system used in the classroom. Classroom management processes fit in this category. How has the teacher organized the class (and students) to accomplish its work? Process improvement (PDSA) is a key part of this category. Also addressed here are ways in which the leader analyzes and supports the development of key suppliers (parents and previous teacher in line).

- *Results.* Results *always* tell the story of the effectiveness and efficiency of the system. They also provide information about the alignment of processes with vision and mission, and how effective the action plans were in addressing strategic goals. Results inform the leadership about gaps in process design and alignment to meet the goals.

HOW DOES IT WORK IN THE CLASSROOM?

Baldrige-based quality (BBQ) is a planned approach to systemic improvement, which leads to organizational performance excellence. Success hinges on complete integration of all the parts. It requires *visionary leaders* who (1) use systems thinking, have (2) a *customer focus* and the humility to realize that (3) *workers* are often in the best position to analyze problems and seek solutions, and (4) are fiercely committed to data-driven *continuous process improvement.* (Students are both customers and workers in the classroom, and therefore play an important role in problem solving.)

When teachers focus on creating a classroom system based on the Baldrige framework, improved student learning naturally follows! The "proof" is demonstrated by districts that have won the prestigious Malcolm Baldrige National Quality Award.

The goal is to improve effectiveness and efficiency throughout the system. This can be applied in any aspect of a school district, individual schools, or classrooms, but this book will focus on the classroom. We'll begin by looking at the key aspects mentioned above, and explore the relationships between each, and finally learn how it all fits together to achieve excellence.

Figure 1.3 shows the relationship between teachers as leaders and the student as customer/worker. It is important to know who your customers are and what they need and expect. When teachers understand this, and are able to create a system to address these needs and expectations, the results are higher satisfaction and an increase in motivation. Naturally, leaders must also have methods to build and sustain relationships with their primary customers. These are the most important customers of any classroom, in priority order:

Figure 1.3 Visionary leaders and student as customer and worker focus.

1. Students

2. Next teacher in line

3. Parents

4. Administration

Remember that students are also workers in a system largely created and controlled by the teacher. Figure 1.4 gives insight into how data are used by and with students and teachers to solve classroom system problems. This demonstrates that the way to continuously improve is to stay focused on customer and worker needs/expectations, knowing that the *only things* a teacher can change are the key classroom processes. But teachers have partners that frequently go undeveloped. It's a pity that too few teachers realize how powerful the partnership with students as workers can become. Provide the students with the skills and knowledge to take personal responsibility for their own learning (data folders and reflection, goal setting, and so on) and help them learn to be "response-able" to the success of the class by collaborating with the teacher and classmates to solve classroom problems. Don't forget, unless data are collected and analyzed, any changes will be based on intuition, which may or may not be accurate and may or may not address the root cause(s) of any problems (instructional or classroom management). That is why teachers must understand that *management by fact* is the approach to use to achieve process improvement. In this way you will achieve and sustain improved learning results and greater student satisfaction.

Most teachers pride themselves on being good problems solvers, yet can you recall a time when you may have reacted to a problem intuitively only to discover that it made the situation worse. Management by fact (data-driven decisions) is the most cost-effective approach to eliminating problems if long-term, sustained solutions are the desired result.

The final chunk is the relationship between continuous process improvement and visionary leaders (Figure 1.5). As Dr. W. Edwards Deming said, "Your system is yielding exactly the results it was designed to get." We don't believe that any teacher would purposely create a classroom system to set students up for failure. However, without an understanding of how every piece of the system is integrated with the whole, and if the system is designed for the teacher's delight, then despite best efforts some students will be unsuccessful. If leaders (teachers) are not able or willing to continuously improve every key classroom process, it is impossible to predict increased learning results, joy of learning, or decreased behavior problems. The continuous process improvement

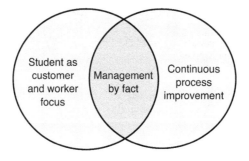

Figure 1.4 Student as customer and worker focus, and continuous process improvement.

model is called *plan–do–study–act*, or PDSA. This is a systematic, structured, scientific approach to identifying root causes and eliminating problems, thus increasing the effectiveness and efficiency of any process. You will learn and practice several PDSA approaches later in this book.

The one exception to the use of PDSA occurs when students and/or teachers are in imminent danger. In such cases, you must react immediately and make every effort to restore a safe environment.

While each circle and its intersections are important, it is not until they are integrated into a whole (Figure 1.6) that leaders know what to do and how to take steps to be able to achieve a highly effective and efficient system. Once achieved, the system must be monitored with repeated cycles of improvement for sustained results.

Figure 1.5   Visionary leaders and continuous process improvement.

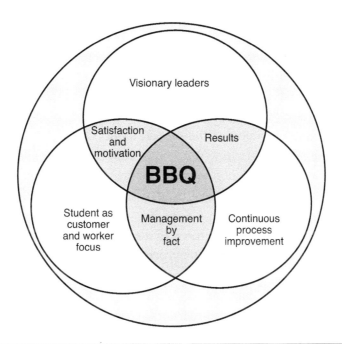

Figure 1.6   A BBQ system.

CLASSROOM SYSTEMS THINKING: DRILLING DOWN

The aim or purpose of every classroom ought to be to facilitate learning and a love of learning among all students. This is important and requires teachers to take a different view of their own purpose. If you have the view that your purpose is to teach, and once taught it is no longer your problem if students don't learn, you will create a classroom system based on the athletic model of winners and losers. On the other hand, teachers who view themselves as *facilitators of learning* realize that their success is measured by how many students gain the skills, knowledge, and abilities required within the semester or school year. These teachers will leave no stone unturned in their quest for all students to achieve success, and will not lower standards to ensure that students gain the skills needed.

A former superintendent from New York, Dr. Al Mammary, once shared this message with his teachers: "Never, ever lower your standards for students who 'won't,' and only after trying every approach would you negotiate standards for students who 'can't.'" Dr. Mammary's message was that most often teachers quickly lower standards and expectations for students who think that they "can't," when really *they just don't want to learn in the ways their teacher wants to teach.* This is an important message for anyone working with students, regardless of ability. Our observation is that many more students fall into the "won't" category than the "can't." History tells us that lowering expectations is a surefire way to get even lower results, so the first axiom is to have high expectations for every student. At the same time, it's important to recognize students who do their "personal best" on assessments and projects. In Chapter 4 we will discuss this in detail as it relates to meeting class goals and performance excellence.

Figure 1.7 provides a bird's-eye view of any classroom system. As you can see, the elements of the system include inputs, key processes, and results. There are arrows connecting these three elements because each one impacts the previous one. The big arrows represent the flow of feedback and results into the system. This informs the teacher and students about how well the class achieved its vision and goals. Notice that the big arrow points directly to key processes and is titled *continuous process improvement*. Take a look at the diagram in more detail.

Inputs into the system are things (people, policies, materials, mandates, curriculum, and attitudes) that influence the system. Note that the second input is *teacher's personal biases, attitudes, knowledge, skills, and feelings of efficacy.* While we often insist that students leave their personal "baggage" outside the classroom, teachers sometimes bring their own personal baggage in, and it *does* matter because it impacts the relationship between teacher and student, and often impedes learning.

When problems arise within the system, or if the results are not as desired, look to the *key processes* for answers. A simple definition of process is "the steps taken to accomplish a task." All processes break down over time, and perhaps one or more of your processes are not capable of yielding the desired results. If this happens, you have three choices: (1) use the PDSA process, (2) benchmark best practice with your peers (district, region, state, or national), or (3) innovate and design a whole new process. In later chapters we'll explain more about these approaches.

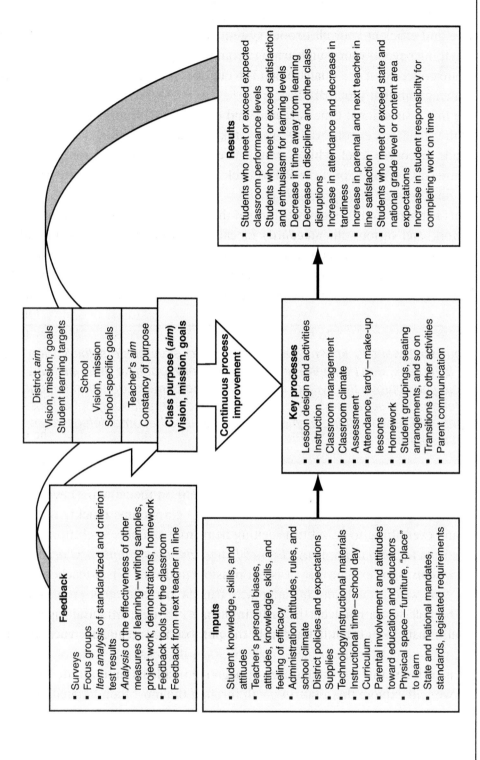

Figure 1.7 Classroom system diagram.

Results are the product of your system. These include student learning results, student and stakeholder satisfaction, student enthusiasm for learning, behavioral results, and attendance/tardy results. These data are used to prepare for the school year and to inform leadership and stakeholders how effective and efficient your classroom system was. Year-end or end-of-course results are not useful for anything beyond your own learning about what worked and what didn't that cycle. By the time results are collected, it is too late to build-in quality. Students will be gone, and opportunities for improvement with that group are lost.

We all agree that instructional time is scarce, and each year the number of students who don't meet or exceed the standards exponentially grows, taking additional time away from learning the skills at that grade or course level. This is why it is essential to collect in-process data (leading indicators of future success) and apply the PDSA cycle of improvement to all key processes *during the school year, on a regular and systematic basis.*

How does this happen? Your system is informed through hard data (for example, quiz and test results, project work) and various other *feedback* mechanisms (for example, quality tools, surveys). The more frequently feedback is sought from students (remember, they are workers in the system created largely by the teacher), the better your chances are of knowing and making mid-course corrections to remove barriers to student success. Feedback is *not useful if it is not used to improve.*

> *If you don't want to know what students and stakeholders think, don't ask. If you ask, don't take the answers personally, but take them as "gifts" to help you improve the system by removing the barriers identified through the feedback mechanisms. In other words, become a leader, not a "boss manager." The worst thing any teacher can do is to become defensive and react negatively.*

The students are incapable of "fixing" the classroom system on their own. They do not have the authority unless teachers give it to them. Teachers in BBQ classrooms quickly realize they have nothing to fear and everything to gain from seeking help from students to eliminate system problems. Asking students for help requires *teachers to listen nonjudgmentally and accept suggestions based on class consensus*, or explain why it is not possible to do so. When teachers become upset and insist on the "my way or the highway" approach, trust is lost, and other problems will surface that may never be able to be resolved. Equally important, though, in a Baldrige-based quality classroom is to eliminate things that detract from the purpose and reduce instructional time, such as interruptions, transitional time, tardiness, and so on. In this case, the goal of an effective and efficient system is to lower the average number of negative incidents until all are extinguished. In the next chapter we will explore this issue in depth through the most foundational of all principles in a BBQ classroom:

- I am responsible for my own learning

- I am response-able to the success of the class.

These principles alone generate significant positive behavior change among students and teachers.

> *System improvement begins with trust. Students must be able to trust their teacher and the other adults they interact with in the classroom. Teachers set the tone and expectations of civility and respect, and must become comfortable knowing that a dynamic system allows for continual improvement and therefore retains the hope and expectation that everyone can succeed. The number one issue of at-risk children is "no hope for the future." Teachers have an obligation to instill hope by changing the classroom system.*

Remember, the aim of education is to facilitate learning and a love of learning. If students are happy in your classroom, but not learning or meeting expectations, there are barriers keeping them from success. It is essential that students leave your classroom with the skills, knowledge, and abilities required to meet future challenges. First and foremost among these are the fundamental skills of literacy, math, and critical thinking. It is also important for students to expand their cognitive and problem-solving abilities and develop emotional intelligence, self-discipline, and civility. In the twenty-first century students will also need to work successfully as members of diverse teams, accept personal responsibility for one's own actions, complete tasks within a given amount of time, and possess the capability to access information and analyze data. It requires a balance between working independently and with others to accomplish difficult tasks. Anything short of this would not be considered success, as these are the requirements for good citizenship and productive citizens.

As you begin to think about the classroom system you've created, it's a good idea to reflect and identify any barriers that might be keeping some students from being successful. Begin the process with Activity 1.1.

Activity 1.1   Identify Potential Classroom Barriers

Directions: Keep in mind that your system is yielding exactly the results it was designed to get. Reflect on how many students are successful in your system, as defined above, and visualize the faces of those who struggle (academically or behaviorally) in your class. Note any barriers you think may exist in your classroom. Barriers to success might include such things as the following suggestions, but are not limited to these: classroom organization, student involvement in decision making, structure, time to accomplish tasks, instructional methods, or instructional materials.

A BARE-BONES INTRODUCTION TO THE CONTINUOUS IMPROVEMENT PROCESS

Plan–Do–Study–Act (PDSA) Cycle

This process requires four sequential steps as shown in Figure 1.8. Note, *plan* takes half the total time, and *study* consumes about 25 percent of the remaining time. Upon hearing this, many teachers and administrators complain, "I don't have that much time to give to this sort of thing; I have a curriculum to cover, and this demonstrates how impractical the BBQ approach is. It's a business model that isn't feasible for education," when, in fact, taking a systems view, people realize that this attitude is what has caused so many recurring failures in education today.

This structured, scientific PDSA problem-solving process uses data and graphical techniques to analyze root cause and produce better solutions than an unstructured process. It recognizes that those involved in the work are in the best position to help resolve any issues because they know (or intuit) what's not working. In the classroom, this means students will be involved in problem solving, and throughout this book you'll discover how this can happen effectively and efficiently. The "how to" details of the PDSA cycle are provided later in this book. Figure 1.9 illustrates a tool selection matrix showing the variety of quality tools from which to choose when using PDSA. Figures 1.10 and 1.11 show thumbnail sketches of each tool, designed as a reminder when you are in the process of selecting a particular tool. (Some tools are not described in detail in this book, even though they have great value. If you are interested in learning more about these tools go to the Recommended Resources section and reference one of the Memory Jogger mini tool books.) At the end of each chapter there is a Toolbox section with detailed step-by-step directions for each tool found in that chapter. Careful selection of the tools saves a great deal of time when determining root cause and problem solving. Even young students can learn and successfully use the tools, including Pareto charts and scatter diagrams, which are the most difficult of them all.

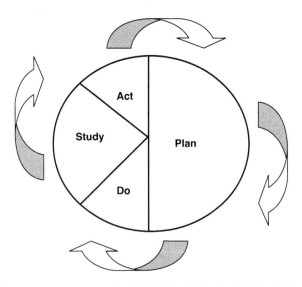

Figure 1.8 The plan–do–study–act (PDSA) cycle.

Tool Selection Chart

If you want to:	Gather ideas	Group ideas	Analyze	Sequence steps	Draw a picture of the data	Track data over time	Prioritize or get group consensus	Show relationships
Use this tool	Affinity diagram page 149	Affinity diagram page 149	Cause-and-effect diagram page 118	Flowchart page 83	Histogram page 271	Check sheet	Multi-voting page 81	Radar chart page 155
	Fishbone diagram page 118	Fishbone diagram page 118	Force field analysis page 219	Gantt chart page 269	Pareto chart page 279	Run chart page 120	Nominal group technique	Relations digraph
	Brainstorming page 80	Lotus diagram page 276	Relations digraph	Systematic diagram	Run chart page 120	Line graph page 273	Relations digraph	Scatter diagram page 282
	Lotus diagram page 276		Pareto chart page 279		Scatter diagram page 282	Pareto chart page 279	Consensogram	E/L chart page 151
	Force field analysis page 219		Fast feedback page 141		Radar chart page 155	Control chart		
			Plus/delta chart page 153		Line graph page 273			
			How helpful ... page 142		Control chart			
			Confidence-o-gram page 268					

Figure 1.9   Tool selection chart.

Tools of Quality

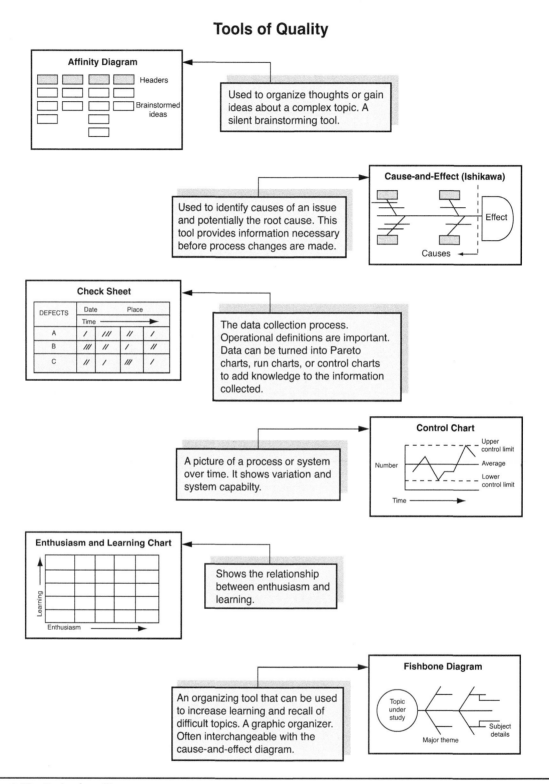

Figure 1.10   Tools of quality.

Tools of Quality

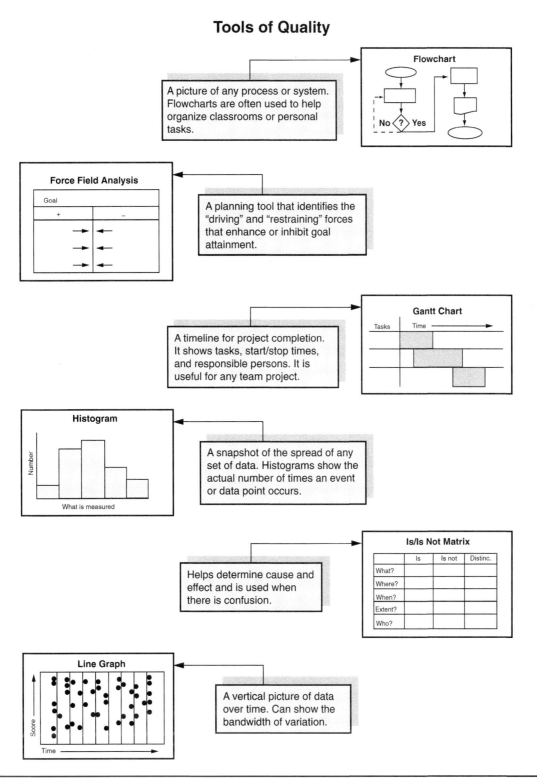

Figure 1.10 *Continued.*

Tools of Quality

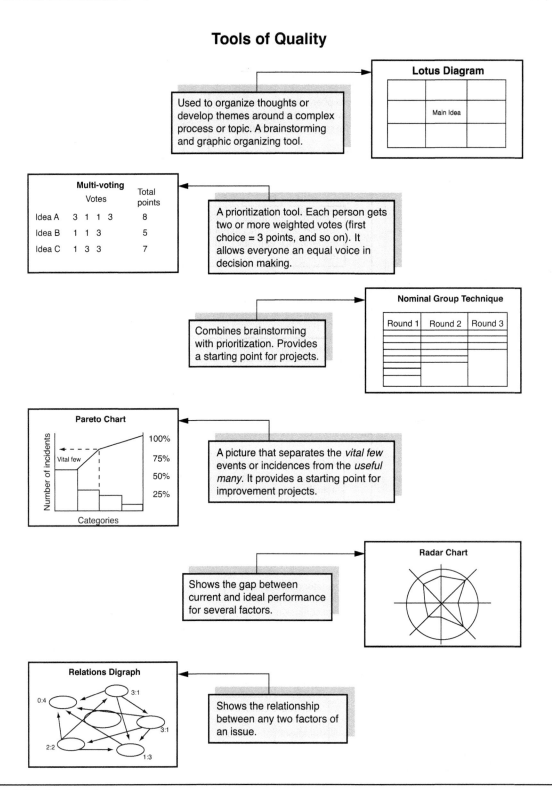

Lotus Diagram

Used to organize thoughts or develop themes around a complex process or topic. A brainstorming and graphic organizing tool.

	Main Idea	

Multi-voting

	Votes			Total points
Idea A	3	1	1	3	8
Idea B	1	1	3		5
Idea C	1	3	3		7

A prioritization tool. Each person gets two or more weighted votes (first choice = 3 points, and so on). It allows everyone an equal voice in decision making.

Nominal Group Technique

Round 1	Round 2	Round 3

Combines brainstorming with prioritization. Provides a starting point for projects.

Pareto Chart

Number of incidents

Vital few

100%
75%
50%
25%

Categories

A picture that separates the *vital few* events or incidences from the *useful many*. It provides a starting point for improvement projects.

Radar Chart

Shows the gap between current and ideal performance for several factors.

Relations Digraph

0:4
3:1
3:1
2:2
1:3

Shows the relationship between any two factors of an issue.

Figure 1.10   *Continued.*

Tools of Quality

Run Chart

A line graph that shows what happens to a process over time. Students can use run charts to track their own progress.

Measure

Time

Scatter Diagram

Variable 2

Variable 1

Shows the potential relationship between one variable and another.

Systematic (Tree) Diagram

End

Goal

Means/end

Means/end

An organization tool. Systematic diagrams provide a picture of the sequence of tasks to accomplish a goal or project.

Figure 1.10 *Continued.*

Informal Tools of Quality

Cups

We have a question

Red   Yellow   Blue

Stop   We get it!

A feedback system for teachers that indicates students' level of comfort with the lesson.

Parking Lot

Questions students have that are not directly related to the topic being studied.

?   ?   ?

A tool to cut down on classroom disruptions. Students write their questions on sticky notes. The teacher clears the parking lot each day.

Plus/Delta Chart

+	Δ
What were the enjoyable things about today, or a certain activity?	What can be changed so tomorrow (or the next time) will be a better experience for everyone?

A feedback tool. It provides the teacher with instant feedback from students and is used to make improvements in lessons or classroom management.

Figure 1.11 Informal tools of quality.

WHAT BALRIGE-BASED QUALITY ISN'T

Simply deciding to take a systems view and use the Baldrige framework is *not a quick fix or silver bullet*. It takes time to align the system, establish a measurement plan, and then integrate the whole system. It is going to require patience and persistence as you release yourself from the traditional ways and move forward. Along the way you will discover amazing things. Among these might be that you don't have all the answers. When you invite all students into the process, you'll have overcome a huge hurdle and are ready to *unlearn* something taught at your university—that *you must take control of the class*!

The use of quality tools in isolation is not a quick fix or a silver bullet, either. In fact, the use of tools does not even equate to systems thinking. You must understand how each piece of the system impacts all the other pieces. The benefit of learning and properly using the tools is that you will save valuable time and provide a picture of the current situation without angst. When everyone (students and teacher) can "see" the situation from a nonemotional perspective, it helps everyone focus on solving process or system problems.

We agree that teachers are stressed today, perhaps like never before in our history. Pressure and stress are linked to feelings of lack of control, which often translates into the concern that there's "not enough time to do this Baldrige thing." Learning takes time, this is true, and to feel comfortable with the system changes takes even more time as you "fall forward" with each cycle of improvement. So, we don't deny that "time" is an issue, but we know that the benefits far outweigh the initial investment.

COMPELLING REASONS TO ENTER
INTO A BBQ APPROACH

> *The decision to create a BBQ classroom is not taken because good things are not happening, but because of a desire to have good things happen regularly, consistently, and predictably.*
>
> *Random acts of excellence have little effect on the desired strategic results.*

Twenty-First Century Skills Demand More of Students

There is no finish line because the world and customer expectations are constantly changing, and the requirements for success continue to increase, thus making it more difficult for under-performing students. Maintaining an awareness of what experts predict students will need in the future prompts you to continuously create new and innovative approaches to learning. This includes using new knowledge in your content area and adapting your instructional activities so all your students are prepared to meet any challenge. Do this with a systems view, while engaging students and your peers to help you remove barriers, and you will be rewarded with increased student motivation and learning.

As barriers are identified and removed, realize that students also have fears that seriously impact their learning, and therefore opportunities for future success. Among these are bullying and intimidation by other students and teachers, too many and too strict rules—or no rules, too much or not enough structure, no freedom to make decisions, expectations from parents and the school that seem unreachable, and the threat of being held back a grade if they fail a course. The greatest fear of all, however, felt by any person is if he/she can not read. The fact that these students even come to school is quite amazing because the fear of being discovered brings not only fear but shame. This fear is compounded each year. Is it any wonder that students who are well below grade level in reading are more likely to act out or drop out? Engaging *these students* as copartners as espoused by the BBQ approach will help improve their confidence and skills over time.

Gain Courage to Overcome Challenges

Dr. Deming advises us and emphasizes that leaders must drive out fear! Teachers and administrators seldom realize how this impacts learning on a daily basis, but the brain research experts confirm how devastating fear is to anyone attempting to learn. What are the causes of fear in school today? One major cause is the high-stakes testing approaches that lead teachers to teach to the test and "cover the curriculum" in response to accountability. In our experience, most teachers are not fearful of standards, but many are confused about how to do their job in predicting success and achievement of the desired results. Many districts have adopted new texts or software in an attempt to reach the state requirements, only to find that progress continues to be sporadic and unpredictable. This leads to the "blame game" directed at students or parents, or even the previous teacher, for the failure to meet grade-level requirements.

Another aspect of this fear comes from the challenges teachers must meet today. Among these is the fear of violence brought on by bullying. Other challenges include the increase in the number of students who lack English-speaking skills, who lack civility, who are undisciplined or disrespectful, or can not read; parents who don't seem to care; and the seemingly constant barrage of new edicts coming from central administration, the state, and the federal government.

Renew Your Passion for the Profession

Add to this the perception of not enough time in the school day/year to accomplish the daunting task of getting everyone to do well on the state standards test and you have teachers who are tense at the start of the year and who become more anxious as deadlines draw closer. Who could think of creating a system focused on learning when they feel the pressure to "cover the curriculum" and "assure high test scores"? How can teachers effectively move students with major deficiencies to subject or grade-level mastery when they work in a system that encourages short-term memorization, as described by Lee Jenkins in his thoughtful book *Permission to Forget*.

We can not guarantee rapid improvement, but if you learn and use the approach with fidelity, you will be amazed at how less stressed you'll feel and how much more enjoyment you get from your efforts. Oh yes, and student learning will go up, too!

IN SUMMARY

You have learned a little about the theory underpinning this approach. Should you need more data and convincing that our *current system of education* needs an overhaul now, we would reference the writings of Tony Wagner, the codirector of the Change Leadership Group (CLG) at the Harvard Graduate School of Education. In his 2008 book *The Global Achievement Gap*, Wagner supports his conclusion that being "standards based and data driven" is not good enough. Teaching to the test is a poor substitute for good teaching that addresses the "hidden gap." Wagner's gap lists *seven survival skills*:

- Critical thinking and problem solving

- Collaboration across networks and leading by influence

- Agility and adaptability

- Initiative and entrepreneurialism

- Effective oral and written communication

- Accessing and analyzing information

- Curiosity and imagination

The above listed survival skills needed by our graduates in today's world can not be mastered by "teaching to the test." *There Is Another Way!* provides a step-by-step approach to establish a system based on continuous improvement and agility. This is your guide for the Baldrige-based quality journey ahead. We urge you to have the courage to *take the first steps* in changing your classroom system. Start now by completing an initial "check-up" of your classroom system and answer the questions on the next few pages.

In this new revision, one of our goals is to recognize that you, the teacher, have a unique learning pattern just like each of your students. There are graphs and charts, and detailed instructions. You, as a learner, may pick and choose the explanation that best fits *your* learning style—just don't skip the steps. The *classroom observables* (see the Introduction) will support your learning and application of the BBQ classroom. You can find the observables in Chapter 8, pages 268–89.

Last, we encourage you to learn from your mistakes, relax a bit, and have fun learning with your students. Above all, *keep going*! Remember, it's all about continuous improvement!

REFLECTION

Peformance Review System—Teachers

Are you . . .	Yes	No
Receiving higher-quality work from your students?	❑	❑
Involving students in planning and decision making?	❑	❑
Seeking feedback from the "next teacher in line" about skills students need to succeed?	❑	❑
Providing learning experiences dealing with real-life application, and using a variety of teaching strategies that address multiple intelligences, incorporate the latest brain research, and use differentiated instruction?	❑	❑
Setting personal goals and measuring progress toward them?	❑	❑
A role model for continuous improvement?	❑	❑
Using quality tools to enhance your effectiveness as a teacher?	❑	❑
Becoming a quality learning "risk taker"?	❑	❑
Sharing your "lessons learned" with colleagues?	❑	❑
Becoming more a facilitator of learning and less a "boss manager"?	❑	❑
Able to analyze data to know "what" to change? Becoming a better problem solver?	❑	❑
Seeking feedback from students regularly to eliminate barriers to their success?	❑	❑

Organizational Review System—Classroom

Does your classroom have . . .	Yes	No
A collaboratively established vision and mission?	❑	❑
Is it signed by all and posted in the classroom?	❑	❑
A climate that demonstrates the two principles of "I am responsible for my own learning" and "I am response-able to the success of the group"?	❑	❑
Measurable class learning goals?	❑	❑
Are the goals posted prominently in the classroom?	❑	❑
Are there charts on the walls showing progress toward the learning goals?	❑	❑

Does your classroom have . . .	**Yes**	**No**
Charts and graphs posted that show evidence of improvement of key classroom processes?	❏	❏
Well-defined procedures that are reviewed for best practice and improved as needed?	❏	❏
Students who are enthusiastic about learning, few discipline problems, high attendance rates, and low tardy rates?	❏	❏
Community members and parents involved?	❏	❏

Performance Review System—Teacher/Students

Are your students . . .	**Yes**	**No**
Involved in planning learning activities?	❏	❏
Setting personal goals? Are they measuring progress toward their goals?	❏	❏
Working cooperatively in teams on projects?	❏	❏
Improving the quality of their work?	❏	❏
Becoming better listeners?	❏	❏
Becoming learning "risk takers"?	❏	❏
Making suggestions to improve classroom procedures?	❏	❏
Using the PDSA process to improve?	❏	❏
Familiar with, and using quality tools to improve learning?	❏	❏
Becoming better problem solvers and making better choices?	❏	❏

2

Setting the Stage for Performance Excellence

CONVERSATION WITH THE TEACHER

Does it sometimes seem that the expectations of policymakers, perhaps at the national, state, or local level, are unrealistic, given the students with whom you work? Perhaps it is the emphasis on accountability and the use of high-stakes testing results that causes you concern. It is our observation that most teachers are doing the best job they can with their current knowledge, skills, and abilities. The difficulty is that traditional approaches work for some students, but not for all. In fact, this has always been the case, but now that educators are being held accountable for the results of all students, the issues have become more prominent.

The lessons learned for education are the same as those for manufacturing, business, and healthcare. Business has learned the necessity to listen to current and future customers and align mission, goals, and action plans to assure success. When business doesn't understand what its customers need and expect, and their products or services are no longer wanted, they go out of business. Healthcare system problems lead to higher costs for malpractice insurance, and higher costs of doing business because of errors and inefficiencies. When doctors make an incorrect diagnosis and/or hospitals don't pay close attention to patient risks and needs, people can (and do) die.

Education's challenges have caused districts to add more complexity to the system in response to governmental or school board mandates. A good example is the curriculum addition of anti-bullying programs or character education programs. In such instances, we say that policy makers have tinkered with the system, not necessarily improved the system or eliminated the problem. The consequences may be different than in business or healthcare, but when educators fail to consider the needs of all students, and students drop out or don't learn all that they need to learn, the results can be just as catastrophic. In essence, we take away their future. The price is simply too high to continue along this path! There is another way to build a classroom culture in which students and teachers work together to support each other in positive ways and where everyone's needs are met; students learn at higher rates and in less time; and where partnerships between parents/guardians, students, and teachers are built and strongly support the purpose of school—learning.

In this chapter you will learn:

- How to set the foundation for excellence with the two principles of a BBQ classroom

- How to listen and learn from customers to meet their needs and expectations

- Ways to engage students and parents as copartners.

THE LEADER "DRIVES THE SYSTEM"

Leadership—Your Role and Responsibility

Your leadership role is to systematically set the tone and expectation that this class will be different from a traditional one. Think first—develop a personal constancy of purpose. Ask yourself if you are paid to teach or to facilitate learning. If you think you are paid to teach, then you'll create a classroom with a teaching focus. In these classrooms, the mentality is "I've taught it. It isn't my fault they didn't learn. Send me the 'right' students and they will learn and we'll all be successful." Or, "These students have so many different needs there is no way I can teach them all." Of course, we know that parents are not holding back the "right" children. Faulty thinking like this reflects a deeper problem for education; that problem is *hopelessness.*

Turn your thinking around, and refer to yourself as a *facilitator of learning.* We guarantee that this one thought alone will make a huge difference in the way you approach your work. Facilitators of learning know that they must create a learner-centered, learning-focused classroom. They also realize that their job is not finished until all students have learned and mastered the skills, knowledge, and abilities required for future success. It *does* matter, and we will show you how to make this transformation in a systematic way. If you follow these steps, it will change the way students act and react, and you'll be pleasantly surprised at the difference in learning and behavioral results.

A teacher/leader takes every opportunity to improve the climate and culture of the classroom and the school—before, during, and after school, every hour of every day. Finally, the teacher/leader looks for ways to continuously improve him/herself as a teacher, leader, professional, and citizen.

Soccer Analogy

You are passionate about soccer and were delighted when the government enacted a law stating that every child from age five through sixteen had to play soccer. You are convinced that this is the way to improve the health of the nation's youth and therefore decrease healthcare costs. The only hitch is that the government has assigned you (the coach) a group of 15 individuals who will form your team. The government has defined the goal, and it's your job to turn these children into an

effective team with a winning record within nine months. The government has also mandated that all players must participate in each game, and no one player can play more than half the game. The imperative for you is to develop each player's skills to the highest possible levels.

You've called a team meeting and only five show up. You observe three to be eager to please and have some skills, and two who have very good skills but don't listen very well. Of the 10 who didn't come, you have been told that six are not interested in soccer. They have potential but would rather spend their time hanging out with friends or texting/tweeting. Four have tried soccer, but have few skills, and previous coaches made them sit on the sidelines. They dislike soccer and don't want to play at all. The other two are non–English speakers and mostly illiterate in their home language. As you observe these two students kick the ball around, it looks like they have great potential, but you are at a loss to communicate with them. The government is insistent that you work with all 15, and they will be monitoring your progress as a coach. Since you can not change the government's ruling, nor can you directly impact the team selection process, you must focus on ways to get the job done quickly and achieve the goals. See Activity 2.1.

SET THE STAGE: THE TWO PRINCIPLES

Right from the first day you begin this BBQ journey it's time to share your expectations with students. This is a *golden key* opportunity to provide the infrastructure for a new classroom culture.

I am responsible for my own learning.

I am response-able to the success of the class.

These two principles are the foundation of a Baldrige-based quality classroom. Everything else is predicated on everyone holding these beliefs and demonstrating them each and every day in the classroom. This includes the teacher, aides, volunteers, and, of course, students. We recommend that teachers make large banners stating each principle, hang them in the classroom as a constant reminder to everyone, and refer to them often. These two principles set the stage for transforming the class into a BBQ class.

A Process for Introducing the Two Principles

Use a whole-group approach if you teach young children, but with students from grades five and up it works well to divide the class into small groups for initial discussion of each principle and then have each group report back to the class.

Activity 2.1   Imagine you are the soccer coach. Answer the questions and fill out the form.

Directions: Answer the following questions using what you've already learned about the Baldrige and its criteria categories. You might want to refresh your memory by returning to Chapter 1, page 4, to review the Baldrige framework.

Reflect for a moment on the current situation—how many students came to the first practice, what their skill level is, and so on. Then reflect on why the other team members chose not to come.

What are some specific things would you do to get everyone to the field?

Once you get all the children to the field, how might you get them motivated to work as a team and continue coming to practices and games?

Once you have the group motivated, what next steps will you take to achieve the goal? Remember, the goal is to have an *effective team with a winning record.*

Task	Approach	How will you know the approach worked?
Example: Get all players to the field and motivate them to play.	*Example:* Host a "welcome to the team" gathering at a local community center. Bring treats and engage some older students to help by talking to the group about how much fun soccer is, and so on. Play a fun team-building activity.	*Example:* Number of players who attend next practice. Number of players appearing to have fun.

Reflect: How do the issues of a teacher or school leader relate to the soccer analogy?

Ask, "How would I know you were being responsible for your own learning? What behaviors would I see?"

Potential answers might include *arrive on time, be prepared with materials, do homework, ask questions,* and so on.

Ask, "How would I know you were being response-able to the success of the class? What behaviors would I see that would show me you were able to respond to your classmates and therefore to the success of the class?"

Potential answers might include *help others by answering their questions if I know the information, work cooperatively with others, help the group stay focused on the tasks, not engage in disruptive behavior*, and so on.

The "response-able" principle usually requires some role-playing and examples as students attempt to define what it means. To be "response-able" means to be *able to respond to others* so the group can achieve success. Do not confuse this with holding students and others *accountable for* the success of the class. No one would expect students to be held accountable for what or how much classmates learn.

To demonstrate this principle you might role-play a student disrupting class by coming in tardy or shoving another student's books aside. In each instance, ask students if this behavior lends itself to being "response-able" to the success of the group. Other ideas to explore include doing one's homework or participating in class discussions. Each time, ask the students whether such behavior lends itself to being "response-able" and, if so, how. Follow this with a conversation about whether helping classmates who are having difficulty or those who don't understand the teacher's instructions would demonstrate being "response-able." We can not overstate the importance of the two principles and how they define student and teacher behavior. They must become the heart of the classroom.

English language learners and some special education students will require patience and more role-playing and demonstrations to help them understand. It isn't fair to assume that *they can't understand*. It may take longer, but the rewards will far exceed the time spent in this activity. Recently, I witnessed a class of severely emotionally disturbed middle school boys who not only understood the two principles but also were eager to help support and encourage each other when a peer struggled to answer the teacher's questions. There were eight students in the class, and all were paying close attention, fully engaged, and were eager learners. I was amazed at the mutual respect in the room and the fact that this class had been able to coalesce as a unit. Right there on the wall were the two principles, and characteristics of a quality student.

How the Principles Apply to You

As the leader, you'll need to embrace the fact that these two principles apply to you—every day, all day. You're not only going to be called on to be a role model for the students, but there's the understanding that if you don't apply these principles to your own actions, you'll be disappointed and frustrated at the sporadic changes in behavior of your students. Activity 2.2 is your opportunity to reflect on this key point.

"I am response-able to the success of the class" implies that teachers understand and act on Baldrige category 3 (Customer Focus) activities to discover the needs and expectations of students, parents, the next teachers in line, and requirements of the district, state, and national policymakers. For teachers working with middle and secondary students, the community, world of work, and post-secondary expectations become more significant and must be considered part of the teacher's learning responsibilities prior to planning instructional activities and developing classroom projects.

Activity 2.2 Embrace the two principles.

Directions: You are the leader and a significant partner in the classroom. Answer the following questions.

What does the principle: "I am response-able to the success of the class" mean? What behaviors would the teacher use that would demonstrate a commitment to this principle?

What does the principle: "I am responsible for my own learning" mean? What are you (the teacher) responsible for learning about? How does this relate to the "response-able" principle?

Remember, teacher bias (see Figure 1.7) is a major input into the classroom system. What is the implication for the teacher/leader in relation to the two principles?

LISTEN AND LEARN FROM YOUR CUSTOMERS

The way to determine customer needs and expectations is to engage often in two-way communication through surveys, focus groups, or face-to-face. Then use the feedback tools that you will learn about in Chapter 5. The way to manage these relationships is to make improvements based on the feedback from students and parents, your PLC, and other stakeholders. First, however, it is important to know who your customers, partners, and stakeholders are.

Figure 2.1 shows the Baldrige categories that make up the Driver Triad. Note: Leadership is number one. To effectively drive the system, your role entails knowing your customers and their needs and expectations, and using that information to feed into a class strategic planning process. This is the beginning of system alignment, which is necessary for excellence.

Figure 2.1 Blazey's Driver Triad.

Identify the Relationship

First, it is important to know who your customers, partners, and stakeholders are. Activity 2.3 is aimed at having you think about the customer/supplier relationships you have with the various stakeholder groups. At the end of this chapter you'll find the answers, but know that in some circumstances each group may take on several roles. (Do the activity on your own before checking the answer.)

Get to Know Your Students

 Another *golden key* opportunity for building a system designed for success is *learn as much as possible about the students—what each needs and expects.* Find out about their interests, learning styles, learning fears, past successes, and problem areas. (You can find survey examples at the end of this chapter. You might also find *True Colors* helpful as it helps identify communication styles. This website is listed in the Recommended Resources section at the back of this book.) Aside from these important things, it is also necessary to learn "how" your students like to learn. This information is used for classroom management, for creating and managing learning activities (often differentiated), and for creating a system that addresses the learning needs of all students. In a BBQ classroom there are often

---

Activity 2.3   Identify relationships of key stakeholder groups.

Directions: Place the following groups into the slots in the matrix below that best describe their *relationship to your grade level, class, course, or services.* Several may appear more than once, but be clear about how you describe and justify the relationship. Depending on your position, the relationship may differ somewhat.

Instructional aides	Parents/guardians	Previous school	Community
Next teacher in line	Student support services	Students	State
World of work	Previous teacher	Administration	District
Pre-K programs			

Internal customers	Partner	Stakeholder	Supplier	Worker
Those inside the system who receive services or products of the system	Individual or group not paid by the system, but who renders services or support	Groups affected by an organization's actions and success	Groups or individuals who provide materials or students	Individuals engaged in processes that affect the finished product

many activities going on simultaneously, with some students doing independent work (not busy work or rework!) while others work with partners or in small groups. Figures 2.2 and 2.3 show two examples of tools that can be used or modified to suit any level (elementary, middle, or high school) at the beginning of the school year or semester (Figure 2.3 is from Teressa DeDominicis, Ninth Grade Academy (English), Potomac High School, Potomac, Virginia). In fact, a way to add value to this tool for older students might be to ask them to prioritize each response to each question. Other "Getting to Know You" examples are provided at the end of this chapter.

Establish Quality Factors for Teacher

Student expectations may be ascertained in several different ways. We recommend this approach for both elementary and secondary teachers. The concept is to seek feedback from students about what they need/expect from the teacher. This is a brainstorming activity that can yield important and valuable information not otherwise readily available. Your goal is to allow all students (even

My name is _____. This is all about me.	
Circle the response that best fits you.	
I learn best	alone
	with a partner
	in a small group
	as part of a large group
I learn best when I	watch others
	read about things
	move objects around
	listen
	talk through what I'm learning
	use the computer
When I am learning I need	someone to work with me
	quiet
	music or noise
	to move around
When I need help	I feel okay about asking the teacher to help me.
	I feel okay about asking a friend to help me.
	I don't like to ask for help.
	I am afraid others will laugh if I ask for help.
Things that get in the way of my learning are	music
	movement around me
	noise
	too complicated directions
	bright light
	too little light

Figure 2.2 Getting to know you—elementary or middle school.

Directions: Answer in complete sentences, using your very best writing skills. Write each question and your responses on a separate sheet of paper.

1. Tell me at least three interesting facts about yourself that make you different from everybody else.

2. What are you most passionate about?

3. Who is the most important person in your life?

4. What extracurricular activities do you participate in?

5. What's your strongest subject? What do you like about it?

6. How do you feel about reading? What was the last book you read? What's your favorite book of all time?

7. How do you feel about writing? What is your favorite writing assignment *ever*? What is the longest essay you've ever written? Have you ever written a five-paragraph essay?

8. How do you learn best? Do you prefer to work alone, with a partner, or in a group?

9. Describe your ideal teacher.

10. What are your goals for this semester?

11. Name at least *three* musical artists or groups who are always on your playlist. You may also list your favorite song(s).

12. List at least *three* of your all-time favorite movies.

13. List at least *three* television shows you enjoy.

14. Describe your family. Who do you live with?

15. How do you normally get to school each day?

16. Do you work? If so, where do you work, and how many hours per week are you typically scheduled?

17. (*Optional*) Is there anything else you need me to know? If so, tell me here.

Figure 2.3 Getting to know you—high school example.

those with few English skills, those with individualized education programs [IEPs], and the shy students) to express themselves freely without judgment on your part. For this reason, it is important to make mental notes of what *each* student says. How you explain this to the students makes a large difference in the outcome; most young children generally like to please their teacher, so most of their ideas will center around concepts like "be nice to us" or "love us." While these are important traits, they are not sufficient. *Remember your purpose—to facilitate learning!*

Some elementary teachers use butcher paper and draw their silhouette on it. Others simply make a bulleted list of traits. Use your creativity and have some fun with the students. Throughout this process, keep a keen ear out and make mental notes of the students who make each suggestion. Naturally, this is easier in elementary classrooms, but not impossible at the secondary level.

Helpful tips for secondary teachers and specialty teachers:

- Purchase a small spiral-bound notebook and divide it into sections that equal the number of classes you teach.

- Transfer any mental notes about specific students' needs to the notebook after each class for reflection and as a constant reminder throughout the school year.

Begin the process by letting your students know that you're starting on a new journey that engages students as partners in their education, and that periodically you are going to ask their opinions. If the school has just started the journey, this approach will be new and you may have to "prime the pump" with your students by offering one characteristic (for example, *be prepared*). However, after the first year of implementation the process will be faster and students will expect their teachers to ask their opinion.

> **Caution:** *The purpose of this activity is to listen (and learn) from all your students about the essential behaviors they need from you, their teacher (facilitator of learning). A one-size-fits-all approach won't be nearly as effective, so we caution you to resist the impulse to "save time" in this manner. Each class of students needs to know you have listened to their voice—a generic list isn't helpful.*

A Process That Works Well for Grades K–5

Explain to the students your purpose. (To *facilitate their learning* and to help make sure each child can learn, have a great school year, and help the class reach its vision.) If your students don't identify the behaviors they need from you *to learn*, it is your obligation to point this out and even make a suggestion. Once you make a suggestion, though, give the students time to come up with their own ideas. In a class of primary students, again we remind you that most of the suggestions may relate to *be kind*, *love us*, *be nice*, *don't yell*, and so on. Write all suggestions down and continue to remind students that the purpose of school is to learn. Also, be certain that all the ideas put forth are in the positive, not the negative. Quality factors are essential elements or characteristics you *want* to have!

It is probable the class will come up with 20 or more things they need from you. But, these will be difficult for you to constantly remember. Therefore, once all the ideas are given, ask the students to prioritize the *four most important things you must remember every day in order that you can help them learn.* Use the multi-voting tool described on page 81, at the end of Chapter 3. We recommend that each student get three or four votes. Total the points and circle the top six quality factors (*essential* attributes) and share the list with the students. Last, the class must operationally define each quality factor.

to a meeting each fall. During that time, she reviewed the curriculum and asked parents for feedback. Not only did she ask them to rank-order their expectations, she also asked in what ways they'd be willing to help. In this way, she made them partners. Many parents expressed these sentiments on their surveys: "No teacher has ever asked me what I expected before. It is a nice surprise and a pleasure."

> **Caution:** *If you don't want to know, don't ask. And, if you're not going to take the feedback and do anything with it, don't ask, as you will surely annoy some parents.*

Candace also followed up with surveys to parents at each marking period, then reported the results back to parents. Building relationships with parents and guardians is an important part of Baldrige category 2. On the occasion that she had to call parents to report issues with their child, she found the parents most willing to listen and help. Figure 2.5 shows the survey Candace gave parents. Examples of other surveys can be found at the end of this chapter.

When you've gathered feedback from all sources and learned about their needs and expectations of you, it is time to share your expectations of each group.

Your student is enrolled in a world geography class for one semester. He/she has indicated his/her expectations and hoped-for outcomes for the class. Because you are most likely concerned about what is taught in the class, this survey is intended to explore those concerns.

Please answer the following questions. Thanks for your assistance. I will send a report informing you of how other parents/guardians have responded.

1. If you were the teacher of a world geography class, what would you think is most important to teach?*

2. Other than content, is there anything else you hope your student will learn? (Skills, attitudes, and so on)

3. Is there any way in which you might be able to assist in the teaching of the class; that is, do you have expertise that might add value to this particular class? Would you be willing or able to help in any particular way?

4. How could I be of assistance in helping to facilitate learning for your student?

5. Other comments, suggestions, expectations, and so on.

Please sign here if you're able to assist with this class. _____

*Candace was able to be flexible because the district did not have a standardized curriculum.

Figure 2.5   Parent/guardian expectations survey—secondary.

Reflect:

- Put together what has been learned from students and make a list of the greatest challenges you face with this group of students. Prioritize the list.

- Put together what has been learned from parents and make a list of their desires and expectations. Prioritize this list. Make a mental note of how many parents responded. We know that as students progress through the grades, fewer parents attend back-to-school nights. The percentage of parents who provide feedback may be as significant as the responses you receive. You may need to be diligent and creative to increase the response rate. Avoid drawing conclusions about expectations based on a small return rate. Likewise, be careful not to fall into to the trap of soliciting anecdotal feedback from parents who happen to be friends. Either way, it's a mistake.

STRONG PARTNERSHIPS FROM POSITIVE RELATIONSHIPS

 There are several ways to develop partnerships with parents. We've already shared Candace Allen's experience at a parent night meeting. Another approach has been modified from an idea we received some years ago from Minuteman Career and Technology High School in Lexington, Massachusetts. It is a teacher/student/parent compact (Figure 2.6). (We were drawn to this example because it demonstrates the need for all parties to share in the responsibilities. If you plan to use this model, we recommend working with a parent group to have them identify those responsibilities they feel are the most essential things a parent can contribute to their child's education. Like all processes, you will want to evaluate the effectiveness of the instrument annually. In later chapters you will learn more about how to evaluate and improve processes.)

Right now, it is important to find a way to communicate *your* expectations (and most likely, this is something to work on with peers) at the beginning of the year. By having all parties sign the document, it cements the agreements in ways that are not otherwise possible.

Note that we've separated the parent expectations for elementary and secondary schools as examples. However, you may want to also develop somewhat different commitments of elementary and secondary teachers—and perhaps even students. This exercise becomes much more powerful and compelling if/when students and parents are engaged in the process of developing the instrument.

Communicate with Parents About BBQ

Baldrige equals a paradigm shift for many schools. That being said, when you embark on this journey you're going to want to be proactive and communicate the differences between a traditional school/classroom and one with a systems-thinking approach. Failure to do this may leave you in

Teacher/Student/Parent Compact

Teacher Agreement

I agree to help students in the following ways:

- Utilizing instructional strategies to ensure learning success for every student
- Focusing on providing instruction based on state/national standards
- Regularly measuring your child's learning and making changes in instructional strategies based on these results
- Creating a warm and friendly learning environment
- Ensuring that safety precautions are taken and students follow safety rules
- Guiding students to analyze their own data and to set goals
- Reporting the child's progress to parents/guardian
- Communicating with the home when any problems of attendance, learning, grades, or behavior arise
- Participating in conferences with and for students
- Providing structured and clear expectations for learning
- Giving parents strategies to assist their child's learning
- Being available to parents before and after school, by appointment

_____   _____
Teacher's signature   Date

Teacher/Student/Parent Compact

Student Agreement

I agree to be responsible for improving my learning in the following ways:

- Attend school regularly
- Study for tests
- Come to class on time
- Listen attentively in class
- Actively participate in class
- Complete assignments on time
- Come prepared to learn with all necessary materials
- Get to bed at a reasonable time
- Respect self and others
- Cooperate with classmates
- Cooperate with teacher
- Ask questions for understanding in class
- Keep my data up to date
- Reflect on and analyze my test results
- Set goals and action plans to achieve my goals
- Adhere to the class procedures and school rules
- Other _____

_____   _____
Student's signature   Date

Figure 2.6   Teacher/student/parent compact.
Source: Modified from Minuteman Career and Technical High School, Lexington, Massachusetts.

Elementary Parent Agreement

Student's name _____

I want my child to succeed in school. I agree to:

_____ See that my child is punctual and attends school regularly

_____ Ask to see my child's data folder weekly

_____ Make a commitment to read with my child ___ minutes per week

_____ Ask my child questions about the story after reading it

_____ Apply what my child learns in school to activities at home

_____ Attend parent–teacher conferences and student-led conferences

_____ Praise my child for progress in setting new goals for improvement

_____ Call my child's teacher if there are important changes in the family

_____ Discuss progress reports with my child

_____ Help my child learn safety rules and how to behave in a safe manner

_____ Establish a time and place for homework, and review it when completed

_____ Listen to my child and contact the teacher with concerns/questions

_____ Be aware of what my child is learning at school

_____ Read, sign, and promptly return any notices from the teacher/school

_____ Monitor time spent watching television, videos, and playing electronic games

_____ See that my child has a healthy breakfast

_____ Ensure that my child gets to bed at a reasonable time

_____ Teach my child how to organize so that s/he is ready to learn

Parent/guardian signature _____ Date _____

Check those that you feel you can support at this time. Thank you.

Secondary Parent Agreement

Student's name _____

I want my child to succeed in school. I agree to:

_____ See that my child is punctual and attends school regularly

_____ Ask to see my child's homework, quiz, and unit test data weekly

_____ Call my child's teacher if there are important changes in the family

_____ Watch and listen to my child and call the teacher if s/he displays any significant and prolonged mood or behavior changes

_____ Apply what my child learns in school to future career aspirations

_____ Attend parent–teacher conferences and student-led conferences

_____ Praise my child for progress in setting new goals for improvement

_____ Discuss progress reports with my child

_____ Expect that my child will behave in a safe manner with other students, teachers, and school staff

_____ Establish a time and place for homework, and review it when completed

_____ Listen to my child and contact the teacher with concerns/questions

_____ Be aware of what my child is learning at school

_____ Read, sign, and promptly return any notices from the teacher/school

_____ Monitor Internet sites accessed and cell phone use for inappropriate/bullying activities

_____ See that my child has a healthy breakfast

_____ Ensure that my child gets to bed at a reasonable time

Parent/guardian signature _____ Date _____

Check those that you feel you can support at this time. Thank you.

Figure 2.6 *Continued.*

a difficult position if parents question you or the administration about changes they see and hear from their children. At issue is that every adult has been to school. Therefore, many hold traditional views on what school and the school experience are supposed to be. It is your responsibility to help everyone understand the new approach and *why it is important to make this change.* You know parents of your students, and know what their educational levels are and something about their needs and expectations of the school. Establishing a relationship takes time, yet the reward is always greater than you may imagine. Positive phone calls or e-mails home help, but going the extra mile to enlighten them about Baldrige and continuous improvement will help even more. As you know, sensitivity to language differences and education levels is essential when preparing written information for your students' parents.

Figures 2.7 and 2.8 show a couple of examples that have worked for us. More examples are provided at the end of this chapter and may be successfully used when modified to "fit" your situation.

Dear Parents,

I am thrilled to have your child in my class this year. You're probably going to start hearing him/her say, "I am responsible for my own learning." Or, "I am response-able to the success of the class." These are the two principles on which we're organizing our class this year. You see, we're on a new journey called BBQ (Baldrige-based quality). This is new to our school district and has proven highly successful with other school districts around the country. What is BBQ and how it is different? For one thing, your child is going to start talking about data, quality tools, and feedback. We'll be introducing student data folders, and your child will be keeping track of his/her own results, learning to reflect on progress, and setting personal goals. Our class also will develop a vision, mission, and goals, and we're even going to establish quality factors for what it means to be a *wow* student. All students will be engaged in data analysis, and we will all focus on continuous improvement. We'll make changes for sure because our goal is to have everyone succeed at a higher level than last year.

Another thing that will be different is that periodically you'll receive surveys from me about a variety of topics. I promise to take your feedback seriously and will inform you about the results in a timely manner.

We are excited about this new journey. I look forward to meeting you on back-to-school night. If I can do anything to help you, please let me know. You can always contact me via e-mail, and can track your student's progress by logging in to our secure server.

Thank you!

Sincerely,
Mrs. Bogan

Figure 2.7   Teacher's introductory letter.

As you know, our school is beginning a continuous improvement journey. Here is some information to help you better understand what this looks like in our Baldrige-based quality classroom.	
Students learn to become independent learners by:	• Writing personal goals based on their needs and the curriculum • Developing action plans to reach their goals • Charting progress • Problem-solving when goals are not being met
Students learn to make decisions and solve problems by:	• Using quality tools such as plus/deltas to examine opportunities for improvement, and force field analysis to analyze what is driving or preventing their learning • Using the PDSA cycle to plan for alternative approaches to learning, followed by analyzing the results
Students learn to take responsibility for learning by:	• Writing personal goals that meet curricular expectations • Exploring their potential by going for "stretch" goals • Monitoring their own progress • Planning for a rapid response if progress is not being made
Students learn how the Baldrige core values and "best practices" will help them achieve by:	• Learning to make decisions based on facts • Demonstrating agility by responding quickly to changing needs • Appreciating and valuing the contributions of others • Focusing on the future by understanding expectations • Practicing and modeling ethical behaviors

Figure 2.8 A back-to-school handout.

IN SUMMARY

In this chapter we have shown you how to start your journey toward excellence by systematically engaging students and key stakeholders as partners in the educational process. Building and maintaining relationships with these individuals (some are direct customers—students and the next teacher in line; some are key stakeholders—parents/guardians, the world of work, post-secondary institutions, the military, community). We have not spent a lot of time addressing the school district as a customer; however, you've learned the necessity of satisfying all key customers, including the state and national policies as they relate to your work.

If you work in a district, you are in a direct customer–supplier situation at each level. At the same time, you are subject to the complexities of the system created by the board of education, superintendent, and other senior leaders. Most likely, the larger the district, the more complex the system is. Likewise, if you teach in a charter school, private school, or small district, there will be less complexity. You are the direct customer of the district senior leaders. In either case, as you learn more about systems and how to create a different culture in your classroom you will begin to recognize any system (district) barriers that keep you from being successful. The significance in terms of your own learning is that you will begin to realize how important the voice of the customer is and use your newfound knowledge to work differently to give "voice" to students especially, and also to engage in a shared partnership with parents/guardians.

You can not predict excellence and improved results unless and until you begin to listen to the needs and expectations of your key customers and stakeholders. Once armed with this information, you can then begin to develop relationships that go beyond the norm, with shared responsibilities spelled out and committed to by all. The two underlying principles on which any BBQ classroom operates are: "I am responsible for my own learning" and "I am response-able to the success of the class." These apply to all students as well as the teacher-leader and any other adults who interface with the class.

Don't let yourself be overwhelmed by new "systems language" or the heavy emphasis we place on building learning partnerships. In reflection, you may already be engaged in some Baldrige in Education (BiE) approaches. Whatever your beginning point, you have begun to flip the culture of the classroom from "you and them" to "we and us." You are a team working together to improve each individual's success and the success of all. It is the beginning of a journey that will reenergize you, and you'll be able to predict improved results.

TOOLBOX

Example—Introductory Survey Sent to Parents of Very Young Students

Getting to Know Your Child

Parents,

Please help me get to know your child. Be as specific or as vague as you feel comfortable with and return this to me by September 8th. *Thanks!*

1. What special talent (sports, music, and so on) does your child have?

2. Any hobbies?

3. What subject area is favored?

4. What is your child's best subject area?

5. What subject is most difficult for your child?

6. How does your child get along with siblings?

7. What does your child do during free time at home?

8. What would you like me to know about your child?

Example—Introductory Student Survey—Grades 2 through Elementary

Getting to Know You

My name is _____ . Please call me_____ .

My birthday is _____ . My phone number is _____ .

I live with _____ .

My favorite color is _____ . Sports I like are _____ .

My favorite sport is _____ .

I don't like any sports. I like _____ .

I have a pet _____ named _____ .

The funniest thing that happened to me this summer was _____

_____ .

I am looking forward to this school year because _____ .

My best or favorite subject in school is _____ .

Why _____ .

My least favorite subject in school is _____ .

Why _____ .

I dread starting school because_____ .

Tell me one (or a lot of) thing(s) you would *really* like to learn in this class. _____

_____

Example—Introductory Student Survey—Middle School Level

Getting to Know You

My name is _____ . Please call me_____ .

My birthday is _____ . My phone number is _____ .

I live with _____ .

Sports I like are _____ . My favorite sport is _____ .

I don't like any sports. I like_____ .

I am a member of the _____ club(s) and participate in _____

_____ after school.

I don't participate in any after-school activities. I work at _____ .

I have a pet _____ named _____ .

The funniest thing that happened to me this summer was _____

_____ .

I am looking forward to this school year because _____ .

My best or favorite subject in school is _____ .

Why _____ .

My least favorite subject in school is_____ .

Why _____ .

I dread starting school because_____ .

Tell me one (or a lot of) thing(s) you would *really* like to learn in this class. _____

_____

Example—Introductory Student Survey—High School Level

Hi,

I am looking forward to having you in this class. Please help me get to know you a little better by completing this survey. I will be asking for your help in making adjustments to our classroom system periodically throughout the semester and your assistance will be greatly appreciated. Thank you.

My name is _____ . Please call me_____ .

My birthday is _____ . My phone number is _____ .

I live with _____ .

Sports I like are _____ . My favorite sport is _____ .

I don't like any sports. I like _____ .

I am a member of the _____ club(s) and participate in _____

_____ after school.

I don't participate in any after-school activities. I work at _____ .

After graduating from high school I plan to_____ .

My career hope is to work as _____ .

The funniest thing that happened to me this summer was _____

_____ .

I am looking forward to this class because_____ .

The thing I am dreading about this class is _____ .

I learn best when I _____ .

The most important thing to know about me is _____

_____ .

It would be really great if we could learn _____ in this class.

Parent/Guardian Expectations Survey—Elementary

I'm delighted to have your child in my third-grade class this year. Because you are most likely concerned about what is taught in the class, this survey is intended to explore those interests.

Please answer the following questions. Thanks for your assistance. I will send a report informing you of how other parents/guardians have responded.

1. If you were the teacher of this class, what would you think is most important to teach? (We typically teach mathematics, language arts, social studies, science, writing, technology, physical education, music, and art.)

2. Other than academic content, is there anything else you hope your student will learn? (Skills, attitudes, and so on.)

3. Is there any way in which you might be able to assist in the teaching of the class; that is, do you have expertise that might add value to this particular class? Would you be willing or able to help in any particular way?

4. What are some things I need to know to help your child learn this year?

5. Other comments, suggestions, expectations, and so on.?

Please sign here if you're able to assist with this class. _____

Answers to the "Identify the Relationship" Activity

Internal customers	Partner	Stakeholder	Supplier	Worker
Those inside the system who receive services or products of the system	Individual or group not paid by the system, but who renders services or support	Groups affected by an organization's actions and success	Groups or individuals who provide materials or students	Individuals engaged in processes that affect the finished product
Next teacher in line District Administration	Parents/guardians World of Work	Parents/guardians Community State World of Work	Previous teacher Student support services Parents Pre-K programs Previous school	Students Administration Instructional aides

3

Establish a Culture of Success for All

CONVERSATION WITH THE TEACHER

You've begun to create a collaborative partnership with students, but the system is not fully aligned. Have you ever wondered what sets champions or other highly successful people apart? It isn't always the privileged ones who end up at the top. So, what is the secret to their success? If you study highly successful people and champions, you'll discover they share some things in common. For example, to a person, they can visualize themselves winning—or receiving an award or recognition, or being at the pinnacle of their career. This ability to visualize a future state is also extremely important for students as it plants the "thought seed" of success. But a vision needs a plan, or it becomes just another dream. The future champion purposefully sets goals and action plans to achieve the vision. Yet, still more is needed to stay on course to achieve the vision, and that is a mission. "Mission" is the path you choose to achieve your vision. Although "luck" may play a role, it is careful planning that carries a person to the top.

Someone once shared with us that three things are necessary to create a different reality. These are (1) having a strong desire, (2) holding a strong belief that it is possible, and (3) acting as if it has happened. When we "translate" these into individual or group behaviors, we can say, (1) establish a vision, (2) stay passionate about reaching the vision, and (3) don't give up—be persistent in the pursuit of your vision, and don't allow anyone to convince you it's not possible. There are many examples of classrooms (and schools) where despite very difficult odds, the achievement gap has been closed and all students learn at higher rates.

As educators, we must accept no more excuses! Instead, align the classroom system to put your students on a trajectory that will lead them to achieve greatness. No shame, no blame! Let go of any old, traditional paradigms you have about teaching and any prejudices you have about any students or groups of students. Instead, be the leader who creates a student/learner-centered classroom. We believe you can do it! Press forward and stay true to systems thinking and you'll be amazed at the difference it makes.

In this chapter you will learn:

- How to facilitate a class strategic plan: vision, mission, and goals

- About action plans and how to set and align them with class goals

- How to help students coalesce and raise expectations for each other by establishing quality factors for students

- How to establish classroom procedures—or processes to improve efficiency and effectiveness

SET THE STAGE—STRATEGIC PLANNING

A strategic plan is a strategic plan—no matter the type of organization (business, hospital, school district, and so on). Can you name one successful, profitable business that doesn't have a strategic plan? We didn't think so. Simply put, those that don't will close for lack of customers or desirable products, or both. Hospitals and nonprofits all have strategic plans. They understand the importance of making certain that all employees know what's important and how to reach their goals. The same holds for all successful organizations. It is impossible to sustain an effort without a purpose, vision, mission, goals, action plans, and a way to measure success.

Public school districts are required to have strategic plans for accreditation, and boards of education use these plans to guide decision making and resource allocation. Private schools have comprehensive strategic plans because continued funding and enrollment depends on their success. Here's a poignant example of what happens when there is no strategic plan. Study charter schools and their success rates. Almost without exception you'll find higher learning results at charter schools with comprehensive strategic plans than at those without. Some charter schools (because they lack decent facilities) have put all their efforts into fund-raising and facility planning, without doing any academic planning. It comes as no surprise that these schools have less than stellar learning results.

It has been well documented that what is focused on "gets done." If there are no efforts to focus on student learning, teachers are left to their own devices for curriculum and learning activities. Is it any wonder teachers, administrators, and parents with children at these schools are frequently dismayed by the results? In the end, these schools will be forced to close, but not before too many students have been let down by the very adults they should be able to trust.

We include this example in the book because of the lessons we can learn at the classroom level. And it is imperative that each teacher (or team) designs a process to collaborate with students to create a class strategic plan. Secondary students should have an opportunity to develop a personal vision, mission, goals, and action plans. This activity helps a person (or a class) stay focused and learn to analyze data, and to make midcourse corrections in order to achieve their vision.

We are aware that classroom strategic planning, as it relates to creation of the purpose, vision, mission, and setting class goals, may seem overwhelming and consume too much instructional time. We suggest chunking the planning process, such as: day 1—purpose and vision, day 2—mission, day 3—quality factors for students, day 4—class goals. Teachers who have been trained on and use this approach *uniformly* tell us that the time spent on this process is regained as "found" instructional time each subsequent day. This approach vastly decreases discipline issues and provides a common language among students and teacher. Even kindergartners are capable of engaging in the process and having their voices heard, despite the conventional "wisdom" of many. For too many years, educators have held limiting ideas about the capabilities of young children that are being dispelled repeatedly by those who operate a BBQ classroom.

The greater challenges come for special education teachers—those who teach the severely or profoundly impaired children. Also, if you work with level one or two English-language learners you have to approach things slightly differently. We will go into more detail about approaching these challenges toward the end of this chapter.

Establish a Purpose

If teachers or students don't know why they are at school or in a particular class, they have no reason to become engaged, eager learners. Further, if *you* don't know what *your* own purpose is, *you will be unable* to stay focused, and a great deal of instructional time may be wasted. There is no getting around this one—every educator has to know his/her purpose (see Figure 3.1). The *5 whys* is the tool to use, and whether you work alone or with a partner it is one of the most significant exercises in which you will ever engage (see Activity 3.1). As one teacher of at-risk teens told us, "This has truly given me a compass for all that I do. I keep my purpose on a 3 × 5 card right on my desk. When the students seem to get off track, I quickly read my purpose and am able to reorient my own thinking."

> Purpose *is the rays of light projecting pulsating energy from and beyond the vision to encompass everyone involved. It is the* aim *of the classroom, or the reason why it exists.*

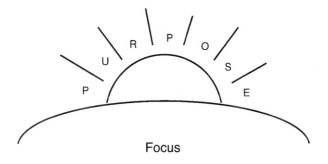

Figure 3.1   Purpose provides focus like the lens of a camera.

Activity 3.1 Practice the five whys.

Directions: Clarify your purpose and write down your response to each question, and then use that answer as the basis for the next "why." Once you've gotten to the fifth "why" your true purpose will be revealed. Is it a noble purpose?

A *purpose* is a short, succinct statement that describes the core reason for what you do. Keep your purpose statement close so you can be reminded of it regularly, as the winds of "life" frequently distract people from their purpose. We highly recommend that middle and high school students create their own purpose statements. It is the beginning of creating a successful future for them.

Why do you teach?

    Why . . .

        Why . . .

            Why . . .

                Why . . .

My purpose is:

Your class purpose can be arrived at in a fashion similar to Activity 3.1. For elementary students, this is probably best done as a whole group, but with older students you might be able to have them work in small groups, then get the whole class together to agree on the best purpose statement. Actually, when the word "learning" is mentioned, you have the central purpose of the class.

Quality tools save time and keep emotions out of the discussion; that's why we highly recommend you use the 5 whys tool instead of simply a broad discussion with the students. As the facilitator, however, you have to be careful not to go down a path that is a dead end. Such responses as shown in Figure 3.2 can lead to a problem.

To avoid this problem, rephrase the "why" questions. For example, the second "why" question in Figure 3.2 could be rephrased as "Why do parents think it is important for students to come to school?" You might want to practice with a friend or colleague before attempting to use the 5 whys with your class to avoid some of these pitfalls. Ask your training partner to respond as s/he thinks the students might respond. A better set of responses is shown in Figure 3.3.

The class purpose arrived at in Figure 3.3 might be: To *learn* the skills taught in this class to improve our chances to be successful in the college and the career of our choice so we can become employed and afford a nice lifestyle, while enjoying our chosen work.

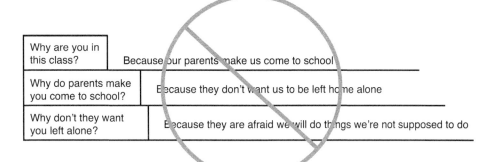

Figure 3.2   Problematic responses to five whys exercise.

Why are you in this class?	Because it is required for graduation	
Why is it required for graduation?	Because it is required to get into college	
Why would a college want you to have this class for admission?	Because we need to have these skills to succeed in college	
Why would these skills help you be successful in college?	Because we need a strong foundation to build on with the new concepts and skills to graduate and get a good job	
Why do you want to graduate and get a good job?	Because we want to earn money to afford a nice lifestyle and enjoy the work we do	

Figure 3.3   Better set of responses to five whys exercise.

Once the purpose has been decided, have the students copy it into their class folder or organizer. It should also be posted prominently in the classroom. Include the class purpose on any communication pieces sent to parents. In this way, the focus of the class becomes indelibly forged in everyone's mind.

Helpful Tip: If the class purpose contains the word "learn," a clear sense of the seriousness of learning will permeate the time students spend in class and completing homework and other assignments.

Create a Class Vision

A *vision* is a brief statement or cluster of sentences that answer the "what" question. Vision is the long-term future. It must be *inspirational*, and lead students to become internally motivated to "live" the two quality principles, stay focused on their purpose, and learn as much as possible.

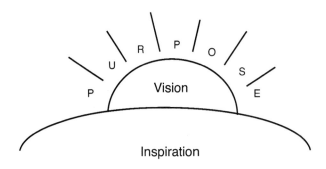

Figure 3.4   Vision provides inspiration for the class.

Teachers, as leaders, provide the passion and inspiration for students to write the vision through their excitement, tonal quality, and passion for answering the "what" question.

Keep in mind that you know the district grade- or course-level requirements and curriculum for your assignment (Customer Focus, Baldrige category 3). This gives you the opportunity to prompt the students with your passion for the subject matter immediately. So much of the visioning process rests on the teacher's ability to express his/her passion for the subject and excitement about learning. Your body language, voice, and enthusiasm are important during this exercise. You know the content of the subject. You know the requirements. You are the one who can bring it to life. For example, instead of simply accepting the idea that "we will learn things," you might add audacious adjectives to the thoughts they have, for example, "We are *superior* scholars or *Einsteins* or *brilliant* mathematicians." These words will lend much more enthusiasm to the class. Of course, you can not use these words unless students concur. It is amazing how much a little passion and teacher enthusiasm lends to capturing students' attention and increasing their desire to learn.

An Elementary Approach

Begin the process by asking the students, "What do we want to achieve in the time we'll be together, what will distinguish our class from all the others, and what will we be noted for by ourselves, parents, and others?" Continue along these lines: "What will we want to be able to do as a result of being in this class; at the end of our time together, what will we accomplish?" "What would make us proud and make others say, '*Wow*, what a great class that was!'" By getting students involved in this activity, you actually are capturing some ideas about students' expectations (Customer Focus, category 3). Even if an individual student's ideas are not prioritized into the final vision statement, you have heard what they've said and can use that information later when preparing learning activities.

At this point, you are asking students to brainstorm ideas. If your students have not experienced this type of activity before, you may need to "prime the pump" by making one or two suggestions. Resist the urge to give your suggestions before allowing at least 30 seconds for students to give theirs. Once they begin providing ideas, stop adding yours and continue only if they seem to get stuck. Capture all ideas by writing them where all can see. Review each idea and, if there are any questions, ask the student who made the suggestion to clarify the idea. If there are like ideas or similar ones, ask for permission to combine them.

Have the students prioritize the remaining ideas to create the vision statement. Use a multi-voting technique as described on page 81 in the Toolbox section at the end of this chapter. Explain the significance of the voting procedure: to ensure that each student's voice is heard and considered. Remember, multi-voting is a silent activity. This is to ensure that each student makes up his/her mind without being influenced by the others. Give students a minute to make up their minds at their desks before anyone starts voting, and then have each place his/her priority votes by going one by one and placing dots next to the corresponding idea(s). Ask several students to total the scores for each idea. Eliminate those without any votes or those with just a few. The remaining ideas will be reworked into the vision by asking the students to help compose them into sentences. If the ideas are already stated in sentence form, they may be adopted as written.

Develop the vision with elementary students or with special education classes as a whole-class activity as outlined above. Once the students have prioritized the lists, you might divide middle or high school–age students into smaller groups. Each group can take the words and compose them into sentences to create a vision. Each group reports out to the class, who can then select the one they like best, or even edit several ideas to create a better vision statement.

Once the vision statement is written, ask for consensus from students, and when adopted, ask everyone in the class to sign it. (Remember, teachers and aides sign too.) Post the signed vision statement in a prominent place in the classroom or outside the classroom above the door where it is visible to everyone. Ask the students to write the class vision in their notebooks. Share it with parents, other classes, and the administration.

Keep in mind that the vision must come from the students and be written in their words, not yours. In this way you are giving students a voice to assure them that it is *our class*, not the *teacher's class*. This helps students feel empowered and take ownership of the class, so motivation for learning begins to flip from external to internal. By asking students to engage in defining the class vision, you are asking them to:

- *Imagine* the result of their efforts—beyond the usual "pass this class" mentality

- *Think* about "excellence" and state it in writing

- *Get involved* in shaping the desired end result of time spent together

An Approach for Those Using a High School or Middle School Team Structure

Prior to doing any strategic planning, the teacher team will need to work together to create a process that is not redundant, that saves time, and can yield the desired result. If possible, get permission to have the entire team of students together so you can work as a large group. You may want to preface the visioning work by having the students name the team. Armed with a team name, you can describe the vision process as defined above.

The team can have one collective vision and mission statement. Some teams manage the time by combining two periods and getting a good deal of the vision work done on the first day. Others choose to break up the time—listing words one day and multi-voting, then dividing the large team into smaller groups and composing the words into one or two sentences on another day. By the third day, the whole team is ready to look at the work produced by each group and multi-vote on a vision for the whole team. The important thing is that this process be inclusive for all students, and that they see their teachers fully engaged with them. Use a similar process to develop the team mission statement described below.

High School or Middle School without a Team Structure

If your school has students divided into grades but not teams, a vision statement can be written for the grade. In fact, given the high numbers of high school dropouts, it would be a good strategy to engage students as support for each other in this way. The process remains the same—brainstorm, then multi-vote on the "best" words that would provide inspiration for achieving at the highest rate. It becomes particularly important to assure that all voices are heard—including those for whom school has not been a welcoming place. It is precisely when students lose hope for their future that we must find ways to engage them more actively. This will be somewhat difficult if the school doesn't have grade-level homerooms. Before you reject the idea outright, work with your peers and administration to seek solutions. Imagine if each grade level had a vision for success! (Followed by a grade-level mission statement, this could be a powerful motivational approach.) A schoolwide data wall might even lend more motivation. Can you think of other possibilities that would help students work and support each other on the journey toward graduation?

   The photos in Figure 3.5 are the work of the sixth, seventh, and eighth grade bands at Graham Park Middle School, Triangle, Virginia. Mr. Brian Heater submitted these photos. He followed the

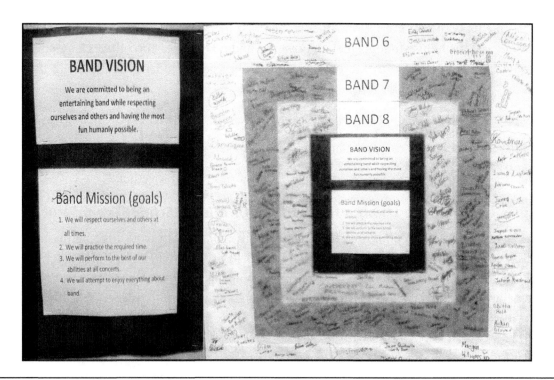

Figure 3.5   Vision and mission statements of Graham Park Middle School students.

brainstorming process for each band, then had the students multi-vote several times. Then each band formed the words into a vision, which was later voted on by all three bands. He followed the same process for developing the mission and goals. When the process was completed, Mr. Heater posted it as shown, and members of each band signed off. Mr. Heater was pleasantly surprised at the impact this had on his students. Even though he'd always taken great pride in the band's accomplishments, never before had the students been so focused on excellence.

Write a Class Mission

A mission is a cluster of sentences that answer the "how" question. It provides the behavioral pathway for the class to achieve the vision and embodies the two quality principles (see Figure 3.6). The mission keeps the focal point on the agreed-on "aim" or purpose of the class.

Teachers begin by drawing a path leading toward the vision. Ask the question, "How will we have to work together during this year (semester) to achieve our vision? What are some behaviors we can use that will help ensure that our vision is accomplished?"

Students follow the same brainstorming and multi-voting approach as they used in creating the vision, although now students will be brainstorming action words. Once again, you may need to prime the pump by making one or two suggestions. Resist the urge to give your suggestions first, as the important thing is that students are empowered to create "their" classroom and not just re-create "your" classroom. Here are some suggestions: cooperate, participate, be kind, have a sense of humor, respect, trust, listen, and so on.

> ***Caution:*** *Make certain all ideas are stated in the positive and not the negative, for example, "Keep hands and feet to yourself" rather than "Don't hit or kick."*

Figure 3.6 Mission is the pathway to the vision.

Throughout this process, you are gaining more and more information from your students (Baldrige category 3) about what they think is important for the class to be successful. It is important to make mental notes of the ideas coming from specific students as this information can help guide you in your approach to these students later, especially if their suggestions are not included in the final version of the mission statement.

Once all ideas are captured, review the list with the class and seek permission to combine like ideas while eliminating duplicates. Now the class is ready to prioritize the list once again using the multi-voting tool. Prior to multi-voting, remind students that their decisions need to be based on the words they believe are *the most important for everyone to remember* in order *to achieve the vision*. Have one or more students total the points and circle the top five words, or more if there is a natural break in point value.

Be mindful that the mission statement can be changed during the school year if it becomes evident that it is not guiding classroom behavior. Having said that, it is necessary to emphasize the importance of having a pathway to achieve the vision. Too many words = too many sentences = too much complexity, and results in a meaningless statement that no one can remember, much less care about. A mission statement ought to be short, powerful, and become the mantra of the class.

After multi-voting, ask students to work together to write sentences that incorporate all the agreed-on words to make a mission statement for the class. Primary grade teachers may take a more prominent role in this process than teachers of students in grades two and up. Still, seek agreement from all students and avoid taking away their voice. Once consensus is reached, rewrite the class mission and have everyone (including the teacher and any other adults who interface with the class) sign it before posting it in the classroom.

Ask the students to copy the mission and put it in a prominent place in their folder or notebook, and send copies home. To solidify the path to excellence, you may want the students to begin the day by repeating the class mission statement.

Helpful Tips:

- When the mission is written, ask the students if they believe it is going to help them achieve the vision.

- If not, find out why, and go back and revise it until everyone in the class is satisfied that it *will matter and help the class reach the vision.*

Caution: *If the mission statement is written by the teacher with little or no input from students, it will not be effective. Time spent in this activity is crucial to aligning the system to reach improved, predictable results. The idea of classroom strategic planning is to flip the power structure from traditional—teacher-led and teacher-focused—to students as partners and learning-focused. Student voice is critical.*

Orient New Students Who Enter the Class

It's rare that a school year begins with the total complement of students that will ultimately enroll, and therefore the natural question is, "What do we do about students who enroll after the class vision and mission have been established?" Add to this the increased number of non–English speaking students who arrive several weeks after school has started. All this can make the process seem overwhelming and too time-consuming. We agree that this is an issue, and we want you to know that the following approach has been successfully used by teachers at all levels.

Assign a two- or three-student leadership team in advance to orient any new students into the class. We call these *BBQ ambassadors*. You might also call them *ambassadors of excellence*. If your circumstances are such that you have non–English speaking students, you're going to want to include one student who is fluent in another language (preferably the language that is most frequently seen among your students). Change the team once a month to give all students an opportunity for a leadership role. The BBQ ambassadors are responsible for orienting new students to the class purpose, the two quality principles, the vision, and the mission. After new students are oriented, the ambassadors seek to have each sign on to the vision and mission. Ambassadors are well trained and taught not to use coercive tactics, but function as mentors to new students about the way business is done in a BBQ classroom.

Help Secondary Students Get on a Positive, Successful Trajectory

As the leader, and with the responsibility for guiding students toward success, we strongly recommend that during language arts classes each student write his/her personal vision and mission statements. This exercise will be invaluable to all students, but especially for those who come from less-supportive families or families where few, if any, have graduated from high school or completed any postsecondary education/training. As noted earlier, at-risk students have little or no hope for their future. This is why personal visioning is so powerful, provided that students also receive guidance to learn goal setting, reflection, and how to measure success. The kinds of questions you'll want to ask students as each envisions his/her future are "What would you like to do—what type of work would you like to do after completing your education? If you could become anything you'd like, what would it be? Do you enjoy working indoors or out? Do you like working with people or alone? Do you enjoy planning more than doing, or working with your hands more than your mind? Do you like to invent things, create beauty, use technology? Do you view yourself as a builder of things? Do you enjoy lots of activity or long periods of time spent thinking? Do you enjoy working with puzzles, numbers, or words? Can you imagine yourself helping those less fortunate, providing for the safety of others, finding a cure for disease, or teaching?"

We recommend that this activity be accomplished in a language arts class because writing is a universal requirement for all students. However, the process doesn't end with a written vision statement. Students can then research the skills, knowledge, and educational level required to achieve the vision. This exercise can be very helpful if teachers are made aware of each student's vision; it is easier to develop learning activities that allow them to make connections between schoolwork and real-life application. We've included a process template used by Ashleigh Burnette, Parkside Middle School, Manassas, Virginia, in the Toolbox section at the end of this chapter.

> **Caution:** *This is an important activity and may even become one of the most important things that can happen in any student's teen years. Each is free to revise their vision (and many will) over and over again throughout middle school, high school, and even in their 20s. We urge you to have each student carry his/her vision, mission, and goals in a prominent place in an organizer or notebook. If you simply ask students to go through the motions of developing a personal vision and mission but do nothing to link them to learning activities, then it becomes yet another "schoolwork" exercise without a hook to anything going on in that child's life.*

An Approach for Special Education or English Language Learner (ELL) Teachers

When students are mainstreamed they will be included with the class as it creates it vision and mission, and additional help with special education students may not be needed.

However, levels 1 and 2 ELL students may require additional help with the words. Teachers might use pictures or role-play the different adjectives and verbs for students. Another approach might be to seek out a volunteer who speaks the primary second language who could be in the classroom to translate the discussion for ELL students. If this is your circumstance, then you're going to need to do additional up-front planning to organize this kind of help. You might, for example, tap into university students, parents, grandparents, or older level 4 or 5 ELL students who can be available to help. The need to hear the voice of and involve every student can not be overstated.

Special needs students with severe or profound cognitive impairments pose a different challenge. In this instance the teacher and any aides in the classroom would develop a team vision and mission. This would not involve the students but will help the adult team (professionals and support staff) focus their energies and aid in their ability to work together closely for all students.

An Approach for Specialty Teachers

Follow the process used to develop the vision. Brainstorm *verbs* one day, and limit the time given to this activity. You may need to prime the pump with specific behaviors critical to your subject matter. For example, in a physical education class *safety* is a key concern. If the students don't mention it, you must. Write down all the words and post them for each grade level or course. Seek permission from the students to combine similar ideas and eliminate duplicates. The next time you meet with the students, reorient them on the purpose of a mission statement and ask them to multi-vote on the most important words for meeting the class vision. It's best if you can have all the words on small pieces of paper or 3 × 5 cards so each student can individually mark the most important four behaviors. Collect these, add up the totals, and circle the top five or six point getters.

Ask students for permission to put these words into complete sentences, or make a bullet point list that says, "As students in _____ class, we will [bullet point the selected words]." Have all students and adults sign the mission statement, then post it in the room and/or on a poster to be carried along with the teacher if shared facilities are used.

Establish Class Goals

Mix *Academic Goals* with *Behaviors*

The last step before proceeding is to establish class goals. Without a way to measure progress toward the vision, it (the vision) will remain a series of words without importance (see Figure 3.7).

Learning goals come from the vision and are measured with "hard," factual data. Behavior and social skills are measured through the mission and quality factors for students (described later in this chapter). Behavior goals can be measured with "soft" perception data. Tools to measure soft data include radar charts, plus/delta, enthusiasm and learning charts, and surveys. Check the quality tools matrix on page 13 to learn where you can find detailed directions about each tool.

Here's the goal-setting process. With the class, review the vision. Then ask, "How can we prove we have reached our vision?" Consider this elementary vision example: *We are super learners and fantastic readers*!

The teacher asks, "How will we know when we are super learners?" From a brainstormed list, the class has agreed on the following:

- When we all turn in our homework for 10 days in a row

- When we can all add single-digit numbers without mistakes

Next, "How will we know when we are fantastic readers?"

- When we know all the sight words

- When we read two books a week at home every week for four consecutive weeks

Naturally, young students will require more prompting and information to state goals than will older students. Have the class write the goals, and post them after you and the students have signed off in agreement.

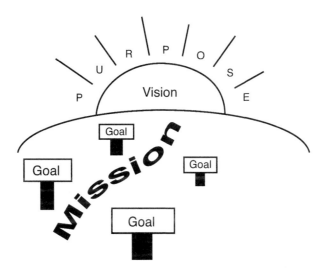

Figure 3.7   Goals are signposts along the way.

Develop Action Plans to Meet the Goals

Once goals have been set, it is the teacher/leader's responsibility to determine initial action plans to achieve the goal. These are the *best strategies and methods* a teacher has available to him/her to teach whatever skills are required by each goal. This would be based on prior experience, discussions with one's PLC, researched best practice, or an innovative, creative approach. Action plans must be fully aligned and designed to meet the goal, otherwise the chances of reaching the goal become less and less. Figure 3.8 shows an example of an action plan, and Activity 3.2 is provided for you to try creating one yourself.

Helpful Tips:

- Keep the goals simple and measurable, focused on the vision and purpose.

- Measure progress toward the goals regularly and display the results.

- When each goal is met, celebrate, and then increase expectations!

Realize that while the teacher sets the initial action plans, students provide input into how they want to learn these skills as the year progresses. In this way, action plans change and reflect student input, thus increasing student motivation to learn. This process (detailed later in this chapter and with an example in Chapter 7) manifests in a learner-centered classroom where student voice becomes amplified toward having the entire class achieve the goals and ultimately the vision. If it becomes apparent that a goal is not going to be met in a timely fashion, you can be sure there is a process problem that must be addressed. When this occurs, the action plans (for example, the process/strategy used to achieve the goal) must be reviewed, and the need to hear the voice of the students as they offer suggestions for improvement must be both encouraged and valued.

Strategic goal (from the vision): 100% mastery of single-digit addition				
Action plan	Current	Sept. 1	Jan. 31	April 30
		Frequency	Frequency	Frequency
Math addition problems to be solved with partners using manipulatives	0	1/week	2/week	3/week
Students silently write math stories from prompts to share with class	0	1/week	2/week	2/week
Two-minute timed quiz of numeric problems	1/week	2/week	3/week	1/week
Two-minute timed quiz of 10 word addition problems	0	1/week	2/week	4/week

Figure 3.8   Example of an action plan.

Activity 3.2 Practice creating actions plans for an appropriate class goal.

Strategic goal				
Action plan	Current	Date:	Date:	Date:
		Frequency	Frequency	Frequency

As you learned in Chapter 2, students are both customers and workers in the classroom. As workers, they must carry out the plans designed by you, the leader. Your action plans may work well for some of the students, while leaving others behind, confused and frustrated. From a systems view, teachers may unwittingly create barriers to student success and then claim, "I taught it, if they didn't learn, it's not my fault." This is vastly different from the paradigm of a facilitator of learning. Facilitators realize the job is not fulfilled unless all students learn. This (creating barriers) is never done with malice or forethought. Instead, it is the result of a faulty paradigm. Remove the old paradigm and replace it with a systems view of yourself as a facilitator of learning. The difference can prove to be amazing as you let go of your need to control and allow yourself to be humbled and made vulnerable by asking/inviting students (as workers in the classroom) for help.

Set Targets As Interim Signposts to the Goal

A semester or year-long goal can seem like an eternity to most students. Therefore, we urge you, with your students, to set some interim targets, certainly quarterly, but for the very youngest children (K–1) you could even set monthly or weekly targets. If you teach a semester course, you may want to set three targets (two interims and at report card time). The point is that students can visually see how well they are moving and have the opportunity to give feedback for making midcourse corrections if it looks like the class is not on track to meet the goal. Naturally, this presumes you are being faithful in charting class data and posting it on your data wall (data walls are described in the next chapter).

Targets are the percentage or number of students you expect to be at a certain level by a certain date. These should be reasonable, yet not set so low as to undermine the students' motivation. Everyone in the class helps set the targets. This comes after a discussion letting the students know that you have high expectations and *believe* they can do it if everyone works together and helps each other.

Elementary example. If the goal is to have all students know math addition facts from 1–10 by the end of the school year, then you could set targets as to how many (or what percentage of students) would know these facts by each target date.

Secondary example. If the goal is to have all students write a five-paragraph essay with no errors of usage and mechanics (conventions and skills), then you would set the targets to the number of students in the class who can produce the work by each target date (see Figure 3.9).

Obviously, if few students have met the target then you can assume your action plans are ineffective. After careful review of the targets, seek feedback from students about what action plans are working and take note of those that are not. Seeking feedback in a structured format, such as the use of a plus/delta chart, allows you to save time and still obtain the information needed. Follow this with asking your students *how they would prefer to learn* the skills required of the goal. Give students the opportunity to brainstorm these ideas and then multi-vote on the one or two they feel would be most helpful. This is how action plans change as *student voice* is taken into account. At this point, we do not recommend you toss out all your strategies (action plans), but give some time to the students' suggestions. Remember, this is not about you; it is about removing the barriers to success that exist in your classroom. If you knew what they were ahead of time, we're sure you would remove them. But, since students are workers in the system you create, they are in the best position to tell you what works and what doesn't. Listen to the voice of your customer (students), who also happen to be the workers. A huge benefit to you comes when they see your willingness to make changes based on their feedback. This benefit takes the form of increased motivation and a desire to be "response-able to the success of the class."

Establish Quality Factors for Students

Similarly to seeking information about the needs and expectations students have of the teacher, you're also going to want to ask students to set appropriate behavior expectations for each other.

Goal: (state the goal)	Targets			
	9/30	11/10	1/10	2/30
Percentage of students who have mastered the expectations. (We recommend using percentage rather than numbers to accommodate student mobility.)	Example: 15%	Example: 45%	Example: 75%	Example: 100%

Figure 3.9 Template for setting targets.

We've already established the significance of asking students to share their opinions. This is especially true in terms of behaviors. In a traditional setting, the teacher (sometimes the school) sets rules, and generally most of them are written in the negative, for example, "don't" or "no." Students receive so many negative messages that over time they simply tune them out. Perhaps you have children of your own and have experienced this firsthand. If you haven't thought of it before, do a little research on how to speak to your own children. Approximately what ratio of negative to positive messages do you give your own children during the period of one week?

In a BBQ classroom, the emphasis is always on the positive. This is what quality factors (QFs) are (see Figure 3.10). They are the *absolute, most essential characteristics we must demonstrate every day in order to be considered quality*! Here, you want students to think about the behaviors all students must exhibit to help achieve the class vision and assure a safe environment for everyone.

An Elementary Approach

Draw an outline of a body on a large piece of butcher paper. Label it *quality student*. Ask students what they need to do to be excellent students and help the class achieve the vision. Write the brainstormed characteristics down on the outlined body in the appropriate places (example: listen—draw a large ear and write "listen" in a bright color).

Continue until all the ideas are represented on the large outlined body. If the word "learn" has not been mentioned, you will need to remind the students of their purpose and ask if their ideas will help them become better learners.

When all ideas are exhausted—there will likely be many—ask whether they will be able to remember them all, or if it would help to shorten the list. Use the multi-voting process again to come up with four to six characteristics that everyone agrees will, if adhered to by all, help keep everyone on the path to success.

Figure 3.10 Quality factors for students.

Total up the points and circle those with the highest number. Redo the chart, this time using only the circled characteristics. Have every student sign the QFs for students. Post this in a prominent place in the classroom.

Provide students with a blank sheet of 8½ × 11 paper. Ask each student to draw a picture of him/herself, label it *quality student (name)* and copy all the ideas from the large butcher paper outline onto their drawing. This becomes a page in the student's data notebook.

A Secondary Approach

Find an inspiring poster (example: someone climbing a mountain) and put a sticky note at the top marked *vision accomplished*. Ask the students to jot down their ideas on sticky notes, or use index cards to identify characteristics they need to have to assure that the class achieves its vision.

List the students' ideas on the poster, with the most frequently suggested ideas on the bottom (to form the foundation), and work your way up to the apex of the mountain. Label it *Quality Student* and post it in a prominent place in the classroom.

Figure 3.11 shows an example from Karen Cunningham, an English teacher at Graham Park Middle School, Triangle, Virginia. After the class voted on the most important characteristics, she divided the class into small groups and had each operationally define each of the QFs using a lotus

obeys	Pays attention	SLANT	Asks kind questions	Respects Classmate	Includes others	neat, without wrinkles	Completes all parts to question	Completely done
Pushes in chair	[7] Respects Teacher	Positive Attitude	Follows COB	Always [8] Friendly	Treats others fairly	checks QF's	Completes [1] HW	legible handwriting
Keep area clean	Turns in HW	Listens	says hi to everybody	Helps friends when asked	Happy Attitude	Tried	Turned in on time	Proper headings
Asks when don't understand	Reads the directions	Listens	[7] Respects Teacher	Always [8] Friendly	Completes [1] HW	actually Reading	Asks questions	Pays attention to what you're reading
Clean underwear	[6] Follows directions	Responds when asked	[6] Follows directions	Quality Student	Reads [2]	Good ideas at book talks	Reads [2]	Understands the book
Courteous when talking	Highlights key words	Focused	[5] Good Grades	Is [4] prepared	Follows [3] COB	More words than pictures	Reads all genres	Challenges you
Tries your best	Extra credit when offered	Good Attitude	Has Homework	Has all supplies	agenda	Follows gum rule	Follows tobacco rule	Follows dress code
A's and B's	[5] Good Grades	Ask ? when don't understand	Is on time	[4] Is prepared	ready to work	Appropriate language	Follows [3] COB	Friendly to all
Finish your work	Studies	S + O in Conduct & work habits	Does locker before class	Used rr + water	Good Attitude	Healthy habits	Honest and caring	Never threatens

Figure 3.11 Student quality factors with operational definitions.

diagram. The class reached consensus on the operational definitions and each student received a lotus diagram and filled it in. This became part of the student's data notebook (discussed in Chapter 6). The directions for a Lotus diagram can be found in the Toolbox section at the end of Chapter 7, page 276.

Similarly to having each student create their own vision and mission, each student can write personal QFs for her/himself. By giving students time to reflect on their current and past behavior, academic success, and his/her vision, each can write those characteristics believed to be the most essential. If you ask students to write their own personal vision, mission, and QFs, the activity becomes much more significant as teachers have a personal conversation with each student to review what they've written. This provides invaluable information to the teacher. It might also become a homework activity to discuss this with parents and have parents sign that they've read their child's vision, mission, and QFs. This should become part of each student's notebook, and report card time offers the perfect opportunity to reflect and make midcourse corrections to assure success.

ALIGN PROCESS WITH DESIRED RESULTS

Rules versus Procedures

When you have completed the preceding steps you will have created a climate conducive to success for everyone. Rules may be unnecessary (except for those mandated by the school or district) so long as the entire class has agreed, reached consensus, and signed on to the purpose, vision, and mission, and quality factors for students have been established and agreed to by everyone.

What may be missing, however, are *procedures*. A procedure is another name for a *process*. A *process* is a sequence of steps taken to accomplish a task. You can tell if any process is effective by answering the question *"Does it yield the desired result?"* You can tell if any process is efficient by answering the question *"Are the desired results generated in a timely manner?"* If your answer to either of these questions is *"no,"* then you have to determine the following:

- Is there a process in place?

- Have the workers (students) been trained on the process?

- Was the process designed taking into consideration customer expectations?

- Who is the primary customer and what are the expectations?

- Have you a way to measure process success? (This will be addressed in the next chapter.)

Classroom management in a BBQ classroom is quite different than what might be seen in a more traditional classroom. This approach goes beyond having students help set the rules. To be "response-able" to the success of the class, you'll need to engage in systems thinking and understand the ripple effects of any and all decisions. Dr. William Glasser, a noted psychiatrist and author (see Recommended Resources), identified five needs basic to all human beings. They are *survival, love and belonging, power, freedom,* and *fun.* Specifically, we need to respond to students' need for *power* (making decisions about things that directly affect them) and *freedom* (within the boundaries of "I am responsible for my own learning" and "I am response-able to the success of the class").

Students are workers in the classroom and, if given the opportunity, can help create an efficient and effective classroom management system that will decrease acting-out behaviors and help you "buy back" valuable instructional time. See Activity 3.3.

Design of Noninstructional Classroom Processes

Remember, a process is a series of steps taken to achieve a task. Examples of classroom procedures include start of class, homework, transition from one activity to another, permission to use the lavatory, make-up tests, and so on. When a standardized process is not designed and used, there is great variation in the activities' effectiveness and efficiency. The object here is to improve both. Effective processes yield the desired results. Efficient processes yield the desired results in a shorter amount

---

Activity 3.3   Reflect on your classroom management.

Directions: Under the microscope of honesty, reflect on your approach to maintaining "order" in the classroom. Do you have a system based on trust and freedom, or fear and coercion? Is your system working? Your answer to this question must take into consideration the amount of time lost due to seeking students' attention and dealing with inappropriate behavior, getting started, or transitioning to another activity. Make notes about any classroom management processes that you have concerns about.

of time. Your goal ought to be to design classroom management processes, such as those mentioned above, that are both effective and efficient. Time spent on the design of these processes will reduce wasted time and therefore give back more instructional time.

Notice that in Figure 3.12 we have highlighted Student as Worker Focus (category 5) as well as Operations Focus (category 6). This is because students are workers in the system traditionally designed by teachers, but in a Baldrige-based quality classroom they become partners with teachers to help improve the key classroom processes.

Each key classroom process can be flowcharted. Table 3.1 shows some suggestions for non-intructional processes. You can fill in the "other" column with those specific to your classroom.

The design of noninstructional processes contains the same essential components as the instructional design process, but they are stated somewhat differently. We recommend that after filling out the chart (shown at the top of Figure 3.13) you flowchart the process. You'll want to train students on the process to enhance success. We recommend selecting the one or two most vital noninstructional process flowcharts and posting them in the classroom. Figure 3.13 shows the process design and a flowchart of the process. Activity 3.4 allows you to practice with one of your own noninstructional classroom processes.

Now that you've identified some key noninstructional processes, choose one and use the universal flowchart symbols on page 83. In the space provided under Activity 3.5, draw a flowchart of the identified process. Ask yourself the questions presented at the beginning of this section. In the past, have you trained the students on this process? Do you have clearly posted flowcharts? A flowchart is a picture of a process. A picture is worth a thousand words. Think about it. Is it your purpose that the students are able to follow the procedure without you?

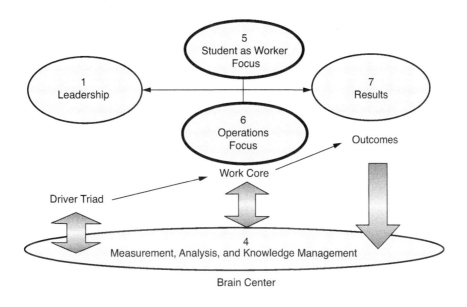

Figure 3.12 The line from leaders to results.

Table 3.1 Examples of noninstructional processes.

Pre-K, kindergarten, SPED (contained)	Elementary grades	Middle or high school
School day	School day	Start of class
Lavatory use	Transitions to recess, special classes	End-of-class process
Transitions to recess, special classes	End-of-day process	Homework
End-of-day process	Transition from one subject to another	Make-up work or tests due to absence
Transition from one subject to another	Homework	Attendance and tardy
Moving through school to cafeteria or playground	Lunch selection/payments for field trips, and so on	
	Make-up work or tests due to absence	
Other	**Other**	**Other**
Physical education	**Music**	**Art**
Start of class	Start of class	Start of class
End of class	Transition back to class (elementary)	End of class
Safety procedures	End of class (middle/high school)	Getting out and putting away supplies
Getting/putting away equipment	Getting out and putting away music	Safety procedures
Attendance and tardy	Handling of instruments	Cleaning up work area
	Attendance and tardy	Attendance and tardy
Other	**Other**	**Other**
Vocational or career classes	**Lab classes**	**Media centers/labs**
Start or end of class	Safety procedures	Safety procedures
Safety procedures	Getting/putting away supplies and equipment	Getting/putting away materials
Getting/putting away equipment	Setting up experiments	Turning on/off computers
Attendance and tardy	Attendance and tardy	Saving files and projects
Getting/putting away materials	Make-up work due to absences	Checking out books, software, videos, and so on
Project work		Book, video, software return process
Make-up work due to absences		
Other	**Other**	**Other**

Process	Process requirements	Success measure(s)	Acceptable tolerance	Quality control strategies: what, who, how often
Example: Start of class	• Minimize lost instructional time • Start the day on a positive note	• Time it takes for all students to be ready to learn	• 15 seconds or less after bell rings	• Flowchart posted in room • Students receive training on process • Timed by teacher or designee each day for one month; thereafter 2× week for two months • Run chart of time posted in class

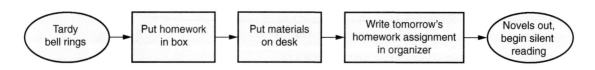

Figure 3.13   Flowchart a simple process.

Activity 3.4   Break Down a Noninstructional Process.

Directions: Complete this chart for one noninstructional classroom process.

Process	Process requirements	Success measure(s)	Acceptable tolerance	Quality control strategies: what, who, how often

Activity 3.5   Flowchart Practice.

Directions: Draw a flowchart of a noninstructional process here.

An Approach to Reduce Transition Time for Pre-K–1, ELL or SPED Inclusion Students

Create and hang process flowcharts to optimize instructional time and minimize classroom management problems.

Materials needed:

- Heavyweight poster board in several colors
- Paper clips
- Lightweight ribbon
- Markers

- Brass brackets (optional)
- Scissors
- Ruler
- Paper clockfaces (optional)

Steps:

1. Draw each process step on different colored sheets of heavy poster board. The optimal size is no larger than 12 inches long; otherwise, the poster board may not support its weight.

2. Arrange the steps in correct order.

3. Open the paper clips to create an S-hook and puncture a hole centered in the top and bottom of each poster board step.

4. Thread the S-hook through one hole and close it; then thread the bottom half through the next process step. Close the ends.

5. Continue hooking process steps together.

6. If there is a feedback loop, gently thread a piece of ribbon through the side of the decision diamond and back to the step that indicates where to regroup. Gently tie the ribbon on the edge of that step.

7. Poke a hole in the first process step with a heavy paper clip and use that to hang the flowchart in the classroom.

An Approach for Nonreaders:

1. Color-code the process steps to the activity. For example, yellow indicates reading, orange indicates math, green indicates recess, and so on.

2. To help students become self-directed, glue a small round clockface to each side of the process step. Use brackets to "set the clock" for start and stop times.

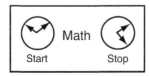

3. Hook the steps together as described above using paper clip S-hooks.

4. Take photos and/or draw pictures of the activity on the poster board at each step.

Design of Instructional Processes

Keep in mind that the way key classroom processes (Figure 1.7, page 9) are designed and used contributes immensely to the results. Whether the workers (students) are able to function in a system traditionally organized entirely by the teacher is the other part of the puzzle.

What is the product of education? Teachers who are biased about using a management model that has been successful in business use this as a hot-button issue. They argue, "Since we don't produce widgets, we can't standardize our processes. Business models don't work for education." This is an excuse for not being interested or willing to use a Baldrige-based approach, indicating a lack of understanding of systems and the continuous improvement approach. Let's be clear about the product of education.

> *The product of education is the total of all skills + abilities + knowledge + wisdom students have when they leave your class, grade, or school.*

Using Baldrige does not imply that innovation or creativity needs to be stifled. In fact, agility is a must, but first things first. *All students* must master the fundamental skills required for success in the twenty-first century as discussed in Chapter 1 and referencing the works of Tony Wagner and Daniel Pink. All the research points to the fact that remediation and drill doesn't dramatically improve results, so teachers must find other ways to reach children who are below grade level. Most certainly, we do not believe that teachers ought to focus on *teaching to the test* rather than facilitating learning and critical thinking. So, what can be done? How would a teacher create a process that reduces variation in student work and results without stifling creativity? First, you must understand that differentiating instruction to meet diverse learning needs is a must. How might you do that? Giving students options for how they want to learn creates immediate buy-in, and students take greater pride in learning.

Figure 3.14 is an example of instructional flowcharts used by Community Consolidated School District 15 (CCSD 15) in Palatine, Illinois, when they received the Baldrige Award in 2003. This school district's board goals were set at 90% of all students who attended school for one year meeting or exceeding grade-level standards on the Illinois state test or the Iowa Test of Basic Skills (ITBS). At first the teachers complained loudly that it was an impossible goal. But district administrators persisted, helping by providing professional development, and ultimately adopting a standard process across all schools. Within two years they achieved their goal.

Activity 3.6 asks you to compare your instructional process with that of CCSD 15. Activity 3.7 gives you the opportunity to put one of your instructional processes under a microscope by drawing a flowchart and looking for any "muddy points."

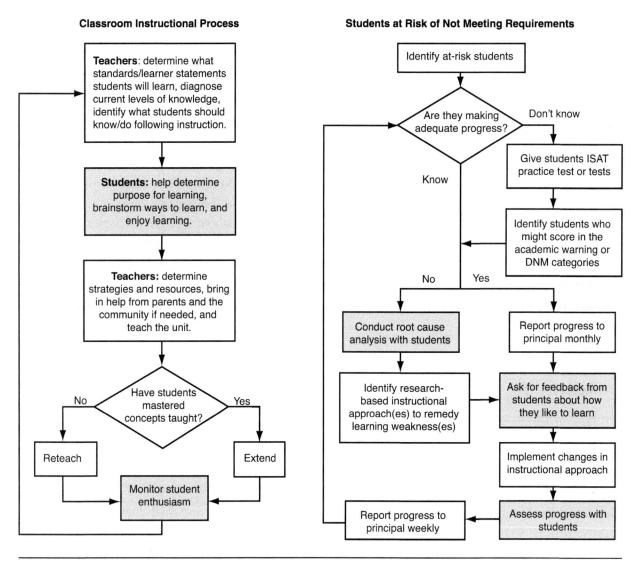

Figure 3.14 CCSD 15 instructional and at-risk process flowcharts.

Helpful Tips for flowcharting:

- Use one sticky note per process step and arrange the steps in correct order before finalizing the flowchart.

- Ask a friend or your students to move through the process in the order steps are arranged to make certain no steps were left out.

- When everyone agrees on the process, have each student copy it, post it prominently in the room, and measure as noted in your design.

- Chart the results.

MULTI-VOTING

What

Multi-voting is a prioritization tool. It helps the group reach consensus. This tool allows everyone to have a "voice" in the decision-making process.

How

1. Explain the tool and the benefits of it to the group.

2. Items to be multi-voted on may come from brainstorming, an affinity process, the items listed on a cause-and-effect diagram, or a simple list.

3. Ask the group to study the list and delete duplicates or combine "like" ideas before voting.

4. The number of votes per person depends on the group size and brainstormed items. Large groups = fewer votes, but at least three per person. Many ideas and a small group = four votes per person.

5. Determine the method of voting (colored markers, colored dots, dimes/nickels/pennies, and so on).

6. Assign a value to the method of voting, for example, red dot = 3 points, yellow dot = 2 points, blue dot = 1 point.

7. Explain the voting procedure. Members may distribute their votes any way they choose. All the votes can go to one item if a person feels it is the single most important. Votes may also be split up among several items.

8. *Members silently vote* one at a time, placing the appropriate symbols next to their prioritized choices.

9. Add the point value of all votes for each item and determine the rank value of items on the list.

10. Record the results and discuss.

When

• Consensus is the desired outcome of any decision

• Some students are shy and would be overpowered by more vocal, assertive students

• It is necessary to determine from the group's perspective the most significant cause of something, or

• There is a desire to have students learn prioritization skills

Example: Field Trip Suggestions

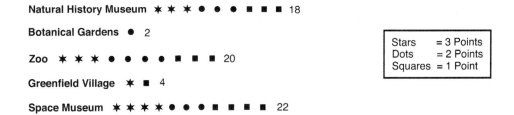

Natural History Museum ✶ ✶ ✶ ● ● ● ■ ■ ■ 18

Botanical Gardens ● 2

Zoo ✶ ✶ ✶ ● ● ● ● ■ ■ ■ 20

Greenfield Village ✶ ■ 4

Space Museum ✶ ✶ ✶ ✶ ● ● ● ■ ■ ■ ■ 22

Stars   = 3 Points
Dots   = 2 Points
Squares = 1 Point

Example: Combine Cause-and-Effect with Multi-Voting—Find #1 Root Cause

This example comes from the results of a cause-and-effect diagram on "why homework is not turned in." The teacher decided to chunk the "assignments" sub-cause responses and ask students to multi-vote only on this group. In this example, students indicated the root cause was *boring homework assignments.*

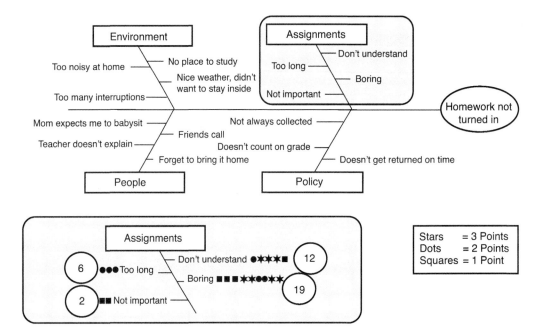

Stars   = 3 Points
Dots   = 2 Points
Squares = 1 Point

FLOWCHART

What

A *flowchart* is a picture of a process. There are three different types of flowcharts:

- Process flowchart shows only the process steps

- Deployment flowchart shows process steps and who's responsible for each

- Deployment/time flowcharts add the anticipated timeline to the chart

Flowcharts can be very complex, showing every small detail of each step of the process, or not as complex, showing only the major steps. When a team selects a less complex approach to flowcharting a process, care must be taken to ensure that everyone understands the smaller tasks behind each major process step.

How

1. Determine the process start and stop points.

2. List all the steps in the process. (It is recommended that this be done using sticky notes or on a separate piece of paper.)

3. Put the steps in proper sequence.

4. Determine the nature of each step, that is, is it a task or a decision? Must a report or form be completed?

5. Use the universal flowchart symbols on the following page to draw the chart.

6. Connect each step with an arrow.

7. If a decision is required, state the question so that it yields a "yes" or "no" response. If the answer is "yes," draw a straight arrow to the next step. If the answer is "no," decide what step must be looped back to in order to resolve the issue.

8. When there are multiple tasks behind a key task, draw shadow boxes to indicate the other tasks.

When

Use flowcharts:

- When devising a new process

- When you desire to study the effectiveness or efficiency of an existing process

- When training new employees or new students, or

- When a "picture" would help everyone involved realize the interdependency of individuals and/or departments to accomplish a complex task

The Universal Flowcharting Symbols

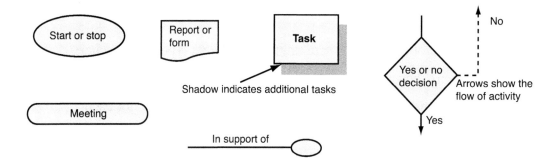

Example: Toothbrushing Process

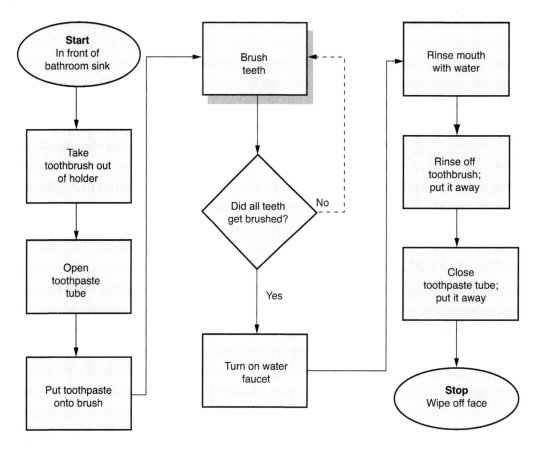

Example: A Day in a Kindergarten Classroom

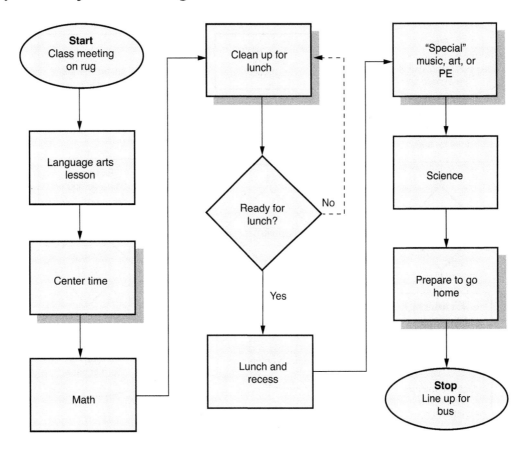

Example: A Writing Assignment

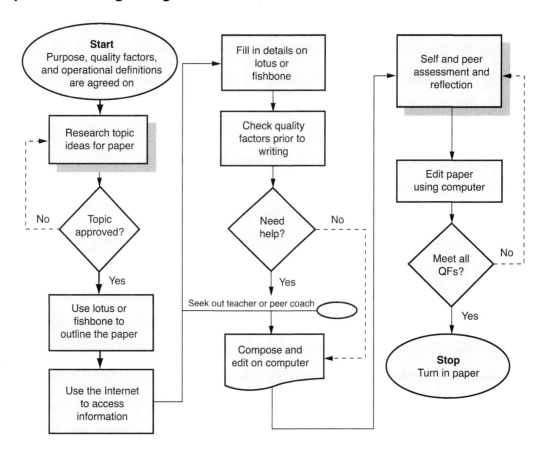

HOW TO CREATE YOUR PERSONAL VISION AND MISSION STATEMENTS—SECONDARY

Vision Statement

1. Think about how you would want us to describe you as both a learner and a person to your seventh-grade teacher. What adjectives (describing words) would you want us to use?

   List three to five of those words: _____

   _____

   _____

2. Now put at least three of these words into a statement (sentence). Keep in mind that you are creating a "vision" for yourself. This is how you want others to "see" you. Here is an idea of how to start your statement:

   I am a student who is _____

Mission Statement

1. Look at your academic goal for this quarter and your vision statement. How are you going to reach this goal and exemplify (demonstrate) your vision for yourself? Brainstorm three to five actions that you can take to help you achieve your goal.

   _____

   _____

2. Now include at least three of these words into a statement (sentence) that explains how you will reach your academic goal and demonstrate your vision for yourself.

   Here is an idea of how to start your statement:

   I will _____ in order to

   _____

4

Management by Fact

CONVERSATION WITH THE TEACHER

There is some irony in the fact that data have been used to denigrate public school teachers and the work they do, causing frustration, fear, and some of the best to give up and quit the profession. Yet, without data there is no way to understand what is really happening or how to analyze the root cause of problems. It is not easy to let down your guard and become comfortable with the notion that you need to rely less on intuition and canned curricula and much more on data analysis to make decisions about instructional approaches and activities—but it must be done.

Here is a word of advice to those of you who find data analysis a daunting task, made only worse when your math-oriented teammates appear to breeze through it all. Take the time to persevere with the challenges this chapter presents. You will not only feel a strong sense of accomplishment, but this may well be the most significant learning curve of your career.

Do you ever think about the consequences of moving ahead while leaving some students behind? Consider the problem that would arise if you were a first-grade teacher with a class of 20, and at the end of the year pass along five students who do not know all their sight words or how to read simple sentences. This leaves the second-grade teacher with 25% or more rework from the first day. If the second-grade teacher does not get all the students up to grade level in math or reading or writing, the third-grade teacher has that much more rework to do. As this pattern continues through the grades, each successive teacher inherits exponentially that much more rework, until finally the learning gaps are so large that it is nearly impossible to close them. This is magnified as students leave elementary school for middle school and then high school. If they don't have the requisite skills, students begin to feel that they can't succeed and stop trying. Dropouts begin in the early grades, and acting-out is often a precursor to dropping out. Each teacher has a responsibility to break the cycle, but how? This chapter will help answer that question.

Many teachers have shared that they spend about six weeks at the start of each school year reviewing what students were supposed to have learned the previous year. The good news is that you're learning about where the gaps in mastery exist. The bad news is that six weeks is a long time to catch everyone up before you can start the grade-level curriculum. Can you imagine the joy of teaching and the saved instructional time if the new class of students had truly mastered the essential skills? You must understand the spread of variation within your class and take appropriate action. This assures that students who are behind make significant gains, and those who are already at grade level are able to significantly improve too. It is simply not acceptable to serve some students at the expense of others.

Unfortunately, we have witnessed many teachers who rely totally on the District Accountability Office or school data person to analyze the data from their students. While we are sympathetic to the time and stress on teachers, we know that unless you dig down and analyze the results of your own students, the impact is lessened. During the data analysis phase you can reflect on the strategies used to teach each skill and take notice of gender differences and subgroups' responses. It will be an eye-opening experience, one that will affirm the strategy or inform you of the necessity to change your approach. Granted, each class is different, but patterns are important.

Aside from analyzing results data to inform planning for the upcoming year, you're going to need a plan for deciding what in-process (leading indicators) data to collect and share with the class. Get used to transparency as it is your friend and allows students to become active partners as you improve the instructional process.

If you have no experience with data analysis, this chapter may intimidate you. The bottom line is that you're learning. Don't be hard on yourself, but keep putting one foot in front of the other. Within a relatively short amount of time you're going to realize that you can not live without analyzing data. Good luck and enjoy the adventure.

In this chapter you will learn:

- The necessity for teachers to know how to analyze results (summative) data and use them to plan for a new school year

- How to use a case study approach to learn the PDSA process

- How to apply some appropriate tools to use at specific steps of the data analysis process

- The importance of data analysis and looking at data from more than one perspective

- How to establish a measurement plan

- The difference between *in-process* measures (leading indicators) and *outcome* measures

- How to create a class data wall

- About your second most important internal customer—the next teacher in line

ANALYZE RESULTS DATA (YEAR OR SEMESTER END) AND USE THEM TO PLAN

As a routine part of planning prior to the start of a new school year, we hope that your school or district administration provides you with the results data from any state or national standardized test(s), including an item analysis of the error types your students made the previous year. If, however, that information is not provided, at a minimum you will want to request the results of your class and grade level. If you teach middle or high school you're also going to want to review (by item) any end-of-course exams. For those who teach K–2, do an in-depth analysis of reading and math assessments that were administered during the year. Any summative assessments can (and should) be thoroughly analyzed prior to the start of the next school year. In essence, we are talking about the Brain Center—Measurement, Analysis, and Knowledge Management (category 4) of the Baldrige framework. From Figure 4.1 you can see how important it is for the leader as it forms the beginning of knowledge that is fed into any strategic planning process. Make no mistake about it, unless you are brave enough to look, analyze, and *own* your students' results, you will never be able to make informed decisions about how to improve instruction so future students can be more successful.

> In an ideal world, you will share your students' results with the next teacher in line. This gives each teacher 20/20 vision about gaps in knowledge among students in the class. Imagine how this information would help when preparing lessons and determining warm-up activities designed to close gaps and cement foundational knowledge necessary to succeed. The value-added exceeds any embarrassment a teacher may feel and acts as an added incentive to "do it right the first time."

If the test has been administered online, check with your testing coordinator to see if reports can be generated immediately after the class has finished the test. The deeper you can drill down in

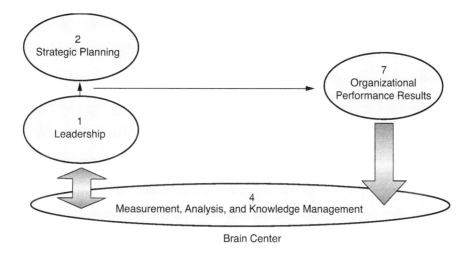

Figure 4.1   Analyzed results feed into strategic planning.

the test itself, the greater your ability to understand what happened. We want to remind you that Dr. Deming was adamant—*your system yields exactly the results you planned for.* Teachers don't intentionally plan for students to fail, or to fall short of expectations; however, some teachers may not adequately "connect the dots" between their instructional approach, learning activities, student engagement, and learning results.

If you look at the results with an open mind—as a facilitator of learning, without prejudgment about individual students—you will discover which methods worked, what strategies and activities were the most powerful, and specifically what must change in order for more students to succeed. Lack of data analysis means making decisions to change based on intuition and not fact. This assumption is always dangerous because you may end up tinkering with the system and make matters worse. Here is a situation where you must embrace the two quality principles—think first of "I am response-able to the success of the class." This alerts you that it is your duty to *uncover the barriers*, while the principle, "I am responsible for my own learning" reminds you that once you have seen the barriers, you must learn how to remove them. This requires great courage! Avoid the temptation to convince yourself that "those students" are the problem. It takes a partnership between teacher and each student to forge ahead. Also, the teacher has to be open to the possibility that each student can help change the system so that everyone can succeed.

Improving the K–12 Situation Is Urgent!

This can not be overstated. Findings from a major study done by the Broad Foundation (http://broadeducation.org/about/crisis_stats.html) reveal the following:

- American students rank 25th in math and 21st in science compared to students in 30 industrialized countries.

- America's top math students rank 25th out of 30 countries when compared with top students elsewhere in the world.

- By the end of eighth grade, U.S. students are two years behind in the math being studied by peers in other countries.

- Sixty-eight percent of eighth graders can't read at their grade level, and most will never catch up.

As referenced in the Broad study, students who leave school early, who don't gain the skills needed to become productive citizens, who turn to illegal means to survive, who cope with problems by engaging in antisocial and/or illegal activities, who are disinterested and/or choose to be uninvolved in the basic responsibilities of citizenship, have the potential to bring our nation down economically. It is the responsibility of each teacher, school, and district administrator to become "chief learners," to put together all the forces of passion and desire, and to promote fact-based, continuous improvement of the instructional process. No one can pass off the responsibility by playing the shame and blame game. If this sounds harsh, it is, because of our deep desire to make a difference in the lives of each and every student.

> *It is not about shame or blame. It is not about the "wrong" or "bad" students or "disinterested," "uncooperative" parents.*
>
> It is about your desire to become a true facilitator of learning and to realize that 90% or more of any problems with the results are because of faulty processes or systems.
>
> *Who creates the system? Leadership (the person in charge).*
>
> You are the leader in the classroom. Therefore, you are the one who must step up to the data and learn how to analyze it from more than one point of view until you know what it really says.

PDSA: ANNUAL PLANNING FOR THE NEW SCHOOL YEAR

An Overview

Plan–do–study–act (PDSA) is a scientific process widely used in Baldrige-based organizations. It is one approach, and we believe that if you review your state's science standards you will find something similar to this: "students will use the scientific approach to solve problems." You can immediately see the value of teaching students PDSA, and the carryover for the rest of their lives. The seven-step process is broken down in the following manner:

Plan has four steps:

1. Define the system (or process) under study.

2. Assess the current situation (collect data from multiple perspectives). Assessment of the current situation is more powerful when data from at least three to five years are used. In this way you can see any trends or patterns. This unveils your opportunities for improvement.

3. Analyze root cause.

4. Write an improvement theory. (An *if/then* statement, or a hypothesis.)

Do—Put the improvement theory into place.

Study—Chart the new data. Did the improvement theory work?

Act—Standardize the improvements and identify a new improvement opportunity, or go back to root cause (if there was no significant improvement).

We like to say that *plan* and *study* are "married" to each other. They go hand in hand and require one to *stop,* learn what the data are telling you, and understand root cause before making decisions about going forward. Similarly, *do* and *act* are married. These are action steps. Remember, it is a scientific process; you must be true to the process and avoid skipping steps. The PDSA process is deliberate but powerful.

Practice PDSA with a Case Study

We believe that the best way to learn the PDSA process and the tools associated with it is through an example. During this case study, assume the role of Lee Brown, a fifth grade teacher at Washington Elementary School. We've added *notes* within the activity for added clarification where needed. Once you go through this PDSA process, and practice using the tools, use your own data to analyze the results of your students.

Plan Step 1—Define the System (Background Information)

Your school is facing some difficult issues with poor student learning results, levels that do not meet state guidelines. On the basis of the most recent state standards test, 34% of all students did not pass and (no surprise) the free/reduced lunch subgroup had the highest failure rate. Attendance is below the expected levels, which may account for some of the low achievement scores, but we can not be certain of this. All we can surmise is that when students are not in school, they miss the benefit of instruction. *What we don't know is whether or not the instruction is effective.*

Your principal has asked you to come in and analyze the test results from your last year's class. You've been teaching in this school for four years, and the principal has given you the data from all previous years.

The results (on page 96) indicate a gap between action plans, instructional strategies, and professional development. Your principal recognizes the problem and is determined to close the achievement gap between subgroups and increase the rates of learning to meet the state standards and grade-level requirements.

The principal has asked you to work with your grade-level peers (professional learning community) to analyze the data for all students after you look at your own class.

The Project Statement. Use a fact-based, data-enlightened approach to improve instructional strategies and activities that result in higher student achievement.

Plan Step 2—Assess the Current Situation

Begin by analyzing results (outcomes) data. These data are the result of previous planning—units, lessons, activities, which were your key instructional strategies. These data inform you, and school/district administrators, about the effectiveness and efficiency of your system. The next teacher in line is a key customer and, as such, will inherit your results, so you ignore this at your own peril. Continuous improvement to increase achievement among all students *is* the personal and professional responsibility of each teacher. This is where the rubber meets the road! This is at the heart of learning to improve so more students can successfully master the skills required and then go beyond to meet the challenges of the twenty-first century. Activity 4.1 allows you to practice using some of the tools.

Activity 4.1   Practice using a run chart.

Directions: Use a *run chart* for these data. Use a different-colored marker for each subgroup in the tables on the next page, with a legend at the side. Place each teacher's data on a separate chart so you can compare the results. Scale the chart as shown in the example below. Each set of data will have four points. Connect the dots for each subgroup.

Draw a line on the chart to indicate any major professional development training.

Put each teacher's data on a separate chart.

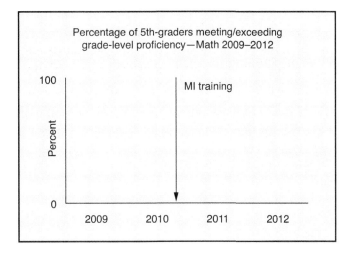

See the run chart instructions in the toolbox on page 120.

Note: We are aware that many educators refer to such a chart as a line graph. Page 273 shows that method #1 may resemble a run chart, while method #2 shows multiple data points and the spread of variation. Both (run and line) display data showing what happens to a process over time. Feel free to interchange names for this tool, if you like, for method #1.

State math results by ethnicity and subgroup—2008–2011. The following are mobility rates for fifth-graders at Washington Elementary School. After you chart the data, reflect on the degree to which you think student mobility rates impacted the results.

- 2008–09—10%

- 2009–10—10%

- 2010–11—17%

- 2011–12—23%

Continued

In 2010, teachers had a week of Math Investigations training. In 2011, each teacher received two hours of Math Investigations mentoring.

Teacher	Washington Elementary School			
Brown, Lee	2009	2010	2011	2012
Native American	10%	19%	11%	25%
White	43%	60%	75%	87%
Hispanic	21%	50%	65%	67%
Black	40%	51%	55%	53%
Free/reduced	35%	40%	48%	50%
SPED	17%	20%	20%	20%
ESOL	35%	30%	33%	37%

Teacher	Washington Elementary School			
Cameron, Sue	2009	2010	2011	2012
Native American	50%	50%	25%	50%
White	38%	74%	85%	93%
Hispanic	28%	49%	70%	79%
Black	37%	51%	65%	79%
Free/reduced	30%	60%	73%	75%
SPED	20%	20%	45%	65%
ESOL	33%	50%	49%	56%

These results are useful for planning for the next school year. The questions to ask are:

- Each fall when you look at your students, how many do you expect to meet/ exceed grade-level requirements? Have your expectations been met each year?

- How well do students in the subgroups perform? Are you closing the achievement gap?

- How well do your students perform relative to other students in the same grade level? Those in each subgroup?

- What professional development (if any) have you received? In general, what were the objectives of the professional development? When did you receive the professional development? Was there any follow-up coaching/mentoring?

- To what extent did you put the newly learned professional development skills into place in your classroom each year?

- How did students in the subgroups respond to the new approach(es)?

- Have the ethnic groups in your classes performed at about the same level as all students in that grade?

- Do you know the preferred learning styles of these student groups?

It is imperative to chart these results as they begin to provide a picture (albeit incomplete) about the effectiveness of your instructional process. It's also important to see your data charted alongside that of your grade-level peers. If you work in a large school district, it would also be informative to compare the results of your class with those of students in other schools of similar demographics, free/reduced lunch, and mobility.

Reflect: Speculate on Washington Elementary School's fifth-grade results. What, in your opinion, would account for these results? What might explain the variation in results for these two classes? Write your thoughts here.

-
-
-
-

As you begin to analyze your own results, respond to the questions at the end of Activity 4.1. Write down your responses to each question.

At the same time, these data do not enlighten you sufficiently to know *what must change*. To gain some insight into this question, you'll need to "drill down" into the data and look at results by reporting category (or strand). Activity 4.2 is a partial example from Virginia. *Note that looking at the results for all students is informative, yet not sufficient to understand specifically where the achievement gaps reside.*

Plan: Step 3—Analyze Root Cause

Look first at the state test trend results from Activity 4.1 overall and discern what you are looking at. A run chart shows a clear picture of a process over time. In this case, what do you notice about both teachers' results? Are there any major changes up or down, year-to-year for *both* teachers that you can see? If so, you're going to want to recall any major initiatives and/or professional development, mentoring, or other events (for example, the state may have changed the test or testing company) that could explain the change in results. If the state made a major change in the test and/or testing company—or if your school simply changed tests—then it is impossible to know how much growth has really taken place. The best thing to do is mark the change on the chart indicating such.

Now take a look at the Number and Number Sense reporting category tables from Activity 4.2, then look at all the charts side by side. What do you see that is important and of concern? What do you see from looking at the subgroup trend data that gives you a different perspective? What would you have thought if you only saw the score for *all* in each reporting category? This level of detail provides important information to teachers that might otherwise go unnoticed.

Many teachers ask why they need to create charts when they can see the data in table format. Charting brings the data into sharper view. All this is made more powerful when you work closely and collaboratively with your peers as part of a professional learning community. For example, if students from a different class attained greater levels of achievement, the opportunity to listen and learn has enormous potential for your success.

Understand Process Capability. Looking at the hard data is necessary but not sufficient to know *what* to change. Are your classroom processes capable of yielding the desired results? Every year (or semester) you work with a different set of students. Therefore, it is natural for teachers to claim

Activity 4.2 "Drilling down" into data for analysis.

Directions: Create a new chart for reporting category. Scale the chart with the total number of problems in the reporting category. Use an arrow to show the direction of improvement.

You're going to want to get a visual picture of improvement by reporting category. Use a *bar* graph to chart these results. In this situation, chart the number of incorrect answers by subgroup.

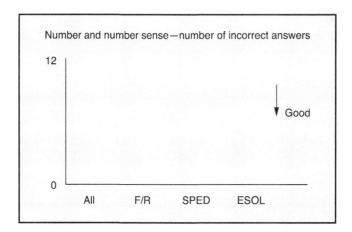

Teacher: Brown, Lee		School: Washington Elementary School				Grade: 5		Reporting category: Number and Number Sense			
	Number of questions in RC	Average number correct in RC				Average number incorrect in RC				Average change in incorrect answers over four years	
Year		All	F/R	SPED	ESOL	All	F/R	SPED	ESOL	All	F/R	SPED	ESOL
2008–09	12	7.8	5.5	3.5	6.7	4.2	6.5	8.5	5.3	–	–	–	–
2009–10	12	9.0	6.3	4.0	7.5	3.0	5.7	8.0	4.5	–1.2	–.8	–.5	–.8
2010–11	12	9.5	8.0	4.0	7.5	2.5	4.0	8.0	4.5	–1.7	–2.5	–.5	–.8
2011–12	12	10.0	8.0	4.5	7.0	2.0	4.0	7.5	5.0	–2.2	–2.5	–1.0	–.3

Teacher: Cameron, Sue		School: Washington Elementary School				Grade: 5		Reporting category: Number and Number Sense			
	Number of questions in RC	Average number correct in RC				Average number incorrect in RC				Average change in incorrect answers over four years	
Year		All	F/R	SPED	ESOL	All	F/R	SPED	ESOL	All	F/R	SPED	ESOL
2008–09	12	8.2	5.3	3.6	6.7	3.8	6.7	8.4	5.3	–	–	–	–
2009–10	12	9.0	8.2	4.1	7.8	3.0	3.8	7.9	4.2	–.8	–2.9	–.5	–1.1
2010–11	12	10.0	9.2	5.8	8.9	2.0	2.8	6.2	3.1	–1.8	–3.9	–2.2	–2.2
2011–12	12	10.2	9.5	7.9	8.8	1.8	2.5	4.1	3.2	–2	–4.2	–4.2	–2.1

"foul" when districts hold them accountable for student learning results. A teacher dedicated to BBQ would want to know and, in fact, has a need to know whether or not his/her system is capable of improved student learning results. While there is a statistical formula you can use to determine whether your key processes are capable of reaching the standards you set, you can deduce this from looking at the results of your classes over time on any normed test, end-of-year exam, and unit test. Another problem is that states change the "cut" score, and sometimes change the testing company and test format. This makes it much more difficult to analyze the effectiveness of your instruction. If this is the situation in which you find yourself, a better approach (and a workable one) is to study the item analyses of *your* students from at least the previous three years. It is even better if you have access to this information from the previous five years. If the analyses provide demographic information about each student, that will allow you to chunk students from each subgroup. This will give you a more focused and accurate picture of what has happened in your classroom. If you continue to drill down into the data and look at the results by gender, you may receive additional insight that otherwise would have not been revealed.

We want to caution you not to make excuses. There is simply no time for this. There are many examples of schools with very high rates of free/reduced lunch students and high numbers of non–English speakers who have closed the achievement gap. It is beyond time to realize that it is the system (not students or parents) that is responsible for poor learning results. You, as the leader, control/manage/lead the system, so let's move on and learn how to find the processes that yielded the results.

The learning gaps emanate from one or more of your key processes. To take advantage of the knowledge gained from data/gap analysis, it's necessary to go back and take a closer look at the key processes that led to these results. Here are some key processes that must be analyzed and linked with the hard data:

Analyze the previous year's lesson plans for the following:

- Alignment with the content standards

- Ways the concepts/standards were addressed in your lesson plans

- Cross-reference student test scores by subgroup and the item analysis with the methods you used to teach the content standards

Analyze the learning activities for the following:

- Relevance to "real life," requiring students to apply basic skills to a different situation

- Requiring rigor and higher-level thinking skills

- Engaging, stimulating, and avoiding repetition (as opposed to "kill and drill")

- Engaging students as part of a group or in partner learning

- Making use of more learning styles, including body kinesthetic, musical/rhythmic, and so on

- Employing a variety of graphic organizers

 *Analyze the ways in which you organized students to do the work, and the connection between this and student results:*

- Reflect on the item analysis you've completed for your students and link together the way students were organized to learn the skills. Your assessment must include effectiveness (how many students learned the skills) and efficiency (how quickly did they learn).

- Do you engage students in partner activities, group activities, and independent activities? How do you determine who works with whom?

 *Analyze the effectiveness and efficiency of your classroom management process.*

- How much instructional time each day (or class period) was lost due to student disinterest or off-task behavior.

 *Analyze your assessment process.*

- Do you use frequent formative assessments?

- Are the unit assessments fully aligned with what was taught and with the state requirements?

- If you use rubrics, are they clearly understood and written so students can see what is required to move from one level to the next?

You may decide there are other key processes that need to be analyzed, and if so, good for you. It is an indicator of your commitment to BBQ. Activity 4.3 asks you to put what you learned about your processes into a cause-and-effect diagram.

For the purposes of learning PDSA, let's assume that your learning activities have the greatest impact on your results. Upon reflection, you've realized that none of your learning activities require any movement. This will be your number one root cause, and the basis for your improvement theory.

It's difficult to do this alone, but in the real world we hope you will work together with peers and/or some students to determine the true root cause and also brainstorm solutions. This is because they have a perspective that you don't. Working with peers would be better than doing it in isolation, but it is much more powerful to have your customers (students) at the table with you.

Plan: Step 4—Write an Improvement Theory

Before writing the improvement theory, you'll need to consider as many specific strategies as you can to eliminate the number one root cause—*lack of movement in learning activities.* Activity 4.4

Activity 4.3   Using a cause-and-effect diagram

Directions: Draw five major "bones" on the diagram as shown here. Assign a key process to each bone. As you reflect on each process, put the cause under the appropriate process. This is best done with your grade-level peers, but not absolutely necessary. The reflection part is what is important. Once all your thoughts are on the cause-and-effect diagram, circle the one cause that seems to stand out as being the most prevalent problem for you.

Use a cause-and-effect diagram to note causes—or potential causes—of process problems leading to the current results. See instructions for a cause-and-effect diagram on page 118.

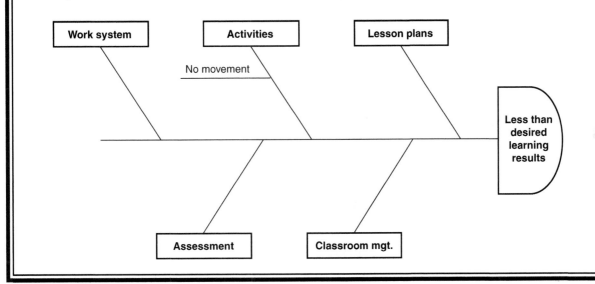

asks you to write an improvement theory. This means you'll brainstorm (use your creative abilities) ways to change your lessons to incorporate movement and then choose two things you are willing to commit to doing for the next school year. These become the improvement theory.

Implement PDSA with Fidelity. The implementation process is going to impact the results, so you'd be wise to systematically track progress along the way. These are in-process data and are leading indicators that allow you to monitor revisions to the process. Using the example, potential *in-process* (leading indicators—predictors of future success) measures would include:

- Number of body/kinesthetic and musical/rhythmic activities per week

- Quiz test results—weekly

- Student satisfaction/enthusiasm for learning/feedback

Do. Try Out the Improvement Theory

Follow the plan as specified. Keep data and chart it regularly.

Activity 4.4: Writing an improvement theory.

Directions: Based on all that you've learned in your analysis, write an improvement theory to eliminate the #1 root cause identified in Activity 4.3. This is a hypothesis—an *if/then* statement.

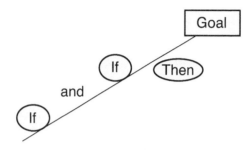

How will the success of the improvement theory be measured? Formative (leading indicators): weekly quiz, and *summative (lagging indicators):* end-of-year.

Example: *If* my lessons are more interesting and I expand the learning activities to include the use of body/kinesthetic and musical/rhythmic intelligences, *then* more students will achieve greater learning gains *as measured by weekly quizzes* and *the yearly state test.*

Study. Did the Improvement Theory Work?

You'll know the answer to this question when you complete a *data analysis* of the following year's test results. Results will confirm whether you understood the true root cause, and therefore your improvement theory worked, or you didn't understand the root cause and your strategies didn't work. Either way, you've learned something.

Keep in mind that a new set of students enters your class each year. If you'll notice, the improvement theory provides several formative assessments (see page 101). These indicators of future success allow the teacher to make midcourse corrections when the data show that many students are not learning at the desired rate.

The BBQ approach does not prescribe *how to change processes.* Your decisions will stem from what you learn from students, peers, and through research of best practice.

Act. Will You Standardize the Improvements?

After implementing the improvement theory during the year and analyzing the student learning results, a BBQ teacher will make decisions as to whether or not to continue with the changes that were made the previous year. If the results have improved, but still don't reach the expected goal, there is more room for improvement, and a focus group of students (those who were not fully successful, but who had good attendance) would be valuable to help you understand the root cause of their lackluster success. this This is how you use PDSA annually prior to planning for the next school year.

MONITOR THE CLASSROOM SYSTEM

To date, everything you've done is going to help, but the question remains, "How will you measure the effectiveness and efficiency of your classroom?" In what ways will you monitor the system throughout the school year to (1) assure that key processes are working effectively and efficiently and (2) predict success at the end of the year? How will you monitor performance throughout the school year? As Figure 4.2 shows, these are significant and important decisions as the Brain Center is vital to the Work Core. If you only collect data at the end of the course or school year (lagging indicators), it is too late for that group of students. You can, therefore, understand the significance of creating a formal measurement system that includes in-process, or leading, indicators. It is no surprise that schools and classrooms with leaders committed to regular monitoring of the system will reap the greatest rewards at the end of the school year. Occasional monitoring is not sufficient or appropriate if you expect to reach performance excellence. It simply won't happen! You must be able to analyze the effectiveness and efficiency of key instructional and classroom management processes routinely during the school year. You, as the leader, can agree to make midcourse corrections to instructional activities and the way students are organized to do their work—if you allow students to help you understand the issues/barriers that keep them from being successful.

It has been said that educators are data rich and information poor. This means that we collect data on everything but mostly *don't use it to inform the system*, and therefore lose opportunities to drive midcourse corrections that lead to improved results.

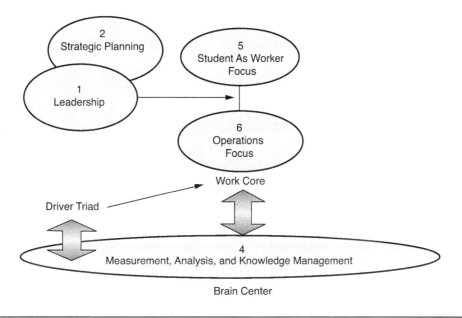

Figure 4.2   Measurement system ties the Driver Triad and Work Core.

> *Collect data only on those things you will use to help you improve. Many teachers track homework (for example) and yet never do anything with the data. For what purpose? Shame/blame students? Point out the obvious? If homework is important, then commit to improving the process and the homework itself so more students will be invested in completing it.*

Keep in mind the need for alignment from the school to each classroom, and follow the lead of your administrators in terms of school improvement goals and any districtwide goals. It stands to reason that you'll want/need to monitor district goals and school improvement plan (SIP) goals (as lagging indicators), but the major emphasis of a classroom measurement plan must be the leading indicators (best predictors of future success). Progress toward the district goals may be measured by unit test scores and/or quarterly assessments of state standards. These are examples of lagging indicators. Leading indicators allow the teacher to make midcourse corrections to build-in better results.

Your class measurement plan will include the broad spectrum of indicators across the content. For example, leading indicators of future reading success include comprehension, vocabulary, fluency, and phonemic awareness. Examples of key indicators of future math success include computing fluency, problem solving, logical reasoning, math operations, and math vocabulary.

Create a Class Measurement Plan

A complete classroom measurement system would include measures from category 3 (Customer Focus), including student satisfaction with class culture or climate, next teacher in line, and parent satisfaction; category 5 (Student as Worker Focus), student feedback on learning activities and the instructional process, materials used, and pacing; category 6 (Operations Focus); and other measures of effectiveness and efficiency such as cycle time, safety, transitions, and so on (see Table 4.1).

You also want to include a combination of hard data (things you can count, measure, time) and soft data (perception) in your measurement system. See the examples in Table 4.2 of leading/ lagging indicators for hard and soft data. The tables also give you suggestions for the frequency and best tool to use to understand the different types of data.

To get started, first determine what data to collect, how often you will collect it, and how the data will be analyzed and used to track and monitor daily operations. The measurement system, a central component of the Brain Center (category 4) of the Baldrige framework, informs the leadership about the efficiency and effectiveness of the system. Activity 4.5 suggests how you might want to organize your measurement system for your subject area.

See the classroom system diagram, Figure 1.7, for other key processes you're going to want to monitor. To learn more about leading indicators (in-process measures), check the examples provided in Table 4.2.

Table 4.1 A classroom system measurement plan.

	Key process	What will be collected	Tolerances	How often collected and studied	How will it be collected?	Who will collect the data?	How will it be used?
Noninstructional processes	Example: tardy	Number of students not ready to learn after bell	*HR* = More than 1 minute *Watch* = More than 15 seconds *OK* = Less than 15 seconds	Daily Studied monthly for trends	Paper/pencil Check sheet	Teacher or designated student	Relationship between tardy and learning; root cause analysis; if school-based problem, information presented to faculty
	Parent conferences	Number of parents who attend	*HR* = 50% or fewer *Watch* = 85%–51% *OK* = 86% or more	Fall and Spring At time of conferences	Paper/pencil Check against student list	Teacher	Planning two-way communication approach(es); improve listening/learning posts
Instructional processes	Writing	Score on prompt	*HR* = 70% at level 3 or less *Watch* = 85% at level 3 or less *OK* = 86% or more at level 3	Monthly Each time data are collected	Paper/pencil QF check sheet	Peer assessment	ID students who need specific help; make changes to student groups; assign peer tutors
	Reading comprehension	Number of correct responses to two implicit questions from short reading passage	*HR* = 30% of students give incorrect response *Watch* = 10–29% give incorrect response *OK* = Fewer than 10% give incorrect response	Daily for both	Student rapid response system	Teacher or aide	Assess overall class improvement; make midcourse corrections to instruction

HR = High risk

Table 4.2   Examples of in-process measures (leading indicators).

Type	What will be studied?	Measure	Tool used	Frequency	Tool used	Frequency
	Absenteeism	Number in class	Run chart	Daily		
	Tardy	Number late	Run chart	Daily		
	Learning gains	Regular quizzes on in-process measures (Example: vocabulary)	Class—line graph	Weekly	Student run chart	Weekly
		Portfolio rubrics	Histogram	Monthly		
		Pre-unit test	Histogram	As appropriate		
		Writing rubrics	Histogram	Monthly	Run chart	Monthly
	Homework	Number turned in on time and accurate	Run chart	Daily or weekly	Bar graph	Daily/weekly
	Relationship between homework and learning	Completed homework and weekly quiz grades	Scatter	Weekly or monthly		
		Completed homework and unit test grades	Scatter	As appropriate		
Hard data	Relationship between attendance and learning gains	Attendance data and pre-post gains	Scatter	As appropriate		
	Reading fluency	Number of words right on timed reading	Run chart	Bimonthly		
	Efficiency of learning	On-time completion of assignments	Line graph	As appropriate		
	Discipline issues (lost instructional time)	Type/frequency	Check sheet	Daily (specified period of time)	Pareto chart	As appropriate
	Failure	Number who fail a quiz or unit test	Run chart	As appropriate		

Table 4.2 *Continued.*

Type	What will be studied?	Measure	Tool used	Frequency	Tool used	Frequency
Soft data	Student satisfaction	Learning climate and rapport	Satisfaction surveys	Weekly		
	Student satisfaction	Effectiveness of resources	How effective were these resources, then Pareto chart of analysis	As appropriate		
	Student satisfaction	Learning activities	Plus/delta chart	Daily or weekly		
	Student satisfaction	Effectiveness of instruction	Fast feedback, then histogram of analysis	Daily		
	Student satisfaction	Effectiveness of teacher	Radar chart of QFs for teacher	Weekly		
	Parent satisfaction	Teacher effectiveness	Prioritization survey	October		
	Next teacher in line satisfaction	Students arrive with necessary skills	Satisfaction survey	Early Fall		
	Learning environment	Faculty and staff trust and respect for students	Student satisfaction survey	At report card time	Histogram	To follow up on survey
	Enthusiasm for learning	Student active engagement in learning	Enthusiasm/learning chart	Daily or weekly end of units		

Activity 4.5   Identify the key predictors of success for your grade or subject.

Content taught	Lagging indicator	Key predictors (leading indicators) tolerances are set for leading indicators
Example: Social studies	*State test results*	*Vocabulary*

Create a Class Dashboard

The power of this approach (measurement plan) is that it yields a dashboard that allows the leader to keep a close eye on the overall health of the organization, which, if used properly, will keep you from "tinkering" with the system. To become useful, though, you're going to need to set tolerance limits for each indicator. Tolerances are determined by you and generally based on three levels (okay, watch, or high risk). Many organizations use red–yellow–green flags to symbolize how well the system is working. See the example given in Figure 4.3.

Because you have set the tolerance level (below which you know you need to use PDSA to uncover process problems), a dashboard gives you peace of mind. You are never left in the dark—wondering, worrying about how well your classroom is running. Just like the dashboard of an automobile, the key indicators of overall health are right at your fingertips. Visibility—line of sight toward the vision and meeting district and school goals—becomes 20:20. Can you imagine the relief you will feel knowing that you have created a system designed for continual smooth running? Of course, this presumes that you not only create a dashboard (based on your measurement plan) but that you are also going to use it regularly.

The dashboard can be made visible for students, peers, the administration, and parents—honoring the concept of transparency—or it can be on your computer. If you decide this is best kept on your computer, then we urge you to include sharing the dashboard with students each month via Smart Board or on a poster hung prominently in the classroom. It's a sure bet that you'll want to share this with your PLC and administration. Our recommendation goes further—and that is to share it with parents, too. You may include the dashboard as information shared at back-to-school night, or include it in a newsletter or via e-mail each quarter at report card time. Many schools have a secure server that could allow parents to access the dashboard in their child's class. Parents can be very helpful if they know what you are measuring. The more transparent you are, the more focused everyone will be. It goes without saying that the dashboard would be shared with students at intervals during the school year, and certainly when one or more triggers is set off. We expect that in these situations, students will become part of the improvement effort—analyzing root cause and helping generate improvement ideas.

Learning goal	Measure	Number of items quizzed	Frequency	70:30 rule?	Tolerance levels		Method of charting
Reading comprehension	Number of students who score less than 80%	10 5 implicit 5 explicit	Monthly	No	High risk	5+	Histogram
					Watch	3–4	
					Okay	2 or fewer	

Safety goal	Measure		Frequency		Tolerance levels		Method of charting
Discipline referrals	Number of students sent to office		Monthly		High risk	3+	Bar graph
					Watch	1–2	
					Okay	0	

Goal		Sept	Oct	Nov	Jan	Feb	March	April
Learning:	Reading comprehension							
Safety:	Discipline referrals							

Figure 4.3 Partial example of a classroom dashboard.

In the event that your district doesn't have the advanced capabilities that allow you to create a system-wide dashboard, do not let this stop you. Excel will do just fine. The important thing is that you set it up with *tolerances*. Figure 4.4 shows a template of a dashboard matrix that could easily be developed in Excel or by hand. Here's a wonderful opportunity for you to exert leadership (demonstrate the principle *I am response-able to the success of my class and the school*) and work with your peers in a PLC to create a common grade-level dashboard, and/or at the secondary level, a content-specific dashboard. Some elements will be standard for all classrooms at any level (primary grades, intermediate grades, middle school, and high school); these are the noninstructional processes. Transitions, for example, are different at elementary than in secondary schools, hence the distinction is made.

Class Data Walls

Transparency and rapid access to data are two elements of a fact-based, continuous improvement model, for example, the BBQ management approach. As we've previously discussed, a significant role of the leader is to monitor the system. What is needed beyond the dashboard is a mechanism for students to *live the two principles* ("I am responsible for my own learning," and "I am response-able to the success of the class") and become partners with you in overall improvement to achieve the class goals and reach the vision. A data wall serves this purpose. It goes beyond any electronic or paper grade book. It is a visible and transparent birds-eye view of class progress. This is true because everyone involved (you, students, and any aides or resource teachers) has a much greater chance of meeting expectations if provided with the data they need and the means and opportunity to work as part of a team to resolve/eliminate any issues. With this in mind, it becomes clear that students must be considered as workers in the classroom system developed largely by teachers. As you've begun to develop a trusting relationship with your students as copartners in their educa-

Class Dashboard Matrix

Teacher name _____Susan Bedazzle_____   School year _____2012_____

Subject or grade _____5th Grade_____

Goals	Measure	# of items quizzed	Frequency	70:30 rule?	Tolerance levels		Method of charting
Learning							
					High risk		
					Watch		
					Okay		
					High risk		
					Watch		
					Okay		
Safety	**Measure**		**Frequency**		**Tolerance levels**		**Charting method**
					High risk		
					Watch		
					Okay		
Student satisfaction	**Measure**		**Frequency**		**Tolerance levels**		**Charting method**
					High risk		
					Watch		
					Okay		
Time on task	**Measure**		**Frequency**		**Tolerance levels**		**Charting method**
					High risk		
					Watch		
					Okay		
Parents as partners	**Measure**		**Frequency**		**Tolerance levels**		**Charting method**
					High risk		
					Watch		
					Okay		

Figure 4.4 Class dashboard matrix.

tion, you can appreciate how important it is to gain feedback and seek help to continuously improve the achievement of the entire class. A significant step in this direction is the development (and systematic use and upkeep) of a class data wall.

A data wall serves many purposes:

- As a reminder to everyone (students, teachers, parents, administrators) of the significant few things the class is working to improve.

- As a motivator for students, *provided* students are allowed to help improve the process.

- To inform everyone about the effectiveness and efficiency of key classroom processes.

- To show progress toward class academic goals as well as social skills (mission specific).

- Makes visible the cycles of improvement and teaches students the scientific process (plan–do–study–act).

- Supports critical thinking, and empowers students as partners in improvement.

- On any given day, any student in the class ought to be able to explain with clarity how well the class is progressing toward its goals and state any changes the class has agreed to use to improve. In many classrooms students are expected to take a leadership role when other adults come into the room. The empowerment of students is an enormous motivator for improvement.

The elements of a class data wall are:

- Class vision, mission, goals, and targets

- Quality factors for students and teacher

- Charts with data measuring progression toward each class goal

- Charts addressing other key noninstructional classroom processes such as safety, transitions, or attendance

- Radar charts measuring mission specificity and quality teacher factors

In short, a class data wall ought to be the hub of the classroom. It is a focal point for class meetings, discussions, and deep reflection on the "health" of the class. Some teachers have extensive space in their classrooms on which to post charts, and so on. Others have scarcely any space, and fire marshals monitor how much is on the walls. Some teachers choose to post data in the hall right outside the classroom. If that's the only space available to you—no problem—so long as you make a concerted effort to gather the entire class around the data wall at least weekly to reflect on progress and to offer suggestions about *what's working* and *what isn't*. Evidence of cycles of improvement using the PDSA process is especially important for everyone to see and celebrate.

Like everything in life, the effort you put into this is directly related to what you and the students will learn and get out of it. To work the system properly, you'll have to commit to starting a data wall and systematically maintaining it. Actually, it won't take that long, and once trained, students can do the charting and graphing. It's a good link to math standards, plus they enjoy being helpers.

As you begin your journey toward full deployment of a BBQ classroom, you'll probably start small. That's fine—just stay open to how you can grow and learn in this area because eventually you will realize you just can't live without it. Remember that you expect all students to achieve at the highest level, and that the class will work together as a high-performing team. Minimally, we would expect to see the class vision, mission, and at least two or three academic goals all signed by students and posted. Select one noninstructional process to monitor as well. In elementary schools this might be time for transitions as that seems to be where a lot of instructional time is lost. In middle and high schools it might be tardiness, or instructional time lost due to student disruptions.

You may choose to monitor homework turned in. If so, choose also to *analyze the data* and *keep an open mind when students give you feedback about* why *they don't do it or don't turn it in on time.* As the school year progresses, you would be smart to create a scatter diagram of grades on unit tests and the number of homework assignments turned in (detailed instructions can be found in the Toolbox section of Chapter 7). If there is little or no correlation, then you've got some thinking/explaining to do with the class. If there is a correlation, then the scatter diagram becomes a powerful tool for the class during a reflection time. In any case, unless you have developed a trusting relationship that values student time and opinions, there is little to be gained from trying to motivate students to do homework if they don't see any value in it.

Middle and high school teachers working in schools using the traditional 45-minute period will have more difficulty finding time to work the data wall regularly. It is, however, a necessity! In such cases, one class goal related to something that can be measured with great frequency and one other that has fewer data points would be better. Keep in mind, the leading indicators are best suited for many data points, while the lagging indicators are unit tests or end-of-course exams. Many middle and high school teachers have shared with us how important it has been to have a classroom dashboard with student data visible to all. Uniformly, they claim that it builds-in healthy competition between sections of the same course. We do not recommend sharing data by student name, but you can be creative about the ways to display data without revealing or identifying any specific student. The case study in Chapter 7 gives more details about ways to chart student data.

Helpful Tip: Rapid response systems are available for classrooms and are reasonably priced, given the "bang for the buck" that you will reap. The use of such systems allows teachers to create their own quizzes. The advantage to using such technology is boundless; you know instantly which students grasp the concept(s), and specifics about the errors.

Measuring leading indicators can be brief. The important part about these indicators is that you analyze the results and turn the data into information, then make midcourse corrections to the process being measured. Obviously, if you work in a school using a block schedule, it will be less frenetic to find the time. Whatever your circumstances, you can take a few minutes to reflect on the most recent data with students. They can provide you with feedback using 3×5 cards or sticky notes as they leave the classroom. This leaves you to organize the feedback into something meaningful and requires that you spend a few minutes the next class period going over the feedback. If you don't share what the students said (yes—the good, the bad, and the ugly) you will betray their trust and get less and less cooperation.

Figure 4.5 shows some photo examples of class data walls we've gathered.

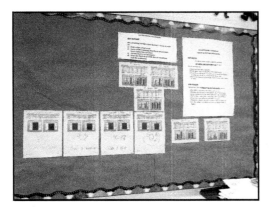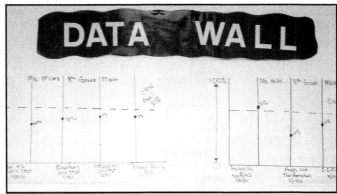

Figure 4.5   Some examples of class data walls.

Class Goals, Data Walls, and Personal Best

Remember in Chapter 1 we quoted Dr. Mammary about the differences between students who *won't* and those who *can't*? It takes on greater significance when we propose class goals and class data walls. Of course you have to be sensitive to those students who *can't* and how they lack self-confidence, making them more vulnerable to the potential for ridicule, hostility, or isolation from their peers.

We'll deal with this issue momentarily, but first we want you to consider this: are you certain that those students who don't do well are incapable of doing the work? Or is it a motivational issue? Perhaps it's a power struggle between you and the student. Whatever the reason, it's important for you to consider the root cause. Is it possible/feasible that your classroom system is not aligned for success for all? How do you know? One way to find out is to go to the students and ask for their honest feedback as advocated in this book. Perhaps these students (those who *won't*) have already become so discouraged that they've begun to act out or opt out and consequently no longer care. We urge you to continue to chart the data (without names) and focus on process improvement.

Now, those students who *can't* pose a different problem when it comes to how you chart the data and track progress toward class goals. Frequently, teachers cry *foul* when we set out the expectation of transparency with data. They'll report, "My students know who is causing us not to meet our goals. How can I handle this?" It's a legitimate concern, yet one that can be overcome if you note which students have done their personal best on any assessment.

As shown in Figure 4.6, the teacher has added *personal best* to the chart. Note that there are no names and no indication of who has scored a personal best that week. In this situation, imagine a student, Viktor, is a level one English language learner. This student is working from a difficult position, and for the past semester has been the student keeping the class from meeting its goal. The teacher, in a private conversation (away from the rest of the class) has negotiated a somewhat lower goal for him (not so low that it takes away his motivation, but not so high that he is going to become frustrated and give up) and this becomes his personal goal. Each time Viktor scores better

Class goal: We will all achieve 90% or better on our weekly vocabulary quizzes. We will celebrate meeting this goal with five minutes to talk with our friends every day for one week.

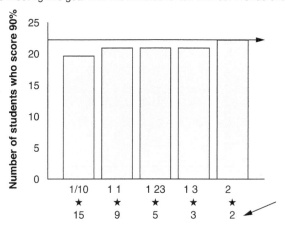

Figure 4.6 Chart progress toward class goals.

than ever, a *personal best* star goes on the data wall chart. Even if he didn't meet his personal goal, he is still recognized (never by name, but as part of the class) so long as he has exceeded the previous highest score. If Viktor meets the *negotiated* goal three weeks in a row, the teacher counts him as having met the class goal for those weeks. (In the grade book, however, the teacher is tracking the actual scores for Viktor and all students.) Keep in mind that Viktor only gets a *personal best* star when he goes beyond what he has ever done before. *In this way, it is the same for all students in the class.* Meanwhile, once Viktor meets his personal goal for three weeks, it is time to have another conversation with him to increase his personal goal, which may still be somewhat below the goal set by the class. This is how the expectations for all students get "ratcheted up," and how a teacher can keep the data wall up without betraying which students are not meeting the class goal.

For those students who fall in the *won't* category, you wouldn't lower the expectations. Again, this is for students who are capable, but for one reason or another are not motivated. This is where PDSA and student feedback are extremely important to system improvement.

The Second Most Significant Internal Customer—the Next Teacher in Line

After the students, the most important internal customer you have is the next teacher in line. He/she receives your students with all their knowledge, skills, wisdom, and abilities. As a practicing teacher, you know the difficulties of bringing students up to grade level. The amount of rework involved in reteaching and remediation is enormous and represents a high cost of not doing it right the first time. A fair concern about using the Baldrige framework for reaching excellence is the argument that "*We don't teach widgets. You can't use a business model for education.*" We are well aware of various arguments about developmental levels and the wide variation in students who come to school not prepared. It is easy to fall into this trap and excuse ourselves and each other as, year after year, students don't achieve at the levels needed to succeed the following year. Yet it has been proven over and over again that using systems thinking and adopting a data-driven, continuous improvement approach works. While there will probably always be a *very small number* of students who get passed on to the next level without the skills, these should be considered the absolute *exception* to the rule.

If your school or school district has a systems view, there is vertical articulation across the grades and elementary/middle/high school; but perhaps this isn't your scenario. If not, we urge you to begin a discussion with your administration about when it can happen. Done correctly, teachers at each grade level will work together to come up with a list of "*must haves.*" These are the skills and knowledge students must have to enter the next grade successfully. We're not talking about the state standards—or the test results. We're talking very specifically about what students must know. For instance, the Developmental Reading Assessment (DRA) has level 4 as the measure of being considered on–grade level at the end of kindergarten. Principals, however, have told us that level 6 is really required for incoming first-graders. This makes the point about the importance of each school and district going through this exercise.

How will you know if your customer (next teacher) is satisfied with the skills, knowledge, wisdom, and abilities of the students you've passed along? Our recommendation is to survey them toward the end of the first month of school. We've included a sample satisfaction survey in the Toolbox section of this chapter on page 122. Keep in mind, the sample is just that—an example. You can feel free to use it as a template, but you're probably going to want to customize it for your use. The important thing is that you take the brave step to do this. As with any type of survey, it's important to be open to the possibility that you can do things better and that your colleague is doing you a huge favor by giving you honest feedback.

Once this becomes part of the culture of your school and district, it is amazing how much help you can receive and give others. Then you can say without hesitation, "We have a true professional learning community, we are all on the same team, working together for the success of all students and to improve the educational system in this town." Of course, these remarks are predicated on the fact that you will take the feedback and use some tools to analyze it and determine the most significant complaints, and to make changes based on the feedback. Two tools that are valuable for this are the *affinity diagram* and *Pareto chart*. You can find instructions for both these tools in the Toolbox sections at the end of Chapters 5 and 7, respectively.

IN SUMMARY

Our experience with teachers new to data analysis has been their fear of getting started. If you find yourself feeling overwhelmed, do not give up. Instead, start small! Look at what data you have available to you and make some smart, lean decisions on what will be most useful starting out. Teachers who are further along in continuous improvement but have more to learn and incorporate into their teaching also find it difficult to turn off the excuse mechanisms that keep popping into their head. For example, "My parents could never provide the extra help needed," or "The class coming up has so many problem students, I could never begin a data wall."

You may also be feeling a bit intimidated regarding the five big ideas emphasized in this chapter. Briefly, they are: (1) analyze results data prior to the start of the next school year in order to make "wise" decisions about changing your instructional approach, (2) track the leading indicators and make midcourse corrections, (3) determine a measurement plan for key processes, (4) engage the next teacher in line by surveying that teacher after a month of school and/or getting together to create a list of "must have" skills that you can address for next year's class, (5) establish a class data wall to maintain transparency and focus on key goals. Let go of your fears and move forward!

TOOLBOX

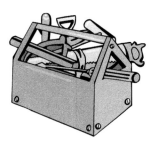

CAUSE-AND-EFFECT DIAGRAM

What

This tool is also known as a *fishbone diagram*, and an *Ishikawa diagram* (named for Professor Kaoru Ishikawa who developed the tool). It is a picture of elements of a system or process that contribute to a problem.

How

1. Draw a horizontal line, which is the center line.

2. At the far right-hand edge of the center line, draw a rectangle, oval, or triangle shape. This will become the "head" of the diagram.

3. Write the *effect* of the problem in the head.

4. On each side of the center line, evenly spaced, draw two (2) additional diagonal lines moving away form the head. Each of these represents a major category of causal factors.

5. Attached to the end of each major causal factor line, draw a box. Label each as one of the major causal factors. It is possible to have more than four, but four is the norm.

6. Brainstorm specific factors relating to each of the major causal lines. The group may decide to write each idea on a sticky note and then place the notes on the line. Individuals may go to the chart and write their ideas at any time on the correct "bone"; or, one person can be designated "writer" while each major causal line is discussed separately. (Keep in mind, this is a brainstorming activity, and the group is seeking to discover *root cause* of a problem. Be certain to record all ideas as valid.)

7. If a cause has other underlying causes, these are recorded as sub-causes and placed on a short line drawn horizontally off the major causal line. Sub-sub-causes may also be drawn underneath each sub-cause. The deeper the team gets into each cause, the greater the chances for discovering true *root cause*.

8. Continue brainstorming until all ideas are on the diagram.

When

Use this tool when:

• Studying a process or system problem

• Many people are involved in the process and it is unclear what the issue is

• Brainstorming root cause of current events, historical events, or the plot of a novel

Example: Generic

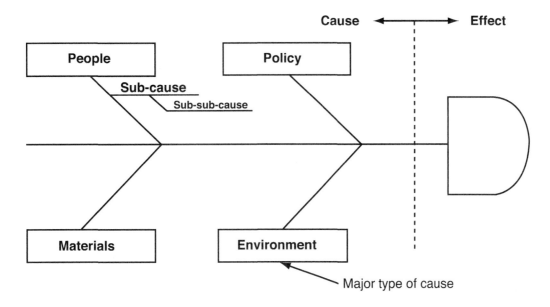

Example: Education

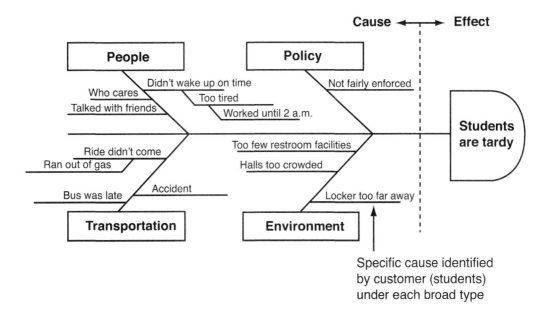

RUN CHART

What

A *run chart* is a picture of a process over time. It is a simple tool to use, and young children from grades one on up can learn to plot and read run charts. A run chart resembles a line graph, method 1.

How

1. Draw the horizontal axis (*x*) and a vertical axis (*y*).

2. Label the horizontal axis (*x*) as *time* (dates, days of the week, months, and so on).

3. Label the vertical axis (*y*) as *what is being measured* (number right on test, number of students, number of sit-ups, and so on).

4. Plot the data by putting a dot at the intersection of the *x*-axis (date) and the *y*-axis (measurement).

5. Continue to plot all the data. When finished, connect the dots.

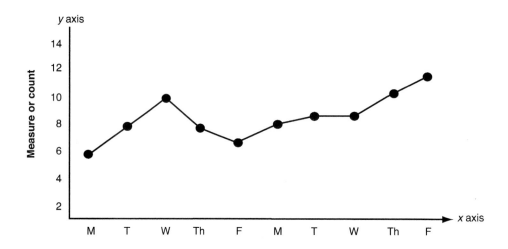

When

Use this tool when:

• You want to see the trend over a certain period of time

• You need to know what the current situation is

• It is important to know if the average is changing

• You want to have students track their own progress

Examples: Classroom

J. Smith's Physical Fitness Record

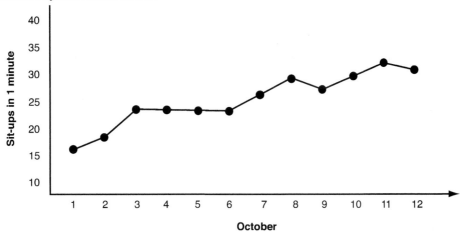

Science

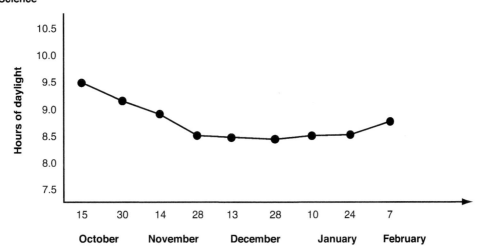

Team "A" Calculus Quiz

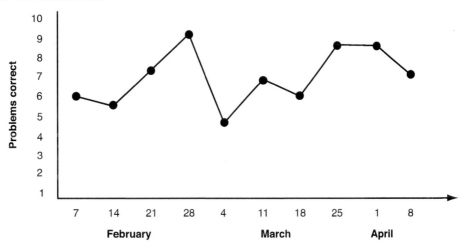

SURVEY THE NEXT TEACHER IN LINE

Example: Elementary

Please rate the skills and abilities of students who were in my class last year. Use the following scale to rate the academic skills and abilities *and* the social skills/behaviors: 5 = Very satisfied, 4 = Mostly satisfied, 3 = Somewhat satisfied, 2 = Not very satisfied, 1 = Unsatisfied.

I plan to take your feedback into consideration as I plan lessons for this year. Thanks for your help.

	Academic abilities	1	2	3	4	5
1.	**Basic math operations—class as a whole**					
1.a	Students on free/reduced lunch					
1.b	Special Education students					
1.c	English language learners					
	Prioritize the need to improve math skills (grade-level appropriate)					
	Addition					
	Subtraction					
	Multiplication					
	Division					
	Fractions					
	Decimals					
	Word problem solving					
2.	**Reading comprehension—class as a whole**					
2.a	Students on free/reduced lunch					
2.b	Special Education students					
2.c	English language learners					
3	**Vocabulary—class as a whole**					
3.a	Students on free/reduced lunch					
3.b	Special Education students					
3.c	English language learners					
4	**Writing—class as a whole**					
4.a	Students on free/reduced lunch					
4.b	Special Education students					
4.c	English language learners					
	Prioritize the need to improve reading/writing skills (grade-level appropriate)					
	Correctly identifies facts in a story					
	Correct response to implicit comprehension questions					
	Able to make inferences based on pictures and/or writing					
	Reading fluency					
	Compare and contrast from a reading sample					
	Word recognition skills—sight words					
	Is able to make predictions based on reading					
	Can write complete sentences with noun/verb agreement, punctuation, capitalization, and spelling.					
	Can write a multiple paragraph story (grade-level appropriate)					

	Behaviors—social skills	1	2	3	4	5
1.	**Follows auditory directions (class as a whole)**					
	Students on free/reduced lunch					
	Special Education students					
	English language learners					
	Students not identified in any subgroup					
2.	**Follows written directions (class as a whole)**					
	Students on free/reduced lunch					
	Special Education students					
	English language learners					
	Students not identified in any subgroup					
3.	**Demonstrate respect for self, peers, and adults**					
	Students on free/reduced lunch					
	Special Education students					
	English language learners					
	Students not identified in any subgroup					
4.	**Helps fellow students when they need help**					
	Students on free/reduced lunch					
	Special Education students					
	English language learners					
	Students not identified in any subgroup					
5.	**Understands the need for behaving in a safe manner and acts appropriately**					
	Students on free/reduced lunch					
	Special Education students					
	English language learners					
	Students not identified in any subgroup					
6.	**Completes homework on time**					
	Students on free/reduced lunch					
	Special Education students					
	English language learners					
	Students not identified in any subgroup					
7.	**Other: please specify**					
	Students on free/reduced lunch					
	Special Education students					
	English language learners					
	Students not identified in any subgroup					

5

Agility: Make Midcourse Corrections

CONVERSATION WITH THE TEACHER

We recognize how precious instructional time is, and applaud you for spending time on data analysis and the PDSA process discussed in Chapter 4. We also understand the data overload that is experienced by teachers in many districts. As funding cuts continue in K–12 education districts, and schools face the pressures of limited resources, larger class sizes, and increasing workloads for staff, the pressures build. The BBQ classroom will provide relief because systems can be continuously improved. Time devoted to learning and practice will bring rewards as long as you persevere.

Now it's time to coach you as you begin to use PDSA on a regular basis in the classroom. Our job is to help you learn to use data selectively, in partnership with your students, to provide critical feedback that helps you create a classroom culture of performance excellence. We know it's possible because it has been proven that the application of the PDSA cycle of improvement to key classroom processes does yield system change and, therefore, allows the teacher to predict improved student learning results. This is, in many ways, a leap of faith because until you have learned the PDSA process and practiced it, you may think, "I can't do this. It takes too much time, and I have to cover the curriculum." Your district may also have a pacing guide from which you are not allowed to deviate. Acting under this assumption, think about how many students get left behind while "covering the curriculum."

As you move forward, remember your purpose and that you are a facilitator of learning. Rely on the two principles of a BBQ classroom ("I am responsible" and "I am respons-able") and let these be a guide for you and your students. Use PDSA to improve every key learning process. Finally, if it becomes evident over time that your strategies, approaches, and activities are not capable of yielding the desired results, you are going to have to engage your students and take some risks—innovate! In a student-focused, learning-centered classroom, it isn't about you, it's about the students—how much they learn and how much they learn to enjoy learning. While frightening in the beginning, this approach becomes very freeing as students become your copartners in every sense of the word. You can do it!

In this chapter you will learn:

- A process to have students provide feedback assessing their teacher on the agreed-on quality factors for the teacher

- How to use a radar chart

- A process for measuring mission specificity

- How to use an enthusiasm/learning (E/L) chart and a plus/delta chart to capture student perceptions about learning, and how those can be weighed with the "hard" data on student learning to improve the instructional process

- How to evaluate and improve noninstructional processes for effectiveness and efficiency

- How to use other feedback tools to improve instructional planning

I AM RESPONSIBLE FOR MY OWN LEARNING

As we discussed in Chapter 1, taking responsibility for one's own learning is an overarching fundamental principle of a BBQ classroom. This is as much the teacher's responsibility as it is the students' and must be lived each day. Actualizing this principle assumes you have not only content expertise, but also a high degree of self-awareness so that you understand your biases about students and parents, peers and the administration, immigrants, non–English speakers, special education (SPED) students, the rich and/or the poor, well, you understand. Biases lead to what we have dubbed "hardening of the categories." Such thinking puts a lid on creativity or being open to the possibility that things can improve when, in fact, things can vastly improve and everyone can have more fun.

We urge you to engage in some real soul-searching about any biases—large or small—and examine their origins. These have become your reality. These biases drive all your thoughts and behaviors—conscious and unconscious. Can you see why it is important to open yourself to letting go of these biases? Henry Ford once said, "Whether you think you can, or you think you can't— you're right." This is true for both you and your students.

Taking responsibility for your own learning requires having a process to *regularly and systematically* understand the meaning of the "hard" data (test/quiz results, project results, tardy and attendance, homework turned in, and so on) and balance that with "soft" data (feedback from students using a variety of tools). The latter requires you to have created trusting relationships with all students, in a safe and caring learning environment. We submit that the aforementioned requirements also impact student learning results in a dramatic fashion. After all, who wants to work hard if the adult doesn't take time to develop a positive, deeply caring relationship? Who wants to work hard if it doesn't seem to matter to the teacher how much, or if, you were able to learn? Who wants to work hard if all decisions are the teacher's, even those that don't make sense to you, but you're told you have to "follow the rules" because the teacher said so? This is probably a tad of an exaggeration, but we're doing it to make a point. It is up to you to decide where you stand on the scale of leadership.

In an earlier chapter you learned to seek information from students about their needs and expectations of the teacher. We call this establishing the *quality factors* for the teacher. This process allowed you to work with your students to whittle down the number to a manageable four or six of the "*most essential things you (the teacher) must remember every day so that everyone can learn more.*" We also suggested that you have the students take time to specifically, operationally define each characteristic. In short, operational definitions are the test or measure used to determine if a certain factor has been met. The QFs and operational definitions allow you to proceed with the confidence that the class will learn more and there will be fewer disruptions.

However, it isn't enough to have students define a quality teacher. A fact-based system of improvement needs follow-up by regularly and systematically evaluating the process for effectiveness and efficiency. In this instance you'll be using a tool to seek feedback from students rating your success on each of the quality factor traits they defined. We highly recommend this as a routine activity at report card time for all regular education teachers. Further, you may want to seek this feedback monthly the first two months of school simply to calibrate students' perceptions with the quality factors and make more-immediate adjustments. Primary grade teachers, or SPED and English language learner teachers who work with small groups of students, will use this approach more frequently. This not only cements trusting relationships and demonstrates how much you value students' opinions, but it also yields invaluable information if done properly. If you're working at building trusting relationships and a caring learning environment, this is one process that will go a long way toward developing deep levels of mutual respect.

The rewards far outweigh the fear of this type of risk-taking.

Caution:

- *If you don't want to know what students think, then don't ask.*

- *If you ask, and then spend your time making excuses, trying to figure out "who said what," then you have missed the purpose of the exercise.*

- *If you ask, and make excuses for some of the comments—somehow belittling the students who took the time and put thought into their response, you have wasted everyone's time because you won't have learned anything, and in fact you'll have damaged your relationships.*

- *If you ask, then you* must share the results—all the results—of their feedback. Students will have deeper respect for you and trust that you want to improve to help everyone.*

Before you engage in this approach, here are some "truisms" about students:

- Very young children (K–3) will often inflate their assessment because of the importance they place on having the teacher "love" them. We refer to this as the "halo effect."

- Some middle school and high school students will not treat it as seriously in the beginning as we hope they would. Some responses will seem to be outrageous, silly, or downright nasty. There may be several explanations:

  - They don't trust that you really will use the feedback to improve.

  - They have had bad experiences with teachers in the past and generally don't like school, so act as if they don't care.

  - The class clown wants attention from his classmates.

  - The students are testing you to see if you really will show all the comments.

It may take a while to build trust, but once they see you gradually make changes based on their comments and feedback, they will realize you are serious and committed to their success. Perseverance is a must. If, over time, there is a student who persists in being frivolous with his/her feedback, you may need to have a little one-on-one conversation for the purpose of trying to find out what his/her purpose is. Remember—no shame, no blame! It takes time for some to realize how important getting feedback is to you. Patience is a real virtue here—as is a sense of humor—but if you maintain your seriousness of purpose, you'll come out okay.

"Allow students to evaluate me? I don't think so," say some teachers. It is such a frightening thought that few are willing to go out on this limb. Yet, those who do so are usually rewarded by increased student participation. To reiterate a common theme of this book—the need to establish caring relationships with all students is vital to everyone's success. It has been said, if students don't think you care, they won't care what you know. This activity is another of those that demonstrates your commitment to the principle "I am response-able to the success of the class." How can one possibly be able-to-respond *to* the success of the class and each individual *unless* there is a mechanism in place to monitor whether you are, in fact, meeting their needs? Each must be aware and fully engaged in "I am responsible for my own learning."

While it is necessary to seek feedback on the teacher QFs, it is not sufficient. You must, absolutely *must*, be transparent and share all the results with your students. In fact, if nothing changes after each assessment cycle, students are likely to get frustrated with you and stop trusting that you truly do care about them and their success. Worse, it becomes a waste of everyone's time, and as we've heard over and over, "I don't have time to do this. I have a curriculum to cover." Ask the students for help and you begin to learn *what* you can do differently to meet the specific QFs where the class rated you lowest. It makes no sense to go through this exercise unless you are willing and open to the possibilities of your own continuous improvement.

Everything you read in this book is designed to help you become more effective and efficient as a leader so that more students can learn at higher rates than heretofore imagined. The significance of sharing the feedback with the students takes on greater importance if you realize this purpose. We know it will take some time, probably about 10 minutes total, to share after you've been able

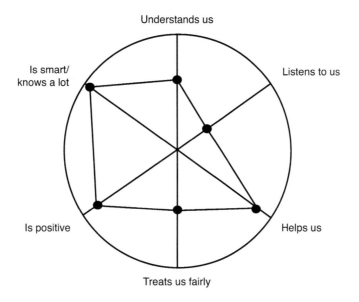

Figure 5.1   Radar chart—teacher quality factors.

to collate the responses and chart them. The use of quality tools can streamline and decrease the amount of time it takes. Once you teach students how to use the tools, even more instructional time will be saved.

We suggest using a *radar chart* (Figure 5.1) for this activity. This tool looks somewhat like the radar scope on an airplane, making it easy to interpret. It shows the gap between where you are and where you want to be. Instructions for the radar chart are at the end of this chapter, on page 155.

A Process for Primary Grades

The process will differ depending on the age and grade level of the students with whom you work. For K–1 students you may want to have another adult (parent volunteer, principal, assistant principal (AP), counselor, an aide, or even an older student) come into the classroom and facilitate the process to diminish the halo effect mentioned above. In fact, it's even better if you are out of the room for the few minutes it will take. This can be done very informally, with students raising their hands when the facilitator reaches the level each child thinks you've attained for each attribute. A more formal approach (Figure 5.2) would be to give each child a small piece of paper with the QF characteristics on it and with a Likert-type scale of numbers (or smiley faces). As the facilitator reviews each QF and reads the operational definition, each child can circle the number (or face) they think best describes the teacher that week or day.

A Process for Grades Three and Up

For grades three and up, you won't need a facilitator, and it shouldn't take more than a minute or two to have all the surveys turned in. Figure 5.3 shows the recommended process explained in a

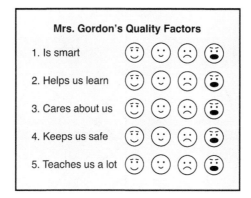

Figure 5.2 Teacher report card—elementary.

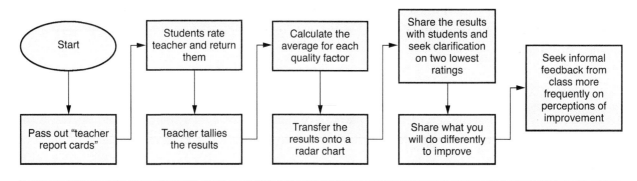

Figure 5.3 Process flowchart—class assesses teacher on quality factors.

flowchart. The same "report card" described for K–2 will work with students in the intermediate grades too. Directions for the radar chart are found at the end of this chapter.

A Process for Secondary Teachers

Perhaps you are more comfortable with asking students to grade you in a report card format. In this case, each QF becomes a separate "subject," and each student will give you a percent (up to 100%) or letter grade for each QF. The following example (story) is from an English teacher at Benton Middle School, Prince William County, Virginia. She gives students a chance to give her a report card on the same day as she does their quarterly grades. Then she follows up with students and asks them to help her understand how to improve.

One issue that became apparent to her was the QF *be fair*. The class operationally defined this as *treat us all the same*. She repeatedly received the lowest score on this QF, yet she remained steadfast about treating students as individuals, some with dissimilar needs. Reality agrees with her, right? The answer to this is to openly discuss it with the students. Engage them, listen to them, and then share your thoughts. Stephen Covey's *Habit 5: Seek first to understand, then to be understood* (*The 7 Habits of Highly Effective People*) hits the mark. The teacher has a good point, and the way forward would be work with students to change the operational definition.

Here's a sad but true story about the consequences of "going through the motions." A high school science teacher shared how proud he was of the "report cards" that he'd amassed from his students all year. Indeed, there they were—hundreds of post card size paper report cards in a big cardboard box. He prefaced his remarks by telling others in training that he was disappointed that some students didn't take it seriously, and sneered at the idea of "wasting all that instructional time" on such an obviously juvenile activity. With that he pulled some of the cards out of the box. "*I know who wrote that. That kid doesn't like anything.*" "*I've had to send that kid out of class at least six times this year. He's going to fail.*" It became obvious that this teacher spent a good bit of energy trying to figure out who authored the comments rather than learning the lessons his students were working so hard to help him understand. A strange look came over his face when I asked how he followed through with the students. That look told me everything I needed to know. He was going through the exercise because his principal said it was required. He learned nothing and very likely turned off at least some of his students.

On the other hand, an excellent example of how a middle or high school teacher would benefit from having students evaluate him/her on the quality factors comes from Ashleigh Burnette, a Language Arts teacher at Parkside Middle School, Manassas, Virginia. Each fall Ashleigh asks her students to think about the qualities of the *best teacher* they can imagine! She uses the multi-voting technique to whittle the list down to a manageable few. At the end of each quarter, on the same day as students receive their report cards, Mrs. Burnette asks her students to evaluate her. Figure 5.4 depicts her current "report card."

Rate Mrs. Burnette on the qualities of a good teacher. 1 is the lowest and 10 is the highest.

Challenging	1	2	3	4	5	6	7	8	9	10
Encouraging	1	2	3	4	5	6	7	8	9	10
Organized	1	2	3	4	5	6	7	8	9	10
Humorous	1	2	3	4	5	6	7	8	9	10
Understanding	1	2	3	4	5	6	7	8	9	10
Intelligent	1	2	3	4	5	6	7	8	9	10

If you rate Mrs. Burnette below a 9 in any category, please give a reason why. This will help Mrs. Burnette better understand what you need in order to feel as if you have a quality teacher.

_____

_____

_____

Figure 5.4 Mrs. Burnette's teacher report card.

To make the most of this opportunity to engage students as your copartners and understand more about the barriers to their learning, systematically follow the "report card" up with a plus/ delta. Figure 5.5 shows an example that Ashleigh Burnette uses. We frequently hear teachers say, "We already do this, but simply by asking our students." This approach may provide useful information for some students, usually the ones who are already doing well and the ones who may be perceived as the "more belligerent" ones. However, if you really are committed to improvement, you will never lose sight of the fact that it is the systematic approach and cycles of improvement that are effective over the long haul. We dare say there are many "average" students and those who are not as successful as they can be who do not feel free to speak up, so the teacher is left with the thoughts of *some but not all students*. An approach like this one will, over time, illuminate other/deeper system problems of which you may not be aware.

Just a gentle reminder! You can not copycat the specific quality factors from either of these examples. This is because the value comes from your students, who determine what they need from you. Each class is different, and therefore this is a process that has to be repeated every year.

As we've said before, if you don't want to know what students think, don't ask. If you ask, don't take it personally and feel wounded when they let you know how they feel. If you ask, you have a responsibility to share all the results and commit to making some improvements.

Benefit of Seeking Feedback

Your students will, at first, think of this as a novel idea. They are not used to being able to assess their teacher. Some teachers are fearful. Interesting, isn't it? You can readily see how the BBQ

Quarterly Feedback Form	
+ Plus	**Δ Delta**
In this column, please list things that Mrs. Burnette did (class activities, lecturers, and so on) that helped you learn.	In this column, please list things that you would like to change in order to make learning easier for you.
Anything else that you would like Mrs. Burnette to know/consider:	
An activity/idea that you have in mind for our class:	

Figure 5.5 Mrs. Burnette's plus/delta chart.

classroom differs from a traditional one. In the former, teachers are "boss managers"; in the latter, students take on a partnership role where teachers and students are all committed to everyone's success and continuous improvement. Everyone embraces the two principles (I am responsible for my own learning, I am response-able to the success of the class).

After being trained, a teacher reported that in a moment of total frustration she chastised her second-graders. A nanosecond later one little girl said, "Mrs. 'X,' that wasn't a very 'response-able' thing you just did." This teacher realized instantly that how she responded to the class and the child who bravely spoke up would be critical to the way the class functioned for a long time. Fortunately, this teacher realized her mistake, *owned it*, and apologized to the class. *We all make mistakes, teachers and students*, it is only human. The way forward is to quickly admit and apologize for your errors. Through your role-modeling of appropriate behavior, students learn how to modify their own behavior. It's an important lesson.

Courage, consistency, seriousness of purpose, and commitment to the two principles are going to carry the day for you. Align everything you do in the classroom with the overarching class purpose, vision, mission, and goals. Give up the old way of the sports model (winners and losers) and focus your personal lens on improving the system so more students can be successful.

The Next Step

After sharing the feedback and coming up with an improvement plan (also shared with students), it's important to check in frequently with students for their perception of the improvement. This can be accomplished by simply asking the class for a thumbs-up or -down at the end of the class period (or day) on whether you stuck with your improvement plan. Amazing things will begin to happen—students *know without a doubt* that you are serious about improvement, that you have a deep respect for their opinions. You hold yourself to the same standard as you do students—you expect and believe that personal improvement is important. Talk about role model leadership!

Radar Charts and Quality Factors for Students

Similarly, students can follow the same process daily, weekly, or monthly (depending on age and circumstances, that is, SPED, secondary, or elementary) to assess themselves on the agreed-on student quality factors. In a BBQ classroom, taking time to reflect on one's results—and what led to them—is considered an important "ritual," a way in which business is done in the classroom. The QFs for students are an integral part of each student's data notebook, making it easy for each student to review his/her behavior in this light. The student can then use the radar chart to see areas of greatest opportunity for improvement. While you are giving up some instructional time having students engaged in this activity, they are learning an important life skill and, hopefully, seeing the relationship between their behaviors, habits, and how much they have learned.

Frequently, teachers ask, "What if students overrate their behavior? We observe them acting in a way that is contrary to the QFs and yet they give themselves top ratings. It isn't right." You may be thinking, "Yes, that's right. That is reality!" In a traditional fear-based environment, you are absolutely right. That would be a typical student response. Yet, paraphrasing Dr. Deming, we must drive out fear! It is the leader's responsibility. Students will not be honest if they fear harm will come to them. Dr. William Glasser (father of responsibility theory and founder of the quality schools movement) echoed these sentiments referring to children and students. Given this, how would a BBQ teacher address this issue? At the beginning of the reflection period, before you ask students to rate themselves, engage your students in a brief discussion reviewing the operational definitions for each QF. Then, when they are rating themselves, you'll walk around the room, and if you see someone has rated him/herself ridiculously high you can ask him/her to explain. No shame, no blame, and no coercion. Over time, they'll mature and improve in their ability to self-assess. Keep in mind there are exceptions to most every rule, but they *are* exceptions.

There are a couple of other things to keep in mind when you're asking students to reflect on their own behavior. First, be aware that you don't know all the intimate details of each student's home life. Some parents expect their children to be *perfect*, and anything less is unacceptable. (One sign of this is the student who receives a B+ on a test or project and bursts into tears or gets extremely upset. It is a red flag for you to consider.) We don't know if there will be consequences for students when they take this home. We hope parents will discuss it calmly with their child, but we can not be certain. As a counselor for children and families, I quickly learned to be cautious in making judgments about student behavior in light of family dynamics.

Weekly, throughout the elementary grades, students plot their behavior using a radar chart in their data notebooks and share it with their parents, who must sign and return it the following week. In this way, communication between school and home increases, and a broader three-way partnership is established. Consistency is important, and this can become a routine on Friday afternoons as students are preparing to leave school. If you have a serious concern about the gap between your appraisal and the student's, then your obligation is to share that with parents. It is the way you approach the issue that is important: *Johnny is learning how to manage his own behavior. He is working to improve. In fact, he is getting better each week.* Notice, this is all written in a positive way and establishes a different tone with parents—one that is hopeful while recognizing there's plenty of room for improvement. Also, it does not inadvertently cast doubt on their parenting skills. (It's a fine line, but an important one.)

In the primary grades it works best when students are asked to reflect twice a day. Some teachers have a little check sheet taped to each student's desk, and before lunch and at the end of the day they rate themselves on each QF. It doesn't take much time and is a reminder to the students. At the end of the week when they reflect and chart it in their data notebook, the daily checks take on added significance and are a good reminder.

Measure Mission Specificity

Keep the mission alive! On a weekly basis ask the students to rate the class as a whole on staying on track with the mission. Remember, the class has agreed that the mission is the *path to achieve the vision.* An opportunity arises during the regular class meeting time. Once again, reflection time is valued and required in a BBQ classroom. A radar chart works really well for this although the process is more informal, using a show of hands instead of cards or an individual assessment.

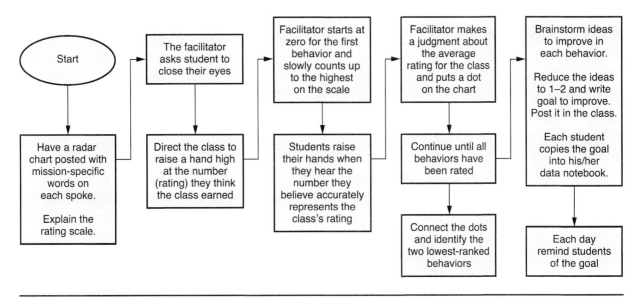

Figure 5.6   Process flowchart—class assessment of mission specificity.

Obviously, the teacher can facilitate this process, but why not empower a student to take a leadership role, with you in a supporting role? Figure 5.6 depicts a flowchart of the process.

Cycles of improvement will become clear on the radar chart. The BBQ teacher will make these improvements to keep the enthusiasm high for reflection and improvement.

Over time, if it becomes clear that the mission is not adequate or the class has outgrown the mission, it can be revised. This is not a waste of time. You'd know that the mission is no longer working if you encounter many disruptions and/or students are not adhering to the operational definitions. You remember the definition of insanity; continuing to do the same thing despite the evidence that it isn't working will cost you valuable instructional time. You don't have time *not* to refocus the class.

I AM RESPONSE-ABLE TO THE SUCCESS OF THE CLASS

The ability to make midcourse corrections is crucial in a BBQ classroom. This is why we urge frequent and systematic approaches to capture student satisfaction with nearly everything that happens in the classroom, including the instructional process. Feedback is perception, and, as we all know, perception is reality in the eyes of the customer, that is, students.

Monitor Instructional Processes

The following case study demonstrates a more informal use of PDSA to make midcourse corrections. As you read the case, note how important it is to Mr. Ortiz to capture feedback from his students to help him understand how to improve the instructional process.

Mr. Ortiz's Case Study

Sixth grade Science teacher Mr. Ortiz was particularly distraught by his students' results on the Watershed Ecology quiz. He gives this quiz halfway through the unit. He is an experienced teacher who prides himself on projects he has designed. The bulk of the work students did to learn these concepts was embedded in a team project. The project was to monitor the water quality from a local lake, which feeds into the Mississippi River. There are several factories located on the lake. Students had to collect water samples, and used a matrix of abiotic factors to determine the quality of the water supply as one of many health-related factors of the community. To accomplish this, the class went on three field trips to the lake (walking distance from the school). Prior to the project, students were given a reading assignment, watched a video, and did some Internet research on the topic to understand its importance. Key vocabulary words and concepts were provided to the students. As a team, they were required to perform experiments that related to filtering sediments, trapping nutrients, and breaking down pollutants, and then write a scientific paper with their findings.

The quiz consisted of 10 questions related to the vocabulary and scientific concepts of the unit. Mr. Ortiz teaches four sections of sixth-graders. He was shocked that fewer than 20% passed the test in his sixth-period class, whereas over 70% of the students in the other sections scored a B or higher. Here's a breakdown of the test results for the sixth-period class:

Score	A	B	C	D	F
# of students	0	0	4	2	24

Mr. Ortiz decided to use an *E/L chart* and a *plus/delta* to get to the bottom of the issue. What he discovered is shown in Figure 5.7.

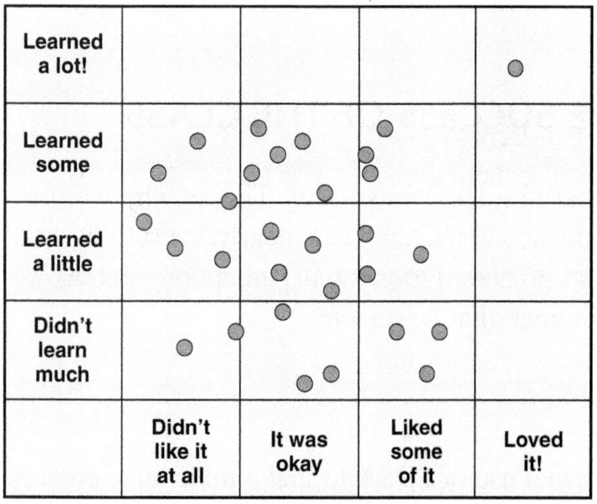

+	Δ
Liked getting the water samples (15) Liked testing the water (26)	Vocabulary list wasn't clear and didn't match the test questions (15) Why is this important (17) You never went over the vocabulary words (20) It was too far to walk to the lake (2) We did this in elementary school (20) You didn't tell us what would be on the quiz (6) Too many bugs (3)

Figure 5.7 Mr. Ortiz's enthusiasm and learning chart and plus/delta chart.

Teacher Δ	Students Δ
• Redirect Internet search for impact on the local community and how poor water quality might affect families. • Give students time in class to learn vocabulary words using their preferred, fun way—make it into a game.	• Give suggestions for how we want to learn the vocabulary and make it fun! • Pay more attention to the Internet research.

Figure 5.8 The changes Mr. Ortiz and his students agreed to make.

Mr. Ortiz was stunned, but didn't share his feelings with his students. After all, he asked the students to be honest because he had a *need to know* what the problem was. When Mr. Ortiz reviewed the results of the plus/delta chart, he realized the problem had to do with his lack of planning. He put the information on another chart to share with the class the changes (Δ) he agreed to make. He then asked his students to give him some more help to know *how to change*. See Figure 5.8.

This is an informal PDSA for improving the instructional process. Mr. Ortiz and his sixth-period class will follow the improvement suggestions, and at the end of the next week Mr. Ortiz will seek feedback once again using the E/L and plus/delta charts. He's going to be looking for a rise in enthusiasm and greater student motivation. He will also give a mini–vocabulary quiz at the end of the week to see if the midcourse corrections yielded an improvement.

Reflection: What are the most important lessons you learned from Mr. Ortiz?

Feedback Tools to Capture Student Perception

In addition to getting information from students about "how" they like to learn, it is necessary to seek more-formal feedback systematically and regularly "in-process" in order to complete the PDSA cycle and make improvements in order to predict better results. The tools most easily used are the following:

- Plus/delta chart

- Enthusiasm and learning (E/L) chart

- Fast feedback

- How helpful were these resources

They are powerful tools, don't take a lot of time, and yet yield a great deal of information. The plus/delta and E/L charts have the added benefit of being easy for students of all ages to learn. It takes some time to teach your students how to use these tools, but once learned they are instructional time savers. We'll look at these tools one at a time.

Plus/Delta Chart

The plus/delta (Figure 5.9, directions on page 153) is helpful for primary students to reflect on at the end of each day, or to reflect on immediately after a lesson. As students get older, it isn't such a necessity at the end of each day, but we recommend it be used weekly, at the end of a unit or whenever you design a new learning activity. High school teachers might only use this tool at the end of a unit or major project. In the end, the decision will be up to you—are you using this tool as an in-process measure to make midcourse corrections, or are you using the tool at the end of a unit? In the latter instance, it is of great value for planning the same unit next time—or for taking into account "lessons learned" in planning for the next unit. Recognize that "end of unit" is not going to allow you to make any changes during the process or allow you to "build in" quality with the goal of more students achieving success on that particular unit of study.

We always like to focus first on the positive. Frame the discussion along these lines: "What did you like about today? What "aha!s" did you have today? What helped you learn today?" Students are then asked to respond (primary students likely will respond verbally while the teacher writes and fills in the + side of the chart. From a teacher's perspective, the plusses let you know overall if your plans worked to help students learn and/or satisfy their needs.

Next is a series of questions about the delta side of the chart. Delta is the mathematical symbol for *change*. Deltas are gifts from students that give insights into potential changes. It is important to frame the questions around change, *not* what we did wrong. The teacher might say, "What could we do differently tomorrow so we could all learn more and have more fun learning?" Remind students that this is not an opportunity to be a tattletale. Focus on process—not individuals. For example, if a student said, "James shoved some of us," the teacher might turn that around by responding, "Are there any words in our class mission that remind us about this kind of behavior?" Hopefully, the students will "see" the words *keep our hands and feet to ourselves.* The teacher would then write on the Δ side, *remember the mission.* (James will get the message; and, James will

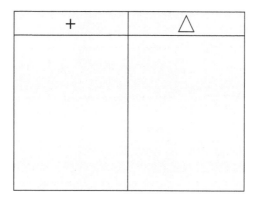

Figure 5.9 Plus/delta chart.

change if he feels part of the class "family." If he feels isolated or disrespected, he will continue his inappropriate behavior.) One of the significant benefits of a BBQ classroom is the common language used by teachers and students.

As soon as students are able to write, they are responsible for putting their ideas on paper, then putting them on the chart. Middle or high school teachers may choose to have several plus/delta charts posted near the classroom door, or just outside the room. Give each student a sticky note and, as they leave the room, they put them on the chart.

Interpreting a plus/delta chart can be tricky. You certainly don't want to draw broad-stroke conclusions using this chart in isolation. It provides limited, but useful, information. We strongly urge its use along with the E/L chart, which will be explained next. But for now, in order to interpret the plus/delta chart you'll need to know how many students share the same issue. This will be no problem for grades two and up, as students will write their responses and place them on the chart. You (or a group of students) can cluster the responses and count how many there are of each. For this part of the process, we suggest using an affinity diagram and Pareto chart. K–2 teachers will ask the class how many "share" the same thought and note the number.

Decisions about *what* to change will be based on (1) how strongly felt and pervasive the issue is among the students, and (2) whether it is an issue within the circle of control of the teacher. School or district policies can not be changed by the teacher (although he/she can be an advocate for the students with the administration), and therefore, while it's nice to know what's on students' minds, you have an obligation to share what's not feasible to change and why. On the other hand, when only one or two students have identified a delta, you're less likely to make sweeping changes. In these cases, we recommend that you become alert to the potential issue growing. If this happens, obviously you're going to engage the class in conversation about the problem. In general, it is never a good idea to make major changes based on limited data such as that afforded by the plus/delta chart. You'll want to consider how enthusiastic students are for learning and take into account the hard data (learning results) at the same time. Bundled together, these data and information can unveil issues that you may not earlier have considered as a barrier.

Figure 5.10 depicts a process flowchart of a useful approach for analyzing the plus/delta chart for grades three and up. Directions for the affinity diagram (page 149) are in the toolbox at the end of this chapter. Directions for the Pareto chart (page 279) are contained in the Toolbox at the end of Chapter 7.

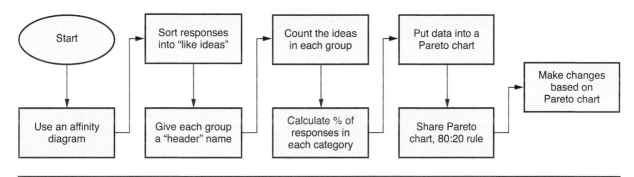

Figure 5.10   Process flowchart for analyzing plus/delta chart.

As useful as the plus/delta chart is, when used in combination with the E/L chart the power is magnified.

Enthusiasm and Learning (E/L) Chart

This chart allows a teacher to get instant feedback from the students about their perception of how much they learned and how much "joy" or enthusiasm they have for the learning. This chart is scaled from highly negative to highly positive on both axes. The vertical axis measures how much each student feels s/he learned, and the horizontal axis measures how much enthusiasm s/he has for the topic and learning. The ideal is to have nearly all (if not all) the dots in the upper-right quadrant on the chart. This would signal that students learned a lot and were quite happy about it (see Figure 5.11).

To avoid some students overly influencing their peers, you can turn the chart around when the time comes for students to put their dot on the chart. Prior to any student casting his/her vote, review the topic(s) covered, the way students were organized to do their work, the assignments, and so on. The purpose of this is *not* to lobby for a positive outcome, but to calibrate their thinking. Ask everyone to think about where they plan to place their dot before beginning the actual process.

Time is saved the more this process becomes a routine part of process evaluation and cycles of improvement. Use this chart at the end of a unit, when you've created a new lesson or activity, or at the end of a major project or demonstration.

Chart interpretation is an important part of this process. If 15% or more of the class places the dot in the lower-left quadrant, the problem must be addressed immediately. A plus/delta is very

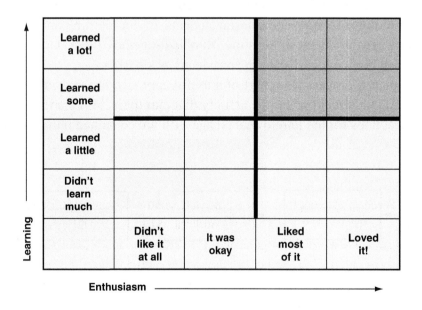

Figure 5.11 Enthusiasm and learning chart.

useful here. If you've just completed a review activity, some students may place the dot below the center line, which makes perfect sense and is no cause for concern. However, if students are saying they didn't learn much and it was "okay" but there was no enthusiasm, you have some work to do.

One approach to recapture student enthusiasm is to invite them to brainstorm how they want to learn something. Students are not given options about *what* they will learn, *but* giving them choices about *how* they want to learn is entirely within the bounds of a BBQ classroom. Differentiation of instruction with a variety of choices of how to experience their learning is almost guaranteed to raise student enthusiasm. Enthusiasm equals increased focus and effort, which equals more learning. This is logical, right? If so, then why aren't more teachers differentiating more and giving students choices? Once you have gained students' trust by implementing change based on their feedback, you will discover they will be more engaged and enthusiastic about learning.

Why is this important? Dissatisfied students = acting out or opting out. As soon as you see slippage and more dots going into the "it was okay" column as shown in Figure 5.11, you must take action to understand why student enthusiasm has not been maintained. (Is it that the activity was a review, or is it evidence of the spiral curriculum from earlier years? Or, are the students simply bored?) In short, don't jump to conclusions before you reflect on what you were measuring. At this point, a formal root cause analysis may not be necessary, but slippage in student enthusiasm for learning means *you must be alert* and remain vigilant in your monitoring efforts. To remain on the path without intervention will eventually lead to lower learning results.

Think about it. When you were in K–12, did you ever have a teacher who was so routinized that every day of the week the pattern was the same: Monday, read the chapter. Tuesday, answer the questions at the back of the chapter. Wednesday, write the vocabulary words in a sentence. . . . You get the idea. This is probably more of an affliction for middle and high school teachers than you find in elementary school. But, if you've ever had this experience, you can readily agree that routines sometimes need change.

Fast Feedback

Use *fast feedback* with older students. Begin by sharing your desire to be the best facilitator of their learning and ask for their help. Explain that this approach will consume no more than five seconds at the end of the class. Put all the names into a box, bowl, or hat, and each day select a random sample of the total in your class or a minimum of five names. These are the only students who will be completing the fast feedback form that day.

Prepare two or three questions that you think will yield the desired information. Your need is to gain insight into whether or not the students understood the material covered that day. Use the same items all semester, so word them generically to fit any content, but specific enough to give you actionable information. Collate and chart the average response to the questions each day and share it with the class the next day. If students respond with specific "muddy" points from the lesson (what was unclear) you know immediately what the start of the next day's lesson will be. Figure 5.12 is an example of a fast feedback form.

Fast Feedback Form—Middle and High School

Instructions: Circle the number that best represents your thoughts on today's lesson.

I understand the logic of today's problem or concept.

	1	2	3	4
	Strongly agree	Agree	Somewhat disagree	Disagree

I could apply this logic (or concept) to another situation.

	1	2	3	4
	Strongly agree	Agree	Somewhat disagree	Disagree

The "muddy" points about today's lesson were:

The pace of this class is (circle one)

Too slow   Just right   Too fast

I'd like some additional help, please. (signed) _____

Figure 5.12   Fast feedback form—example.

How Helpful Were These Resources

This tool is used at the end of a unit of study. It is not helpful if you are working on improving student learning in-process, but is highly effective when you have a desire to improve the unit for the next group of students. Process evaluation and cycles of improvement are important every year. This tool can become a regular part of the debriefing process for students immediately after they've completed a unit test. It's not geared directly for primary students, but can be highly effective with students from grades three and up. This tool verifies the importance you place on student feedback, and how much you depend on them for insights into ways to improve. We have a lot to learn from students; they are the ones who have to work in the system you've developed.

This tool seeks information about the text and any materials students had at their disposal during the learning process. Because it is unit specific, it's not possible to copy the tool as shown in Figure 5.13. Instead, you can make a template and fill in the materials and other resources specifically used. Students have been known to say they thought the field trips were excellent, yet there never were any field trips. You'll want to avoid any of these missteps. If it is at all possible, we recommend that you allow students to tabulate the results. Following tabulation, you will want to seek further information on those resources the majority of the class thought were "a waste of time." For example, if students rate your lectures *W* (waste of time), you'll want to find out if there is a way to improve the lectures so that they are deemed worthwhile.

Notice the wording of the Helpful scale. It is important. No one likes to have their time wasted, and we need to put this into "student" language, not teacher language.

How Helpful Were These Resources				
Class:	Year:	Project or unit:		Date:
Rating scale: E = Excellent, couldn't have done without it G = Good, was a big help O = Okay, wasn't that much help W = Waste of time, was no help whatsoever				
Please rate each of the following resources on how much it helped during this learning experience.				
	E	**G**	**O**	**W**
Lecture				
Textbook				
Library books				
CD				
Internet				
Video				
Class discussion				
Print media (newspapers, magazines)				
Outside experts				

Figure 5.13 Example of "how helpful were these resources" tool.

Monitor Noninstructional Processes

The classroom system is complex, with many instructional and noninstructional processes. The noninstructional processes are frequently the source of inefficiency and lost instructional time. Knowing that, you will want to learn how to monitor this aspect of your system. You will recall, in Chapter 3 you learned how to flowchart a noninstructional process. By now it is clear that processes must be aligned to achieve the purpose of the organization. Imagine a straight line of sight from the vision through the mission, goals, and action plans. The more aligned your key processes are, the more effective and efficient the organization will be. In plain language, make it easy for the students—as workers in the system—to do the job right the first time. The classroom system diagram (Figure 1.7, page 9) lists some noninstructional processes. There are, of course, many more.

To help you put it all together, we invite you to learn from the following case study.

Mrs. Molly—A Case Study

Let's get a bird's-eye view of what has transpired in Mrs. Molly's class. She was experiencing trouble with students transitioning from one activity to the next. Her process flow is a simple one, as shown in Figure 5.14. What should take the class two minutes has begun to take five. You may not think this is serious enough to warrant our attention; Mrs. Molly didn't at first. Mrs. Molly decided to do the math. Each transition took an additional 3 minutes × 3 transitions a day = 9 minutes of lost instructional time per day. Mrs. Molly was curious about what this meant over the course of the school year. Nine minutes a day means 45 minutes per week. Over a 180-day school

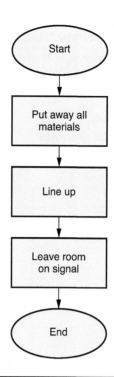

Figure 5.14   Flowchart of Mrs. Molly's transition process.

year, 1620 minutes, or 27 hours for the year. A typical school day is six hours long, and at this rate Mrs. Molly would have lost almost a week of school. Still think 9 minutes a day isn't something to be concerned about? It certainly got Mrs. Molly's attention!

Figure 5.14 is a flowchart of the transition process in her class. At least, this is what she thought was the process. She drew the flowchart onto her Smart Board.

Mrs. Molly gathered the students together and shared the current situation with them. She told them she'd noticed that it was taking them longer to get ready for lunch, to go home, and to go to specials. Then, she told the students she started timing them to make sure her intuition was right—and sure enough, it was!

The students were given the "nitty-gritty" of the problem—how many instructional minutes were being lost, which spurred a discussion about the importance of learning and *how much there was to learn this year.*

Then, she turned on the Smart Board and showed her students the flowchart. She asked the students to work in small groups to discuss where the "muddy points" were. Once each group made their decision, they were asked to put a cloud around the step that was causing the increase in transition time. Each group came up with the same issue (see Figure 5.15). There was a pretty dark cloud about the step *put away all materials.*

Mrs. Molly began to ask the students to think about why this was such a big problem. Here are some reasons cited by the students:

1. Some kids hop out of their chairs and block our way.

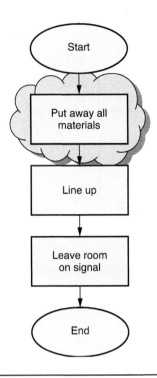

Figure 5.15 Flowchart muddy point.

2. The boxes we have to put our stuff in are too close together.

3. Sometimes we're not ready to go because our work is not finished.

Mrs. Molly had been given an opportunity to learn how to change the transition process, but she wanted to empower students even more so that they would have a vested interest in reducing the amount of time spent. She asked the students for suggestions about how to resolve the three problems. The first was addressed instantly—pushing chairs in under the table will be an expectation of the process. After capturing their ideas, students multi-voted on the ways to best resolve the problems. It was agreed that students would rearrange the positioning of the student boxes in clusters around the room. This would allow easier access. To address the third problem, the students asked Mrs. Molly to give them a two-minute warning to finish up their work before transition time. After the boxes were rearranged, the students were ready to try out the new process. A new flowchart was agreed on, and everyone practiced. Figure 5.16 shows the new flowchart for transitions in this class.

Mrs. Molly gave students the challenge of improving by reducing the transition time from five minutes to two minutes. She reminded students of the class mission and need for safety above speed. Each day for the next two weeks she timed each transitional process and charted it. Students were excited to be back "on track," and to assure that this process didn't deteriorate quickly, they decided to write a song that would last exactly two minutes. During the transition time, the class was committed to singing their song. When they finished singing the song, all

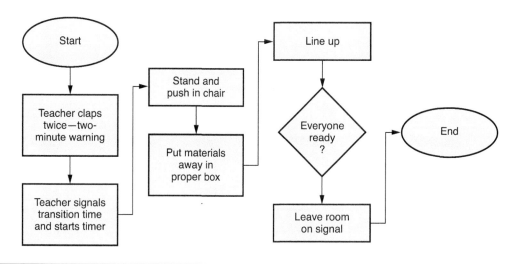

Figure 5.16   Flowchart of Mrs. Molly's revised process.

students had to be lined up and ready to move. It worked, and Mrs. Molly didn't have to admonish or discipline anyone.

Reflection: Go back to Chapter 3 and look at the noninstructional process you flowcharted (page 73). Is the process as effective (meets your requirements and expectations) and efficient (in a timely manner) as it can be? If not, where are the "muddy points"? Circle these and make a note to yourself that you're going to work with the students to see what can be done to increase effectiveness and efficiency. Why? To save valuable instructional time.

Many of your noninstructional processes are more complicated than this one, which means if they are inefficient, you're losing even more instructional time. (Start timing the transitions in your classroom and chart the data, but out of view of the students. After two weeks, share the data with them. And follow this process to improve efficiency.)

Take time to share your concern with the students. In many elementary classrooms, there are regular Friday meetings. This is a super opportunity for this type of improvement work. In a secondary setting you'll want to address transition issues (or other noninstructional processes that are inefficient and therefore causing you to lose instructional time) quickly. Time spent doing this will reap rewards every day. To claim you have no time—you have to cover the curriculum—is foolhardy if you know there is a problem within the classroom system that can/must be fixed. Not addressing the situation means you are willing to allow it to further degrade, which it surely will.

IN SUMMARY

As you implement suggestions from this chapter in your classroom, you will understand more clearly our absolute commitment to the concept of a teacher–student partnership for learning. Learning-centered classrooms are indeed partnerships that allow you to make midcourse corrections with your students instead of waiting until the end of the term or unit when it is too late. In this chapter you learned to get feedback from your students linked to teacher quality factors that they helped identify at the beginning of the year. We would point out, however, that it is possible to introduce QFs (quality factors for teachers and students) as you begin your journey to a Baldrige-based quality classroom. Don't wait until "next year" if your school situation is one where you can ask for student and parent cooperation as you embark on your own continuous improvement process.

This chapter stresses the value of using the radar chart, plus/delta chart, and E/L chart to capture student perceptions. These are quality tools that are easy for students to learn, and instructional time is increased with regular use. Over and over again you have heard us say, "It takes courage and perseverance to open yourself to improvement, especially if you are making the transition from 'boss manager' to 'learning facilitator.'" It's not easy to admit mistakes and errors, but when you do, you will be building the trust and close relationships that lead to students being responsible for their own learning and response-able to the success of the entire class. Take the necessary time to reflect on the contents of this chapter and what is being asked of the BBQ teacher. The payoff for you and your students will be huge!

TOOLBOX

AFFINITY DIAGRAM

What

An *affinity diagram* is a silent brainstorming tool that allows groups to identify and organize large quantities of information or ideas in a short time.

How

1. Clearly state the topic and write it down for all to see.

2. Pass out five or six 3 × 3 sticky notes or index cards to each group member (more if available).

3. Each person will write one idea per note until he/she has run out of ideas or the allotted time has passed. *This is to be done silently.*

4. When finished, each person places his/her ideas on the board or in the middle of the table for all to see.

5. Silently, the group then begins moving like ideas into categories. Generally, groups put like ideas into vertical columns.

6. Individuals may continue moving cards from one grouping to another until everyone is satisfied. Ideas that don't seem to "fit" any category can be placed into a miscellaneous one. Individuals can ask for clarification about the meaning of any idea they are unclear about.

7. The group as a whole will determine titles or "headers" for each category. Headers ought to be noun/verb phrases for greater understanding and clarification.

8. Each agreed-on header is written on a sticky note of a distinguishing color and placed at the top of its respective column. To complete the affinity diagram, each group of ideas is enclosed in a rectangle.

When

Use this tool when:

- One or more individuals in the group are very assertive and others are quiet and shy

- It is important to learn what individuals' ideas or thoughts are about a complex topic

- You want to know how much students know about a topic

- The class is studying categorization or classification

Example

Topic

What are the elements of a successful field trip?

Permission slips   Adults to help   Cooperation from everybody   Lunch or snacks

Learn a lot   Go to a fun place   Admission money   Nice weather   Ask questions

Good manners   Friendly bus driver   Buddy system   See interesting stuff

Don't climb on stuff without permission   Don't fight   Be good listeners

Affinity Diagram

What are the elements of a successful field trip?

Things to remember	We wish for	We want to	Help we need!
Permission slips	Nice weather	See interesting stuff	Adults to help
Admission money		Go to a fun place	Friendly bus driver
Ask questions		Learn a lot	Cooperation from everybody
Be good listeners			
Don't fight			
Buddy system			
Lunch or snacks			
Good manners			
Don't climb on stuff			

Other Educational Topic Ideas

- Characteristics of a "quality" student

- Things that fly

- Modes of transportation

- What do you know about your state?

- What keeps students from doing homework?

- Animals with four legs

- Characteristics of the major characters of a novel

ENTHUSIASM AND LEARNING (E/L) CHART

What

The *enthusiasm and learning* (E/L) *chart* gives feedback to the teacher about the relationship between student enthusiasm for learning and how much was learned. This provides an important means for teachers to gain input from students about what to change so they can learn more and enjoy it too.

How

The steps to creating an E/L chart are:

1. Create a matrix like the one shown, with the learning continuum along the left vertical and enthusiasm horizontally along the bottom.

2. At the end of each day, week, lesson, or unit, ask students to silently reflect on their learning and the activities they were engaged in to learn it.

3. Pass out colored dots or provide colored markers to the students. (If the chart is laminated it can be used over and over throughout the school year.)

4. Each student will silently come to the chart—preferably without the teacher present to preserve anonymity—and put a dot or marker in the square that best represents his/her feelings about the classroom experience.

When

At the end of a day, week, lesson, or unit.

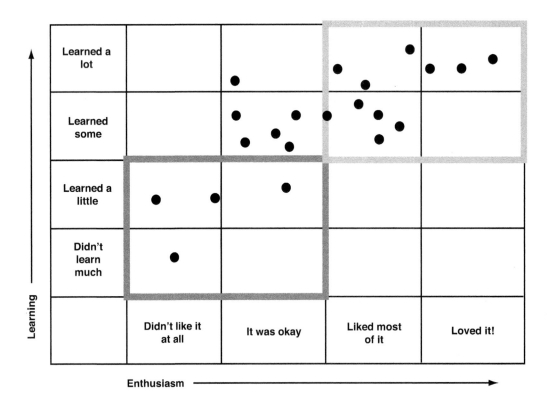

	Didn't like it at all	It was okay	Liked most of it	Loved it!
Learned a lot				
Learned some				
Learned a little				
Didn't learn much				

Learning →

Enthusiasm →

Example

Relationship between Enthusiasm and Learning—Ninth Grade Social Studies

Learning

Enthusiasm →

PLUS/DELTA CHART

What

A *plus/delta chart* is a simple feedback tool that can be used at the end of each day, unit, or after any lesson. It provides teachers, team leaders, and others with valuable information about how to improve.

How

1. Draw a vertical line in the middle of a piece of flip-chart paper—or on the chalkboard.

2. Approximately four inches down from the top, draw a horizontal line across the paper.

3. In the upper-left rectangle, draw a large "+" sign.

4. In the upper-right rectangle, draw a large "Δ" sign (the mathematical symbol for "change").

5. Explain your desire to gain feedback in order to improve the class, assignment, unit, test, meeting, and so on.

6. *Wording is very important.* Say, "Please share with us what worked for you today, what was good about the day, perhaps an "aha!" you had today, or maybe what you learned today. What was good about today?"

7. When all the good news is exhausted, go on with the deltas. "Please tell me what we can do differently tomorrow so we can all have a better day." Or, in the case of a plus/delta after a test, you might say, "What could we do differently to prepare so that we could all do better on the test." Remind everyone that this is about *how to change, and not what was done wrong.*

8. Give the group sticky notes to write their comments on. Ask them to write a "+" or "Δ" at the top of the note and then one comment per note.

9. Or, write all ideas on the chart if the group is unable to write their own feedback.

10. Take each delta into consideration for the following day, unit, and so on. Let the students know how you've changed things in response to their requests for change. This will help build trust and student buy-in to the quality effort.

When

Use this tool:

- After completing any unit

- The last three minutes at the end of the day

- At least weekly in high school, at the end of each class period if operating on a block schedule

- When there is a need to determine issues students have after taking a test

What helped you learn? What did you like? $+$	What kept you from learning? What is a better way to learn? Δ
I loved the experiments	I didn't feel like anyone listened to me
The way we were able to work with each other	Reading too hard
Neat video	Not enough time to finish everything
	Lectures were not interesting

RADAR CHART

What

A *radar chart* shows the gaps between current performance and ideal performance using a number of previously agreed-on key criteria (from the multi-voting technique).

How

1. Select and operationally define the characteristics to be rated. The chart can handle up to 10 characteristics.

2. Construct the chart:

   • Draw a large wheel with as many spokes as there are characteristics.

   • Around the outside of the wheel, label each spoke (characteristic).

3. Scale the chart. If the desire is to increase the behavior or results, do the following:

   • Mark a "zero" at the center of the wheel and "100%" at the outside end of each spoke.

   If the desire is to decrease the behavior or results, do the following:

   • Mark "100%" at the center of the wheel and "zero" at the outside end of each spoke.

   For all charts:

   • Along each spoke, put hash marks indicating percentages moving toward the desired outcome, either 100% or 0%.

   An alternative way to scale the chart is from 0–10.

4. Put the data on the chart:

   • Put a dot along each spoke corresponding to the numerical value of the data.

   • When data are on the chart, connect the dots in circular fashion.

5. Interpret the chart:

   • The radar chart shows the gap between the optimal and the current reality.

   • Each radar chart can handle up to four different sets of data for the same characteristics. It is suggested that a different colored marker be used each time data are put on the chart. The value of this is to show growth or growing gaps that must be addressed.

6. Act to improve:

- Look at the gaps between the optimal rating and actual rating for each characteristic being measured.

- Engage students in a brief brainstorming activity to address the lowest area of performance.

- Ask for clarification regarding student suggestions and determine what will be done differently the following week.

- If there is little or no improvement in the way the radar chart looks, engage students in a cause-and-effect diagram to discover what is keeping the results stagnant.

When

Use this tool when:

- There is a desire to look at more than one characteristic at a time

- You want the class or individuals to see the gap between current and desired performance

- You have a desire to have the group become more aware of where they need to improve

Example: Mission Specificity

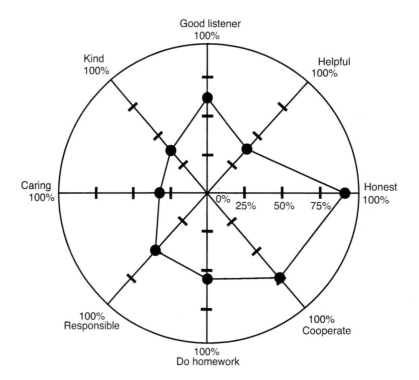

Example: Weekly Timed Math Quiz

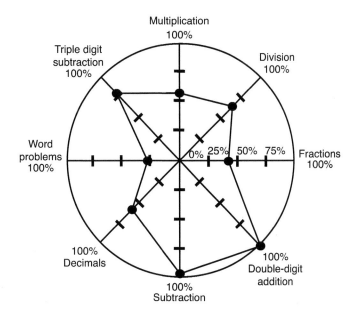

6

Student As Worker Focus

CONVERSATION WITH THE TEACHER

Have you ever had the feeling that you were working way too hard, putting a great deal more energy into the classroom than your students? Do you ever leave school at the end of the day feeling exhausted, knowing that there is a stack of papers to grade and return the next day? We believe you are absolutely right—you are doing too much work, carrying too much of the burden for student learning, not knowing there is another way!

Now, more than ever, our country needs exemplary teachers who create classroom systems that are fully aligned and integrated with the vision and mission of the district and school. It starts with trust. How much do you trust your students to help create the class-room climate and culture of success? Students, yes, even kindergartners, are capable of being responsible for their own learning and demonstrating it. You must trust and continue to build relationships. (Yes, we know some students will test your patience.) Remember— no shame, no blame! As you first find and remove the barriers to success in partnership with your students, look to rekindle your flame for learning so that you can rekindle the flame for all students. We urge you to resist the temptation to "just do it" by yourself— because it's easier, faster, and so on.

How will you discover the barriers? In the last chapter we addressed a noninstructional process in which the teacher engaged the students in identifying the "muddy points" of the process. In another example the science teacher addressed an instructional process problem and was able to make a midcourse correction. Both teachers sought feedback from their students and made changes based on their suggestions. It becomes clear that when teachers listen and respect students' opinions based on their classroom experience(s), barriers to learning can be eliminated. This chapter builds on what you learned in the last one.

In this chapter you will learn:

- About student data notebooks

- How to reduce variation in student work using quality factors

- To replace your reward and recognition system with a celebration system

STUDENT DATA NOTEBOOKS

If students are to be our partners in their education, they have a responsibility to know how well they are doing. The idea that students can or will keep track of their own data helps them realize that the teacher does not "give" grades arbitrarily, but rather grades are "earned." Another reason to have students keep track of their own progress is to teach them how to reflect, set goals, and create personal action plans for improvement. This is an important life-long skill.

When students track their own data, each can say s/he has understood and is demonstrating the first principle: *I am responsible for my own learning.* In elementary schools (at least the primary grades) student data notebooks are generally kept at school in a special place in the classroom. "How much time will it take?" and "Can young children really chart their own data?" are two frequently asked questions. Anything new takes time, but once you train the students and provide them with some guidance, not only even the youngest can do this, but we have seen many special education students track their own data too.

We say *data notebooks*, but they can just as easily be folders or pages in an organizer. Many middle and high school teachers prefer to establish data pages in spiral notebooks for each subject. Loose papers are the least efficient method simply because it is too easy for individual papers to get lost. The benefit of a three-ring data notebook or folder with brackets is that pages can be added as the school year progresses. Some schools have students keep an electronic data notebook or porfolio and these are accessible to teachers, administrators, counselors, and parents. It is the wave of the future.

Warning: This can be a messy activity. That is, the youngest and perhaps some special needs students will have trouble *staying within the lines* of the various charts. Teachers who are fastidious about neatness and organization have a difficult time "letting go" of the need for perfection. (Think about your own early learning experiences. Were you always "neat" and "inside the lines"?) It's a maturation process and, in the end, having students take the responsibility is the fastest way to ensure that students connect the dots between their work, work habits, and how much they learn. Teach them as early as kindergarten how to chart data. Charting is a math standard too, so this is not time wasted. Later in this chapter you'll see examples.

You may want to discuss this with your administrator and/or PLC peers in a conversation about the value and purpose of the notebooks before designing a process of implementation. (Refer to the model for process design on page 72, in Chapter 3. Here are some important considerations:

- Where will the notebooks be kept?

- Will students be allowed to take the notebooks home for parents to review?

- What will the notebooks look like?

- Will the notebooks be standardized across grade levels, or middle/high school courses?

Some teachers keep the notebooks on a shelf; others allow students to keep them in their cubbies. Secondary teachers who've decided not to allow their students to leave the room with their binders establish a filing system in the back of the room. Others, as we indicated earlier, have organized data pages in each student's spiral notebook where everything is kept together—class notes and learning results. We've seen a first grade teacher line the notebooks up on the floor, and fourth grade teachers who have students keep their binders in their desks. There are probably as many options as you have imagination. The vital thing is that a system be put into place prior to starting this process, and that you spend time having students practice charting learning and behavior. Don't forget to decide where to put the notebooks when finished. It will save you a lot of headaches down the road if you front-load the system with proper planning. Just don't insult the students by assuming they can't or won't be responsible if you set a clear expectation.

Another consideration is *when* students will be given time to record results in their notebooks. There are several schools of thought. Some teachers believe strongly that recording data should be done on the same day, at the same time, every week. Others think it best to have students record their results immediately after receiving them. In either case, you'll want to make certain that students have enough time to chart and then reflect on the results. The reflection piece can not be understated as it is a twenty-first century skill that needs more emphasis. Once again, make a decision before implementing this process. The important thing is that students in your classes start keeping track of their own results.

In Chapter 7 you'll see that student data notebooks can be a precursor to student-led parent conferences. When students have to explain to their parents/guardians how well they are doing and what plans they have for improving, it emphasizes the importance of learning.

Basics of Student Data Notebooks

- Class purpose, vision, mission, and class goals

- Quality factors for a student—operationally defined

- Two principles of a quality classroom (I am responsible and I am response-able)

- Some kind of learning styles awareness chart or sheet

- Sheets for weekly quizzes by subject—generally set out for the semester or grading period (bar graph, run chart, or radar chart format)

- Sheets for monthly assessments for the entire year by subject (bar graph or run chart)

- Goal-setting sheets with action plans for improvement (one per subject per week for primary grades or per month for grades 3–12)

- Blank radar charts for social skills improvement—quality student or mission

- Parent review and signature sheet—elementary and middle school

- Record of required skills/concepts needed to master for the year or semester

Added features that can make the experience more powerful:

- For students in grades three and above, a personal mission statement.

- *I am proudest of* . . . sheets (one per subject per marking period).

- Copies of any and all rubrics or QF checklists used for grading purposes. This should include the district or school writing rubric (restated in child-friendly language appropriate for the grade level and easily understood by parents) and other project rubrics with clearly spelled out operationally defined quality factors.

- Other?

What follows are some examples that might prove helpful to you. Select from the laundry list of examples and see what works best for you. There are also numerous school district websites with examples. We've included two that we believe are very helpful and insightful: Cedar Rapids, Iowa and Montgomery County Schools, Maryland. See the Recommended Resources for URLs that link right to the examples. Above all, feel free to modify anything you see. *Caution:* be careful about copyright laws when you download anything off the Internet. We'd love to have you share your thoughts and examples with us. Figures 6.1, 6.2, and 6.3 are examples of student data notebooks, one suitable for students in primary grades and the others for secondary.

It is so important to help young children understand how their behavior impacts the class and learn ways to become independent, and at the same time develop relationships to become interdependent with others. Stephen Covey (*The 7 Habits of Highly Effective People*) rightly points out the importance of working together for greater success. Be mindful about Dr. Glasser's theory of the five basic human needs that drive all behavior (survival, love and belonging, power, freedom, and fun). Some days it is very difficult to maintain this perspective with patience and calm. We hope it is becoming clear how you (the leader) have to be vigilant and embrace the two principles (I am responsible . . . I am response-able . . .) every day. Students, too, must learn to embrace and practice the two principles. Some elementary classes, after morning announcements, recite the class vision, mission, and the two principles. The structure of the school day lends itself to this approach. At the end of the day the students work in their data notebooks to reflect on their work and behavior. It makes a difference. If it is your desire to have the students become independent learners, critical thinkers, with the ability to work together, then there must be a noncoercive way to reach that goal.

It is true that any students who have not had their basic needs met or learned how to develop healthy, productive habits present a variety of nonproductive and often disruptive behaviors in middle and high school. This poses a dilemma for many teachers, who are already stressed from the pressures of high-stakes testing in the "real" world of diversity (not simply ethnic or economic

This data notebook belongs to:

Our Purpose

We are here to LEARN and HAVE FUN!

Figure 6.1   Student data notebook suitable for primary grades.

Our class vision is: _We are the smartest 1st graders ever!_

_____

_____

_____

Our class mission is: _We will be kind to each other, offer help_

when needed, do our best work every day, listen carefully, and have

fun learning!

_____

Our class reading goal is: _We will all know 100 sight words_

by January.

Our class writing goal is: _We can all write a complete sentence_

before the end of March.

Our class math goal is: _Everyone will get at least 7 out of 10_

addition problems right on each weekly quiz for 5 weeks.

Figure 6.1 *Continued.*

I _____ will work hard to be a quality student.

Figure 6.1 *Continued.*

I learn best when:

It is quiet so I can read or look at books

I can talk in a small group with a teacher

I am alone using a computer

I can move around and manipulate things

Figure 6.1   *Continued.*

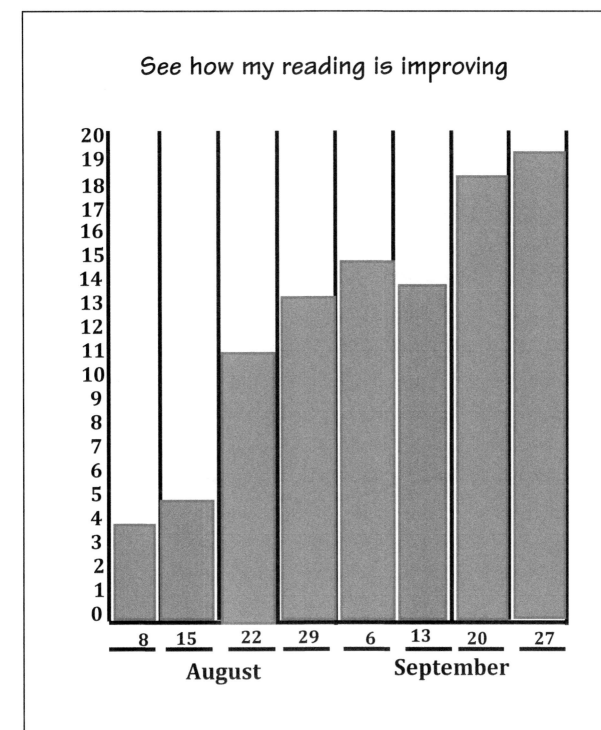

Figure 6.1 *Continued.*

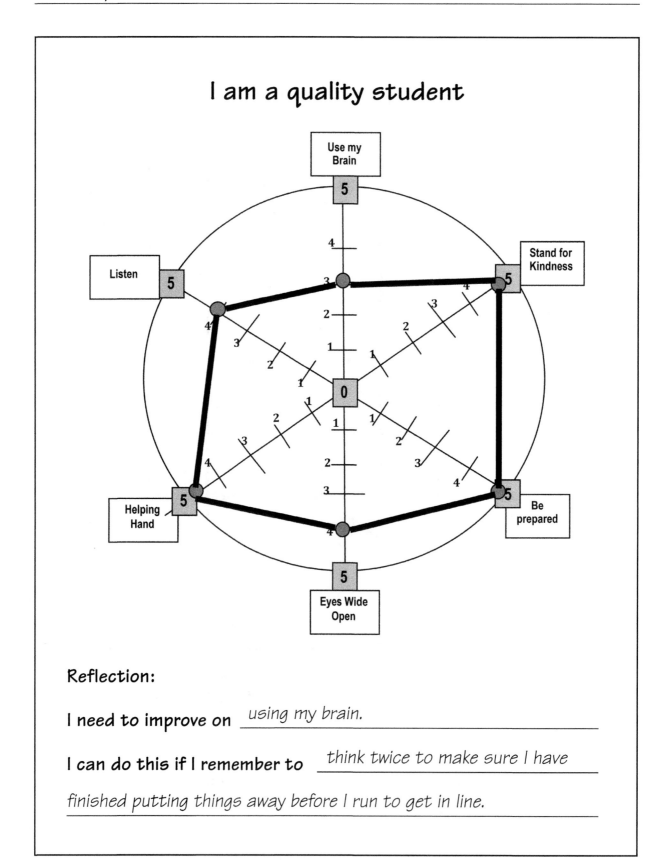

Figure 6.1 *Continued.*

See how my writing is improving!

	Upper case letters	Lower case letters	Use "." and "?"	Spell 25 sight words	Write a complete sentence
May					
March					
January					
November					
September					

Figure 6.1   *Continued.*

Dear _____ (Parents or Guardian),

Please review and discuss these results with your child. Please feel free to contact me anytime via e-mail _____ or by telephone at _____.

Your child will ask you to initial this form indicating you've chatted with your child about his/her results. I'll ask your help to assure it goes into _____'s backpack and is returned to school on Monday.

I am so pleased to have _____ in the class this year. Thanks for being a great partner.

Sincerely,

_____

Date	Initial	Date	Initial	Date	Initial	Date	Initial
9/5							
9/12							
9/19							
9/26							
10/3							
10/10							
10/17							
10/24							
10/30							
End of 1st marking period		End of 2nd marking period		End of 3rd marking period		End of 4th marking period	

Figure 6.1 *Continued.*

situation, but also personal responsibility for one's own actions). While we are sympathetic to this, we are also aware that trying to solve today's problems with previously tried tactics (many of which added to the problem) is foolhardy. Understand your system, together with the five basic human needs, and put it all together with Covey's *7 habits*. You are the leader—you are in charge of the classroom system—you are the one who must recognize barriers (learn from the students) and remove them to create a classroom culture of success for all (as you learned in Chapter 3).

Having each student chart his/her own data goes a long way to helping them learn to manage themselves. For the very young students, reflection at the end of the day on the quality factors for students is a good idea. Waiting until the end of the week is too long. They will not be able to remember. So, in order to be noncoercive, simply make this a part of the daily routine—something you do as part of the process of getting ready to go home. You see from the "reflection" part of the *I Am a Quality Student* page in Figure 6.1 that you have the children focus on one thing at a time. It may take a few minutes, but keep the end in mind. If this is a part of school routines, then students will learn to become personal problem solvers much earlier. Our suggestion is to add chart templates as the school year progresses in order not to overwhelm anyone with the volume of pages.

We've been pretty focused on early elementary thus far, but the same principles apply to all students. Figure 6.2 is an example of a data notebook suitable for secondary students, and Figure 6.3 is a middle school data notebook example from Ashleigh Burnette, sixth grade Language Arts teacher, Parkside Middle School, Manassas, Virginia.

In addition, at the end of each quarter, students are required to complete the form shown in Figure 6.4 and turn it in to the teacher. It clarifies and drives home the principle "I am responsible for my own learning." She uses this when holding individual conferences with her students.

STUDENT AS WORKER: DEFINE QUALITY AND REDUCE VARIATION

Most teachers we know are puzzled and deeply concerned about the wide range of variation in student work. If you think about it, the range for "accepted work" can vary from 100% correct to 60% correct. To unravel this puzzle, you need to understand the two types of variation (see Figure 6.5). Common cause variation represents the biggest problem for teachers and therefore requires further study as it indicates one or more problems with your process(es).

Variation causes rework. How much time do you spend reteaching because students don't "get it right" the first time? Just as unfortunate is the amount of time students spend doing things over again because they didn't understand exactly what was required the first time. Frustration is felt by both groups, and you're probably asking yourself what the remedy is. Teachers who are knowledgeable about Baldrige and have embraced the quality process do not accept sloppy, incorrect student work, but build-in processes that support excellent work and high-performance results. Let's delve deeper into this issue.

Have you ever wondered why there is such variation in completed assignments after you've given everyone the same instructions? Instructions that may seem clear to teachers are often ambiguous or not clearly defined for all students, and, unfortunately, some students do not feel

2012

Data Notebook

High School Freshman Academy

Name_____

Homeroom_____

Figure 6.2   Student data notebook suitable for secondary schools.

Table of Contents

Freshman Academy High School Team Vision

FA Team Mission

FA Student and Teacher Rights and Responsibilities

FA Teacher/Student Agreements

My Purpose, Vision, Quality Factors, Mission, Goals

My Skills and Knowledge Worksheet

Action Plans and Force Field Analysis

Core Subject Standards and Data (Example Sheets for All Core Subjects)*

PWCS Language Arts Benchmarks and Evidence—Grade 9

Weekly Homework Log

Quiz Results

Language Arts Unit Test Results

Electives—Standards, Assignments, Grades*

PDSA Reflection and Action Plan Sheets

*For brevity, not all are included here.

Figure 6.2 *Continued.*

Freshman Academy—High School

Team Vision

_____

_____

_____

Team Mission

_____

_____

_____

_____

Student and Teacher Rights and Responsibilities

_____

_____

_____

_____

_____

Example—Teacher/Student Agreements

- We agree to be mindful of the two principles—"I am responsible for my own learning" and "I am response-able to the success of the class"—the FA Team, and the entire Freshman Academy.

- We will be respectful partners committed to continuous improvement who analyze data to improve the instructional process and to improve personal learning results.

- We are committed to excellence and are not satisfied with mediocrity in instructional activities, participation, or the products of our work.

- We are committed team players, and agree to work with each other to support success for all.

- We will maintain an open mind and listen carefully to each other's suggestions for improvement.

- We recognize, appreciate, and honor diversity in backgrounds and experiences, and believe that each has something to teach one another. Therefore, we will listen first before imposing any judgments or solutions to problems that arise.

Figure 6.2 *Continued.*

My *purpose*—*Why* I am in school.

_____

_____

My *vision* for my life's work—*What* I want to become.

_____

_____

_____

My *quality factors*—A personal commitment to achieve my vision.

_____

_____

_____

My *mission*—*How* I will function to stay focused to my vision.

_____

_____

_____

Goals—*What milestones* must I reach to achieve my vision?

Long term (1 year)

_____

_____

Short term (1 marking period)

_____

_____

_____

_____

Figure 6.2   *Continued.*

List of Skills and Knowledge Needed

To become a successful _____ (career) I will need to acquire these skills and knowledge.

Personal skills	Skills and knowledge to "do the job"	Classes where I can learn these skills and gain the knowledge

Figure 6.2 *Continued.*

Action plans to reach my goals:

- Come to class on time
- Turn in all homework on time
- Ask questions if I don't understand
- Read and complete all assignments on time
- Eat properly to stay healthy

- Take notes in class as appropriate
- Listen attentively
- Work cooperatively with classmates
- Study before taking tests
- Get adequate sleep

Other_____

_____

Force Field Analysis

Goal	
+ Driving forces	**– Restraining forces**
Action plan to remove/diminish restraining forces:	
Who will help?	I need this kind of help:
Date to review progress	

Figure 6.2   *Continued.*

PWCS Language Arts Benchmarks and Evidence—Grade 9

Communication

Benchmarks: At the end of grade 9, students will demonstrate they can:

- Develop interpersonal communication skills as well as formal public speaking skills by making planned oral presentations independently and in small groups **9.1**

- Continue developing media literacy by producing, analyzing, and evaluating auditory, visual, and written media messages **9.2**

- Use the PWCS Communication Process

Benchmark evidence: Minimum number and types

- Four small-group oral presentations with each group member contributing by active speaking during the presentation, and two formal individual speaking presentations

- One of the presentations must involve poetry, a monologue, scene from a play, or other literary form

- Analyze and evaluate persuasive methods in at least five media messages

- Make and publish a media message

- Note-taking and questions/response to speaker to demonstrate consistent active listening

- Use the PWCS Communication Rubric

Reading

Benchmarks: At the end of grade 9, students will demonstrate they can:

- Expand general and specialized vocabulary through understanding of cognates and application of roots, affixes, and derivations that focus on Greek forms **9.3**

- Analyze the literature of a variety of cultures and eras to ascertain similarities and differences in artistic expression, societal institutions, and patterns of belief **9.4**, **9.5**

- Apply knowledge of figurative language and literary terms to the analysis of literature and other print materials **9.4**, **9.5**

- Continue developing reading comprehension skills, recognizing main ideas and supporting ideas, and the effect of formats and text structures **9.5**

- Use the PWCS Reading Process

Benchmark evidence: Minimum number and types

- A variety of evidence indicating that a student can use cognates, roots, affixes, and Greek forms to determine or clarify the meanings of words.

(Permission to print granted from Prince William County Schools, Manassas, Virginia.)

Figure 6.2   *Continued.*

- A variety of evidence, both spoken and written, that illustrates student growth in vocabulary and in analyzing world literature, literary forms, and elements. Evidence could include journals/learning logs, classroom discussion, presentations, essays and tests, and blind reading assessments.

- A variety of evidence, both spoken and written, that illustrates student growth in analysis of nonfiction texts and in the use of text features to locate information.

- Use the PWCS Reading Rubric.

- Minimum of 30 minutes of reading daily, applying critical reading skills at the independent level. Evidence to include reading logs, desk-side conferences, teacher–student book talks, and/or class discussion.

Writing

Benchmarks: At the end of grade 9, students will:

- Produce narrative, expository, and persuasive papers with an emphasis on analysis **9.6**

- Develop an individual writing style by analyzing and imitating models of narratives and analysis **9.6**

- Use writing as a tool for learning **9.6**

- Use the writing process effectively and demonstrate an understanding of correct grammar, capitalization, punctuation, spelling, sentence structure, and paragraphing **9.7**

- Use the PWCS Writing Process

Benchmark evidence: Minimum number and types

- Two narrative, two expository, and two persuasive writings with emphasis on analysis per semester

- A variety of daily writings as evidence of student thinking and learning

- A writing sample at the beginning and end of year that demonstrates by comparison student growth in grammar and writing skills

- Use the PWCS Writing Rubric

Research

Benchmarks: At the end of grade 9, students will demonstrate they can:

- Produce a well-documented research paper by locating, evaluating, synthesizing, and documenting information, following MLA and ethical and legal guidelines **9.8**

- Use the PWCS Research Process

Benchmark evidence: Minimum number and types

- One research paper, two to four (2–4) pages of body text

- Use the PWCS Research Writing Rubric

Figure 6.2 *Continued.*

Weekly Homework Log

Overarching homework goal: ___*I will turn in all homework on time.*___

Algebra assignments turned in

Assigned?	Day/date	Yes	No
YES	Mon, Oct. 1		
YES	Tues, Oct 2		
YES	Wed, Oct. 3		
YES	Thurs, Oct 4		
YES	Fri, Oct 5		

Biology assignments turned in

Assigned?	Day/date	Yes	No
YES	Mon, Oct 1		
YES	Tues, Oct 2		
YES	Wed, Oct 3		
YES	Thurs, Oct 4		
YES	Fri, Oct 5		

English assignments turned in

Assigned?	Day/date	Yes	No
YES	Mon, Oct. 1		
YES	Tues, Oct 2		
No	Wed, Oct. 3		
No	Thurs, Oct 4		
YES	Fri, Oct 5		

World history assignments turned in

Assigned?	Day/date	Yes	No
No	Mon, Oct 1		
YES	Tues, Oct 2		
YES	Wed, Oct 3		
YES	Thurs, Oct 4		
No	Fri, Oct 5		

Spanish assignments turned in

Assigned?	Day/date	Yes	No
No	Mon, Oct. 1		
YES	Tues, Oct 2		
YES	Wed, Oct. 3		
YES	Thurs, Oct 4		
No	Fri, Oct 5		

Band practice time

Assigned?	Day/date	Yes	No
YES	Mon, Oct 1		
YES	Tues, Oct 2		
YES	Wed, Oct 3		
YES	Thurs, Oct 4		
YES	Fri, Oct 5		

Figure 6.2   *Continued.*

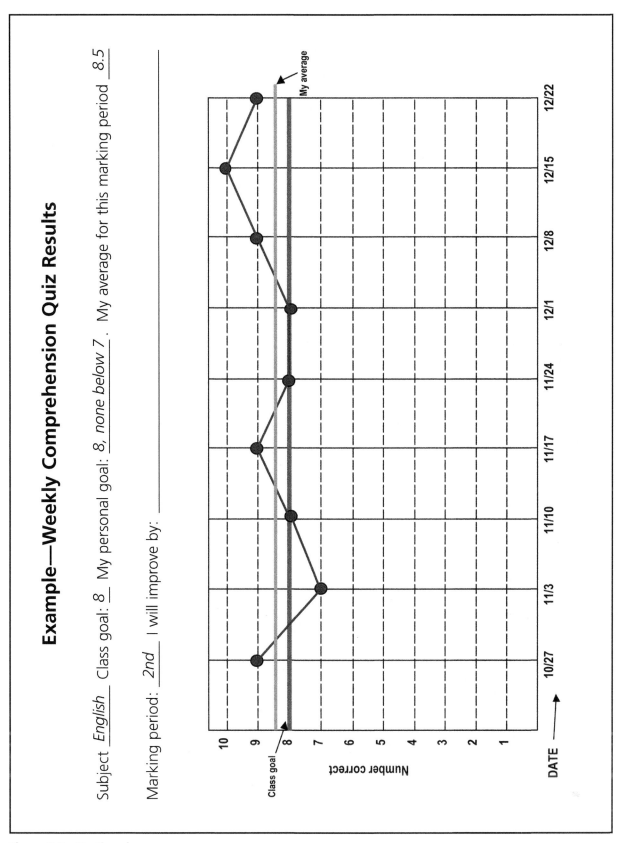

Figure 6.2 *Continued.*

Language Arts Unit Test Results

% Correct	Date	Time spent studying	Date	Time spent studying	Date	Time spent studying	Date	Time spent studying
100		1 hr. + 30–60 min. ≤ 30 min.		1 hr. + 30–60 min. ≤ 30 min.		1 hr. + 30–60 min. ≤ 30 min.		1 hr. + 30–60 min. ≤ 30 min.
90		1 hr. + 30–60 min. ≤ 30 min.		1 hr. + 30–60 min. ≤ 30 min.		1 hr. + 30–60 min. ≤ 30 min.		1 hr. + 30–60 min. ≤ 30 min.
80		1 hr. + 30–60 min. ≤ 30 min.		1 hr. + 30–60 min. ≤ 30 min.		1 hr. + 30–60 min. ≤ 30 min.		1 hr. + 30–60 min. ≤ 30 min.
70		1 hr. + 30–60 min. ≤ 30 min.		1 hr. + 30–60 min. ≤ 30 min.		1 hr. + 30–60 min. ≤ 30 min.		1 hr. + 30–60 min. ≤ 30 min.
60		1 hr. + 30–60 min. ≤ 30 min.		1 hr. + 30–60 min. ≤ 30 min.		1 hr. + 30–60 min. ≤ 30 min.		1 hr. + 30–60 min. ≤ 30 min.
50–below		1 hr. + 30–60 min. ≤ 30 min.		1 hr. + 30–60 min. ≤ 30 min.		1 hr. + 30–60 min. ≤ 30 min.		1 hr. + 30–60 min. ≤ 30 min.

Figure 6.2   *Continued.*

Reflection and Improvement Plan, Project, or Writing Assignment

Date: _____   Class: _____

Grade: _____

I met my goal for this assignment.   Yes ___   No ___

This represents my personal best.   Yes ___   No ___

I can improve my:

❏ Time management skills

❏ Organization

❏ Focus and following directions

❏ Attention to details

❏ Writing skills

❏ Creativity

❏ Presentation skills

I specifically plan to reach—or exceed—my goal for the next assignment by:

_____

_____

_____

My "quality control buddy" is _____ .

We are committed to helping each other and achieving our personal goals.

_____   _____

Signed: Student   Signed: Quality control buddy

Figure 6.2 *Continued.*

Personal Improvement Plan

Subject: _____   Date:_____

My vision: _____

My goal for this class: _____

My weekly data tells me:
- ❏ I am "on track" to reach my goal.
- ❏ I am not "on track" to reach my goal.

Homework completed and turned in on time _____   Homework grade _____

Unit test _____   Quiz _____   Project _____   Writing assignment _____

In class every day _____   On time every day _____   Participated _____

I realize I need to continue doing the following: _____

_____

_____ to reach my semester goal.

To get back "on track" I must begin doing the following: _____

_____

_____ to reach my semester goal.

I am committed to doing these things this week:

_____   _____

_____   _____

_____   _____

Signed: _____   Date:_____

Figure 6.2   *Continued.*

Middle School Example

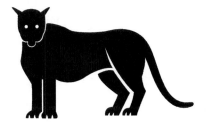

Name _____

Homeroom _____

Team _____

Figure 6.3   Student data notebook suitable for middle schools.

Vision and Mission Statements

Our team/class vision statement: _____

_____

_____

_____

Our team/class mission statement: _____

_____

_____

_____

I understand completely the vision and mission that we have set as a class/team and have committed myself to working hard to achieve these standards.

Signed: _____   Date:_____

My personal vision statement:_____

_____

_____

_____

My personal mission statement: _____

_____

_____

_____

I will work diligently so that my work/behavior will reflect my personal vision and mission statements.

Signed: _____   Date:_____

Figure 6.3 *Continued.*

My Academic Goal for _____ Quarter

I, _____ , plan to earn a grade of _____ in my Language Arts class for the second marking period, November _____ to January _____ .

Students who want to improve their grades, maintain high grades, improve their understanding, and show excellence in their work should consider the following:

❏ *Improve attendance* (do you miss school on a regular basis?)

❏ Complete *all* homework

❏ Taking steps to make sure you understand the material. These steps should include:

  ❏ Use *active listening skills*

  ❏ Make a point to listen and *follow directions carefully and completely*

  ❏ Ask the *teacher* for clarification when needed

❏ Use our *"Chunk, Click, and Clunk"* reading strategy when reading/studying

❏ Finding strategies to *stay focused* during class

❏ Improving *organization* of notebooks (See a teacher if you need help with this)

❏ Getting *more sleep* on school nights (turn off the games, TV, iPods, cell phones!)

Think about the items on this list. Put a check mark in the box next to the ones that you think will help you reach your goal in this class.

Figure 6.3 *Continued.*

My Reading Goals for the _____ Quarter

Number of pages read									
More?									
100									
90									
80									
70									
60									
50									
40									
30									
20									
10									
Week	1	2	3	4	5	6	7	8	9

Figure 6.3 *Continued.*

Week 1

I did/did not reach my reading goal this week. In order to meet my reading goal next week I will:

_____

_____

_____

Week 2

I did/did not reach my reading goal this week. In order to meet my reading goal next week I will:

_____

_____

_____

Week 3

I did/did not reach my reading goal this week. In order to meet my reading goal next week I will:

_____

_____

_____

Week 4

I did/did not reach my reading goal this week. In order to meet my reading goal next week I will:

_____

_____

_____

Week 5

I did/did not reach my reading goal this week. In order to meet my reading goal next week I will:

_____

_____

_____

Week 6

I did/did not reach my reading goal this week. In order to meet my reading goal next week I will:

_____

_____

_____

Week 7

I did/did not reach my reading goal this week. In order to meet my reading goal next week I will:

_____

_____

_____

Week 8

I did/did not reach my reading goal this week. In order to meet my reading goal next week I will:

_____

_____

_____

Week 9

I did/did not reach my reading goal this week. In order to meet my reading goal next week I will:

_____

_____

_____

Figure 6.3 *Continued.*

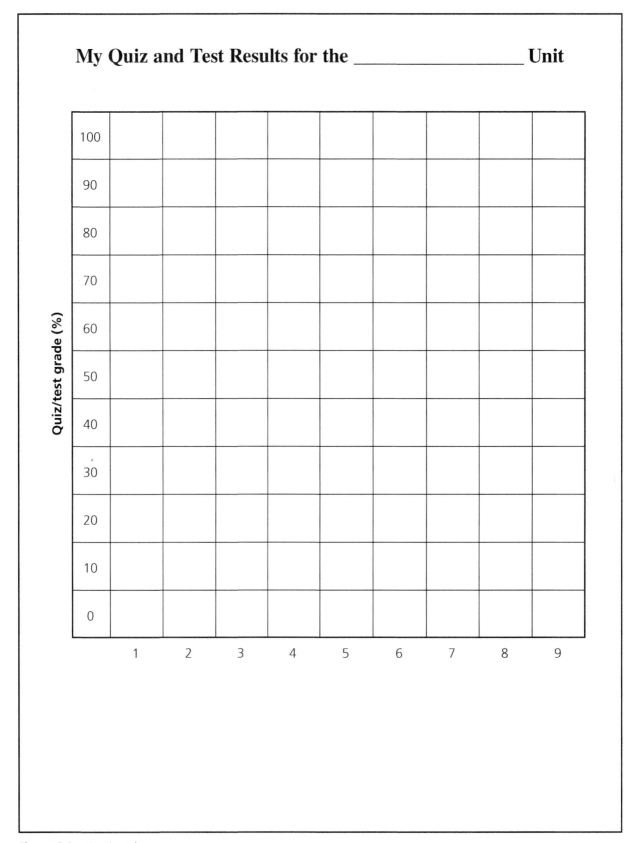

Figure 6.3 *Continued.*

Unit Test Reflection Sheet

Unit test _____

Grade received on test _____   Number of incorrect answers_____

I earned this grade because_____

_____

_____

_____

Test Question Corrections

_____ The correct answer should be _____ because _____

_____

_____

_____ The correct answer should be _____ because _____

_____

_____

_____ The correct answer should be _____ because _____

_____

_____

_____ The correct answer should be _____ because _____

_____

_____

I plan to improve my grade for the next test by _____

_____

_____

Figure 6.3   *Continued.*

Name: _____ Class period: _____ Date: _____

End of _____ Quarter Self-Evaluation

1. My final grade for this quarter is: _____

2. Did I meet my _____ quarter academic goal? _____ Yes _____ No

3. Looking at my _____ quarter action plan I can see that I: _____

_____

_____

_____

_____

_____

4. I am working toward achieving my vision for myself every day.

_____ Yes _____ No

5. Overall, I feel as if I gave my very best effort this quarter.

_____ Yes _____ No

Note from Mrs. Burnette: *You are an amazing Wolverine student! You can achieve anything you set your mind to. I am here to help you reach your goals. Please let me know what I can do to help you during the next school quarter.*

_____

_____

_____

_____

Figure 6.3 *Continued.*

Name: _____

End of Quarter Self-Assessment

Things that helped me reach my academic goal:

_____

_____

_____

_____

_____

_____

_____

_____

Things that kept me from reaching my academic goal:

_____

_____

_____

_____

_____

_____

_____

_____

Figure 6.3 *Continued.*

Name: _____

End of Quarter Data/Self Reflection

1. My personal goal was to make an _____ in this class for the _____ quarter.

2. My final grade for the _____ quarter was a _____ .

3. My grade on the _____ quarter benchmark exam was a _____ .

4. My personal reading goal for the _____ quarter was _____ .

5. I met my reading goal _____ .

6. Quality student:

Rate yourself from 1–10, just like you did for Mrs. Burnette. If you give yourself lower than a 9, explain why and what you can do in order to achieve a 9 or higher next quarter.

Respectful	1	2	3	4	5	6	7	8	9	10
Trustworthy	1	2	3	4	5	6	7	8	9	10
Participating	1	2	3	4	5	6	7	8	9	10
Prepared	1	2	3	4	5	6	7	8	9	10
Organized	1	2	3	4	5	6	7	8	9	10
Goal oriented	1	2	3	4	5	6	7	8	9	10

_____

_____

Figure 6.4   Student self-reflection form.

comfortable asking for clarification. (If this describes your classroom, it is necessary to understand what has driven fear into the classroom.) Or, do you wonder why some students don't seem to care about the work they turn in? Perhaps it is because when previous assignments were returned, students realized certain things went unnoticed and were, therefore, not considered important enough to remember. *The cumulative effect of this over time lends less credibility to the need for giving careful attention to work before it is turned in to the teacher.*

For example, a teacher might say, "Students, your book reports will be due on Monday. Remember to write your report in paragraph form and use proper punctuation, and include everything you have learned about good book reports."

Immediately, this teacher has invited trouble. In this example, one can not assume that all students can/will interpret the definition of "good book reports" exactly the same way. *Variation begins when there is no clear, concise definition of quality work.* To reduce the variation and to assure that more students meet the district, state, or national standards it is necessary to help students define *quality* in schoolwork, in their lives, and in their daily choices. Without ever thinking about what quality means, many students go through life with vague ideas and few discriminating habits. Quality factors and operational definitions set specifications and help reduce variation in students' work.

Common cause variation

Results from system problems and can only be eliminated by changing the system.

Example: The average number of students coming to first period class after the bell rings is 6. (Teacher is frequently late and doesn't take roll until the end of the period.)

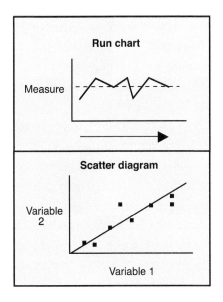

Special cause variation

Results from unpredictable and sporadic circumstances; not due to system problems but must be eliminated or addressed without changing the system.

Example: A spike in tardiness to class on a specific date. (A traffic accident resulted in 6 of 10 buses arriving late for school.)

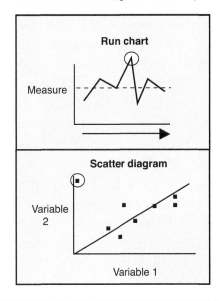

Figure 6.5 Types of variation.

Quality Factors and Quality Features

Quality factors are the absolute essential elements of a product or service. They are the *wow* factors, or the standard way to measure excellence of a product or service. Quality factors are determined by the customer—people who use the product or service and therefore constantly change.

All of us must be concerned that students understand quality work. The reasons that stand out most are:

- Too many students graduate without the minimal skills to succeed in the workforce or in postsecondary education.

- The extraordinarily high cost of rework and "educational scrap" drains instructional budgets. (Think remediation.)

- Unless all students understand what quality work is, they will be inadequately prepared to meet the challenges of their adult life.

- Students who can define and understand quality work are more discriminating about other areas in their lives.

In contrast to quality factors, students must understand *quality features. Quality features* are nonessential elements of a product or service that *delight the customer, going beyond meeting customer needs and expectations.* You must understand that today's quality features are tomorrow's quality factors. For example, think about video games from the early days of Pong (1972) and Pac-Man (1979). They are a far cry from the realistic, multi-layered, and challenging games of today. Some are violent, while others allow you to become a virtual team player in a sporting event. There is no end to the variety and levels of difficulty of video games these days. Who do you think has driven the movement toward more-complex games? The customer, of course!

The evolution of every product has been based on customer demand. What starts as the brainchild of the engineer/inventor becomes an upward spiral as consumers expect more and more. This even plays out in sports. Think for a moment about professional golfers. In the days when Arnold Palmer and Jack Nicklaus dominated the game in the sixties and seventies, golfers were not especially physically fit. They focused on their swings and putting. In the late 1990s, a young man named Tiger Woods came onto the scene and in 1997 won his first PGA championship—the U.S. Open at the age of 21. Tiger revolutionized the game of golf because he not only made incredibly difficult shots, but he also was the first golfer to engage in a rigorous exercise program to strengthen all the muscles in his body. He understood that the power of a golf swing (translate into length of drive) comes from leg and arm strength and flexibility in the torso. Why is this example appropriate for this book? Tiger Woods single-handedly raised the quality bar/expectations for every other professional golfer. This is how quality expectations get ramped up.

It's important to have the discussion about quality work—what it means, what it looks like, and why it matters—with students of all ages. Once they have a clear understanding of the specifications, then they can work to meet the expectations. Activity 6.1 provides a suggestion about how to begin the dialogue with your students.

Helpful Tips:

- Guide the discussion along when students define quality factors to avoid getting bogged down in the activity.

- Always use a product with which the students are familiar when doing this activity.

- Avoid using "class specific" products such as designer clothing or athletic shoes.

- Use a product in which many students would be interested. Older students may be more concerned about cars or trucks, video games, or the latest app, but be careful when choosing one of these products.

- You may need to come back and use a similar activity just to remind students to more clearly define quality.

- Make the leap to the curriculum quickly so the lessons learned in Activity 6.1 are not lost on students. The next section will help you with the transition.

Activity 6.1   Define quality (more suitable for elementary students, though you could use different types of food and have success with older students too).

Teacher prep work:

- Gather materials

  - Three (3) different varieties of apples (one set of apples for each table group of students); I generally use Red Delicious, Fuji, and Granny Smith apples, but you can use any product with which all students are familiar. Food seems to work out well, but we know some teachers have used bubble gum, and pencils. Avoid using any product that would discriminate against students of lower socioeconomic status or other cultures.

  - Napkins—one per person.

  - Small paper plates (mark each plate with an A, B, or C). Each table will have one set (A, B, and C) of plates.

  - Decide which variety of apple will be A, B, and C. Organize the apples on the plates, for example, all Red Delicious will be A, all Fuji will be B, and so on.

  - A plastic knife on each table (if you are uncomfortable having students cut the apples, you can cut all the apples).

  - Pass out a copy of the *data collection form* (DCF) for each student.

  - Use the Elmo, or Smart Board, or make a transparency of the *data collection plan* (DCP) template.

- Explain to the students that for this activity they will be *quality inspectors*, an important scientific job. Their task is to discover the *wow* or quality factors for an eating apple, and to test each apple to see if it meets expectations. Remind students that the factors for an eating apple are different than those for apples used in baking, for example.

Steps:

1. Ask the students to go back into their memory and visualize the *best* eating apple they've ever had. Visualizing helps bring the senses into play to articulate quality factors.

2. Capture all brainstormed student suggestions on the chart or smart board.

Continued

3. After all ideas are exhausted, review the list and ask, *"Are there any ideas on this list that may not be* absolutely essential *characteristics of the* best *eating apple?"*

4. Eliminate those that the class agrees are not absolutely essential, but remind the students that these qualities are individual preferences and, therefore, are quality features that delight them, making them important but not essential to a *wow* eating apple. An example might be *shiny* or *caramel dipped.*

5. Ask, *"Can any of the remaining ideas be combined?"* If so, put them together.

6. Explain that for the purposes of this experiment, the group should consider only three quality factors. Also explain that you've selected three different varieties of apples, so that eliminates taste and color from becoming quality factors. Taste is a factor (sugar content) for the wholesale buyer and does impact the amount of money paid to a grower, but this class doesn't have the capability of measuring sugar content. Therefore, for our purposes, taste (sweet or sour) becomes a quality feature. The same goes for color, which is important when the buyers set the price to the growers.

7. Explain the necessity of establishing a data collection plan. (Create a transparency similar to the data collection plan below and project it for the class to view.) DCPs answer key questions about what the quality factors are, how they will be measured, and specifics about what data are to be collected. *The teacher completes the DCP.* Have the class operationally define each of the quality factors and completely fill in the DCP.

Data Collection Plan

Quality factor	Operational definition	How measured?	When?	By whom?
Example: Juicy	*Example:* Juice is visible on plate immediately after apple is cut	*Example:* Visual test	*Example:* Immediately after cutting apple	*Example:* Everyone on the team will do the test. The team leader or aide or teacher will cut the apple

Continued

8. Ask students to take out the data collection form (as shown below). As a class, decide which of the three quality factor tests need to be done first, second, and third. The type of test (visual, tactile, audio, and so on) and what is being measured determine the order of tests. Students individually fill in the quality factors in the order each will be tested.

Data Collection Form

Name: *Suze*   Date: *9/12/12*

Quality factor	Operational definition	How measured?	When?	Sample A	Sample B	Sample C
Example: Juicy	*Example:* Juice is visible on plate immediately after apple is cut	*Example:* Visual test	*Example:* Immediately after cutting apple	Q	Q	–

9. Each student completes his/her data collection form, paying close attention to the agreed-on operational definitions for each quality factor.

10. Give the students 10 minutes to perform each quality test individually and to chart the data. Each apple is to be judged independently from the others, and only as to whether or not it meets each quality factor—based *solely* on the operational definition. Students should mark a "Q" if it meets the operational definition, or "–"if it does not. Do this for each apple and each quality factor.

11. Allow five minutes for teams to come to consensus on *each* quality factor for *each* variety of apple. It is possible that none of the apples will meet all the QFs. Likewise, it is possible that all of them will. Remind students that the only "test" is whether or not each apple meets the precise operational definitions for each QF.

12. Debrief with these questions:

Continued

- How many teams had complete agreement before the team discussion? *Variation* in the results of team members depends on the completeness and clarity of the operational definitions. (This is one significant cause of variation in student work.)

- What were the benefits to having you (students) determine the quality factors?

- What are the insights you have gained about the differences between quality factors and features?

The customer defines *quality*. This is a central reason to engage students in helping to determine quality factors. They, the students, are customers in the classroom. By engaging them in this manner, students are active rather than passive, and further embody the two principles: *I am responsible for my own learning* and *I am response-able to the success of the group*. It requires students to think critically about what quality is and to be precise in their thinking. We recommend you not overwhelm students in the Fall with a long list of QFs (especially in primary grades), but that as the weeks and months progress, the expectations rise and more QFs are added. For example, in the Fall a kindergarten teacher may have one QF for assignments turned in—name on paper. But quickly the bar is raised. Kindergartners would be expected to write upper- and lower-case letters, eventually write words, then simple two-word sentences, correctly spell a number of sight words, and so on. It is the same for all grades and all disciplines. We call this "ratcheting up" quality expectations, and students can, if given the opportunity, help.

By-products of this type of thinking spread to their personal lives, and we have heard stories of students teaching their parents about quality when they go to the grocery store. It is a great way to get parents involved in discussions about quality and quality work.

Teachers play a customer role too, and represent the needs/expectations of customers not present, such as the next teacher in line and the district. When it comes to learning activities, teachers must also participate in establishing quality factors, especially when students don't always come up with what the teacher knows is expected.

Establish Quality Factors for the Assignment and Create Clear High-Performance Expectations

Like all states, Hawaii uses a rubric to assess students' abilities to meet writing standards. The rubric uses a five-point scale with these five dimensions—meaning, voice, clarity, design, and conventions. We submit that teachers may want to change the way they approach writing and set the expectations for all students at the highest level, then help students reach the goal through QFs and repeated cycles of peer assessment with coaching from the teacher.

It doesn't matter how your state has defined the writing dimensions, what matters is how you guide students to raise expectations over the course of a school year. We highly recommend beginning the school year with the expectation that all students will write at a score point of four (on a five-point scale, or three on a four-point scale) and then quickly raise the bar to the highest level for all students. Impossible, you say? Perhaps in a traditional classroom, but how can you be sure? Teachers in a BBQ classroom will have a much greater chance of having more, if not all, students reach the highest levels. Figure 6.6 shows our suggestion, and a partial example is given in Figure 6.7.

Example: Goal (Language Arts)—Write to communicate for a variety of purposes and audiences.

Duty of the teacher:

1. Identify the state standards to be addressed. Example: Compose a well-organized and coherent writing sample for specific purposes and audiences.

2. Establish the purpose of the assignment. Example: To write an expository essay.

3. Determine the assignment. Example: Write a story about people close to you.

4. Determine the quality factors. See the example in Figure 6.10.

Duty of the teacher and students together:

Determine, through a brainstorming process, the operational definitions *for each of the standards to be addressed.*

Figure 6.6 A process for determining QFs for learning.

Quality factor	Operational definition	Q? / NY?	Coaching tips
Explains or describes the topic	At least 3 valid points		
Length	5 paragraphs		
Paragraphs	All—topic sentence		
	All—supporting details		
	#1 Introduces the topic and intent of entire essay		
	#2–4 Relate to and elaborate on the introduction		
	#5 Conclusion—summarizing points		
Grammar	Spelling		
No errors	Subject–verb agreement		
	Punctuation		
	Capitalization		
	Parts of speech		
	No sentence fragments		
	No run-on sentences		
Neatness	No smudges or erasures		
	No wrinkles		

Figure 6.7 Writing QFs—a checklist and peer coaching guide.

In Figure 6.7, the fourth grade students helped determine the quality factors and the operational definitions. This is just a partial list to demonstrate how students helped and came up with definitions in their writing assignment. This allowed everyone to know precisely what the expectations were. Students self-assessed their writing, and then everyone had a "buddy" who reviewed, assessed the writing, and gave coaching tips to explain what was needed to improve to meet the quality factors. Students then had an opportunity to edit their work before turning it in.

In a BBQ classroom, the peer assessment process is considered very important, and students and teachers take it seriously. This relates to the principle of *"I am response-able to the success of the class."* It is not only the accomplished students who participate in this process; everyone is responsible for being a coach. Students learn to improve their own skills every time they are required to give coaching tips. Teachers, as facilitators, move around the class and easily can see when individual, small group, or whole class direct teaching is required.

We suggest that schools and grade-level teams adopt a standardized best practice writing process and expectations. Activity 6.2 allows you to practice, then answer the questions posed within the activity. If every teacher (regardless of subject matter) expected the same degree of expertise in writing, students would learn, variation would vastly decrease, and we submit that many more students would reach level 5 on any writing sample. This expectation, however, is not just to satisfy state requirements. Writing is an important life skill, and vital for anyone entering the job market. It is time to set the bar high for all students and then help them reach it.

Teach Students to Reflect on Their Own Work and the Work of Their Peers

Steps:

1. Put one of the work samples (see the examples in Figures 6.8 and 6.9) on the Smart Board (or any type media you have available) and draw everyone's attention to the first quality factor. Ask the students to reflect on the sample and determine whether or not the QF is visible. Get a volunteer to come and point out where the QF is in the document. If it is not there, describe the problem and what needs to be done to meet that particular QF.

2. Repeat this with the other work samples, different student volunteers, and other quality factors.

3. Show another sample and ask the students to rate it for each quality factor. If the sample meets any quality factor, students can put a "Q" in the appropriate box. If it does not, write "NY" (meaning *not yet*) in the appropriate box and provide coaching tips.

4. For each writing or project activity, have students reflect on their own work for quality, and if any QFs are missing, revise the work. Before turning any work in, ask students to give their papers to another student for peer reflection and coaching, if necessary.

Friends

A friend is someone who is there for you and cares about what you do. Some people even have friends to help them do things like homework. I have friends so I won't get lonely or sad. A friend is a very special person. Sometimes they are friends you go to birthdays or sleepovers. Friends are people you can tell anything that you can't tell others. Sometimes you can tell them things you can't tell your family like if you got a bad grade in school.

Friends are people that are special to you. Sometimes people get there friends to do chores for them. But sometimes you just have to let them go and not bother with them. Or like myself I just ignore them to get more work done, but sometimes you need them to help you.

The kinds of friends you would like is friends like Mohala, Krystal, Elizabeth, and Lehua. You would like that kind of friend because they all have a sense of humor. They all are this type of friend.

Figure 6.8   Student writing sample—third grade. (This sample has been retyped exactly as the anonymous student author wrote it.)

My Sassy Sister

I have a sassy sister. She yells at me so loud by ears come off. She bosses me around and I hate it because, she declares "You don't do anything around the house." But I clean the house every Wednesday. What else does she want me to do? She thinks she own my mom's house. But she is not paying the T.V. bill, the phone bill, the water bill, and the electric bill. Man I hate my sister. When we both disagree on something we fight and talk back like this "Am I talking to you, No!" I reply. She grumbled. "Did I say anything, No!" Then she teases me and say Jennifer Pest the door." You see my last name is Pescador. I cry and slam my door behind me because I'm mad. Man I really hate my sister but if I get in trouble she will always be by my side so I guess she isn't bad after all.

Figure 6.9   Student writing sample—second grade. (This sample has been retyped exactly as the anonymous student author wrote it.)

Activity 6.2   Assess the writing samples

Directions: There are two writing samples provided (Figures 6.8 and 6.9). Use Figure 6.7, a QF checklist (made from a rubric and turned into user-friendly and explicit QFs) and assess one or both samples for quality. Do this by yourself, with a partner, or your PLC. Then, look at the writing rubric you use and answer these questions: Are the requirements (QFs) stated in student-friendly language? Would a student in your class know clearly how s/he can get from one level to the next? How might you put your rubric into a checklist to make it easier for your students to achieve greater success?

Helpful Tips:

- Avoid overwhelming students in the beginning of the year with too many QFs. Begin small and add more with each assignment. Soon, the students will uniformly be achieving more than ever before.

- Teach reflection skills often in the beginning, and especially when the quality factors are "ratcheted up," as this means there is a higher level of specifications to which students are going to be held.

After years of using this approach, we've come to realize the importance of having all teachers calibrate how the writing is scored. Enjoy!

Now, let's look at two other examples for secondary students. Figure 6.10 is an example from Christine Don's middle school Social Studies class at Voyager Charter School, Honolulu, Hawaii. This assignment not only differentiated instruction, but also provided very specific QFs for any of the approaches a student decided to do. If you were a student in this classroom, would there be any doubt you would know the exact path to take to receive all the points?

(Note: We have included the entire project *selection packet* to dispense with confusion about what differentiation means and what it "looks like" in a real setting. The significance of the range of choices students have and the quality factors and explicit operational definitions (expectations) set by Mrs. Don can not be overstated. You can see QFs for the flag and trading cards. We think this is an exemplary example of addressing different student interests and abilities while at the same time holding all students to high expectations. By the way, all students were given the same Revolutionary War unit test.)

Figure 6.11 shows a unique high school English project example from Teressa De Dominicis, English teacher at Potomac High School, Dumfries, Virginia. She created this approach after the ninth grade students' request for some "fun" activities. It has been wildly successful for her and it accommodates different learning styles. Can you think of a better way to teach "*voice*"?

In both the Revolutionary War Project and the *Odyssey* Postcard Project, the quality factors are operationally defined. When you make it easier for students to clearly understand the requirements, variation in the products received by teachers is narrowed and more students succeed. The process becomes even more powerful when students are empowered to participate in operationally defining the quality factors as buy-in rises exponentially.

APPROPRIATE CELEBRATIONS (REWARD AND RECOGNITION SYSTEM)

Students are workers in the classroom system, and learning can be hard work. It's often hard to keep the energy level high, and even more difficult to maintain high levels of student enthusiasm and motivation or desire for learning as students struggle to master increasingly difficult material.

A Differentiated Social Studies Project:
Choices and Expectations

Generously shared by:
Christine Don, Middle School Teacher
Voyager Charter School
Honolulu, Hawaii

Figure 6.10   Example of project expectations and QFs.

Dear readers: Midway through my classes' unit on the American Revolution, I introduced a project that would be a good portion of their grade (100-point project). The project ideas were found at the Highland Park Middle School (Dallas, TX) website. I changed some of the projects and rubrics to fit the resources available to my students.

1. *Introduce the project choices*: I distributed the project choices to the whole class. The options were read aloud and discussed. I tried to identify which projects required more writing, and which were more technical.

2. *Introduce project rubrics*: Each project rubric was passed out to the students. These were read aloud and discussed as a whole class. I wanted the kids to be sure they knew the expectations up front.

3. *Establish project checkpoints and deadlines*: We identified checkpoints and the final due dates, and the kids wrote these on their project choice sheet.

4. *Parent discussion and involvement*: The students brought their project packet home to discuss it with their parents. Both students and parents had to sign off on the project, and the choice made. Once the student had chosen a project, they were not allowed to change their minds. I counted the signed, returned choice sheet as a quiz grade.

Checkpoints: The kids had four weeks to complete the project. I allotted 30 minutes per class period (90-minute blocks) for the kids to research and work in class on their project. I established checkpoints (two for the 7th and 8th grades, three for the 6th) where the kids had to bring in what they had completed up to that point. I counted these as 5-point quiz grades—they either had made progress (5 pts) or they had not (0 pts). This was used to help ensure that the kids did not wait until the last minute to begin. It also helped ensure they were productive during class time.

Oral presentation: To help offset the weight of this project on their overall grade (if they failed the project, they were at risk of failing the trimester), I introduced a presentation component to their grade. The kids would have to present their project orally to the class. Again, I distributed the rubric beforehand (rubric was made at http://rubistar.4teachers.org). I told the kids that their oral grade would count as a 20-point test grade (tests and projects weighted the same). They would receive three evaluations—teacher, peer, and self. They could choose the peer. The three evaluations were averaged together. I copied the evaluations on different colored paper in order to distinguish between evaluators. If the student did not have their copy of the evaluation, then only two were averaged (teacher and peer). I did not provide additional student copies.

Analyis and reflection: When all the projects were graded, I created a stem-and-leaf plot for each class (refer to Project Scores). I then displayed these so that the different classes could analyze the data. The students were able to see how they compared to their peers, as well as identify which scores were outliers. The projects were displayed throughout the class, and since the kids had access to all the rubrics, they could easily identify which projects met quality standards. The kids also reflected on their work habits compared to other students—they said they were reflected in the grades.

Christine Don

Voyager Charter School, Social Studies Teacher

Figure 6.10   *Continued.*

AMERICAN REVOLUTION PROJECT CHOICES

This is a project worth one major grade, so make sure you choose a project that you can do well on and be proud of. I have offered many selections so that there will be something that appeals to everyone. These are just the descriptions of the projects; you will receive a detailed rubric that you must follow once you decide which one you want to do. Choose carefully; once you have turned in what project you are doing, you will not be allowed to change. Show your options to your parents and discuss it with them. They must sign off on what project you decide to do.

There will be checkpoints for each project along the way that will be announced at a later date.

1. Flags of the American Revolution

Research and make a replica of any American Revolution flag. It may be any of the following types of flags: Regimental, Artillery, Cavalry, Infantry, Company, Militia, or Battle. The flag can be either American/Patriot or British/Loyalists. You will then write a two-page paper on the history and details of your flag. Your research must include what group the flag belonged to, the reason behind the design of the flag, and battles in which it was flown. You may include any other interesting facts or details relating to your flag or the group that it belonged to. You must also include a bibliography documenting the sources you used. You must use at least five sources, two not being from the Internet.

- Dimensions should be approximately the following: width 21" and height 16" after being hemmed (no raw edges). Please stay within the size dimensions requested.
  You can use fabric, canvas, or any material besides paper.

- 40% of grade on the written research paper (must be typed—double-spaced, Times New Roman, size 12 font)

- 60% of grade on the flag (accuracy of design, color and neatness, historically accurate)

2. American Revolution Battle Chart and Map

Create a battle chart and map, which is accurate and gives full descriptions and locations of battles preselected by the teacher. Must include information on the selected battles; therefore, you must do research. It should be neat, colorful, and include appropriate drawings, pictures, and map to demonstrate battles in an interesting and educational manner. Your chart and map should correspond. You will need to include a bibliography that documents the sources you used. You must use at least five sources, two not being from the Internet.

- Chart must include the following information about the battles (name of battle, date, location, casualties, leaders, and outcome).

- Map must include the location of battles, a key denoting British and American victories, and important places (cities, headquarters, and so on).

- Map = 40%, Chart = 60%

Figure 6.10   *Continued.*

3. PowerPoint Media Presentation

Create a media presentation using the PowerPoint program. Your presentation will include various aspects of the American Revolution. You will have a total of 12 slides with an original script to accompany each slide. You will do the voice-over for each slide using your script. The categories you must include are: 3 Important People (1 Loyalist/British, 1 Patriot/American, 1 female), 3 Battles, 3 Events Leading to the Revolution, and 3 Interesting/Unusual/Fun Facts. The slides and script must be organized in either a chronological or topical fashion. You will need to include a bibliography that documents the sources you used. You must use at least five sources, two not being from the Internet.

4. American Revolution Trading Cards

Many people collect and trade baseball, football, and other sports cards. You will create a collection of Revolutionary era trading cards. You should have a total of 5 cards—2 British/Loyalist, 2 Americans/Patriots, and 1 woman. You will fill out a brief biographical information sheet as you research each person. Then you will incorporate important facts from the information sheet to create the back of your trading card. You will make your trading cards in "baseball card" style with a picture on the front and the written info on the back. You will also be required to turn in your research sheets. You must also include a bibliography listing the sources that you used for your research. You must use at least five sources, two not being from the Internet.

5. American Revolution Board Game

You will design a kid-friendly, colorful, and interactive board game based on events leading up to the American Revolution or on the battles of the Revolution. You have creative freedom in creating the type of game as well as the name of it, the game pieces, and how it is played. You will need to have a game board, game pieces, questions and answers, and rules. People must be able to play this game without you having to explain it in great detail (examples—Candyland, Monopoly, Clue, Trivial Pursuit). The questions you use in your game should be upper-level questions related to the Revolutionary era. You must also include a bibliography listing the sources that you used for your research. You must use at least five sources, two not being from the Internet.

This project is due _____. I have chosen to complete project #_____ and agree to turn in a finished project on the due date. I know that I must complete the project I have chosen and may not do a different one once I turn in this form. If I do not turn this project in on the due date, I will lose 10 points each day it is late. Also, I know that if I never turn this project in, it will result in one major grade zero. This form needs to be signed by my parent and me and returned by _____. Turning in this form will be my first grade for the project, and every day this form is not turned in, points will be taken off. I am fully aware of my responsibilities for this project.

_____   _____
Student name (printed)   Parent signature

_____
Student signature

Figure 6.10 *Continued.*

REVOLUTIONARY FLAG RUBRIC

Flag: The flag will be worth 100 points and will be 60% of your project grade.

30 total points—Follows design instructions

_____ 5 points—size 21 × 16 (or very close to)

_____ 5 points—anything that is attached to the flag is securely glued or sewed on and not falling off

_____ 10 points—material used (no paper flags)

_____ 10 points—hemmed edges

50 total points—Historically accurate

_____ 25 points—color(s) are accurate

_____ 25 points—design matches original flag design

20 total points—Neatness and effort

Total for flag _____

Research paper: The paper is worth 100 points and will be counted as 40% of your grade. You will write a two-page essay including the following information: unit flag belonged to (that is, what Regiment, Company, Militia unit, and so on), where they came from, reason for the design of the flag, what designs/images or words mean, battles or places it was flown, who designed it, which side it was flown for. Also include any other interesting information you can find on your flag.

_____ 2 points—Typed

_____ 2 points—12-point font

_____ 2 points—Times New Roman

_____ 2 points—1-inch margins

_____ 2 points—double-spaced

_____ 5 points—Title page (name, date, class, teacher, assignment title)—do not put a title on the actual essay pages or you will lose points!

_____ 5 points—Picture of the original flag

_____ 10 points—Bibliography in proper format (MLA, titled, all sources cited properly including pictures, minimum of five sources—two not being from the Internet)

_____ 70 points—Research (historical accuracy, biographical information, interesting facts, battles flown in, information in the instructions is included)

***Note: I will take off one point for each spelling or grammar error made.

Research paper grade _____

Overall project grade _____

Figure 6.10 *Continued.*

REVOLUTIONARY TRADING CARDS

Biography Research Sheet and Bibliography—The research portion of this project is worth 100 points and is 40% of the final project:

_____ 75 total points—15 points each for completed Biography Research Sheet

_____ 10 total points—Proper Bibliography (five sources, two not from the Internet)

_____ Biography #1

_____ 15 total points—neatness, effort, historical accuracy

_____ Biography #2

_____ Biography #3

_____ Biography #4

_____ Biography #5

Total for research _____

Trading Cards: The cards are worth 100 points and will be counted as 60% of your grade

Card #1—American/Patriot

_____ 5 points—Clear, color picture (drawn, copied, or printed) on front of trading card

_____ 2 points—Name of person on front of card

_____ 10 points—Minimum of 10 facts from your research sheets per person on each card (you may be creative in how you list your facts)

_____ 3 points—Neatness and creativity

Card #2—American/Patriot (Not from class)

_____ 5 points—Clear, color picture (drawn, copied, or printed) on front of trading card

_____ 2 points—Name of person on front of card

_____ 10 points—Minimum of 10 facts from your research sheets per person on each card (you may be creative in how you list your facts)

_____ 3 points—Neatness and creativity

Trading card total _____

Overall project grade _____

Card #3—British/Loyalist

_____ 5 points—Clear, color picture (drawn, copied, or printed) on front of trading card

_____ 2 points—Name of person on front of card

_____ 10 points—Minimum of 10 facts from your research sheets per person on each card (you may be creative in how you list your facts)

_____ 3 points—Neatness and creativity

Card #4—British/Loyalist (Not from class)

_____ 5 points—Clear, color picture (drawn, copied, or printed) on front of trading card

_____ 2 points—Name of person on front of card

_____ 10 points—Minimum of 10 facts from your research sheets per person on each card (you may be creative in how you list your facts)

_____ 3 points—Neatness and creativity

Card #5—Woman (from either side)

_____ 5 points—Clear, color picture (drawn, copied, or printed) on front of trading card

_____ 2 points—Name of person on front of card

_____ 10 points—Minimum of 10 facts from your research sheets per person on each card (you may be creative in how you list your facts)

_____ 3 points—Neatness and creativity

Figure 6.10   *Continued.*

AMERICAN REVOLUTION TRADING CARDS
BIOGRAPHY RESEARCH SHEET

Full name: _____   Title or nickname: _____

Date of birth: _____   Place of birth: _____

Date of death: _____   Place of death: _____

Cause of death: _____   Buried: _____

Educational background (describe in detail): _____

_____

Occupation before the war: _____

Describe your occupation (accomplishments, responsibilities, duties, training, and so on): _____

_____

_____

Name of spouse(s): _____

Date of marriage: _____   Number of children: _____

Are there any other famous relatives in your family (past or present)? If so, who? _____

_____

Which one are you?   Loyalists   Patriot   British   Other: _____

What beliefs led you to support this side? _____

_____

Where do you live during the time period (1750–1783)? _____

What is your role in the American Revolution or the events leading up to the war? Describe it in detail.

_____

List three ways and describe how your life was remarkable, eventful, or special:

1. _____

2. _____

3. _____

Did you make any major mistakes or bad decisions in your life? If so, what were they and how did they

turn out? _____

Are you considered a hero?   ❑ Yes   ❑ No   If so, by whom? _____

Why are you or why are you not a hero? _____

_____

What do you think it means to be a hero? _____

_____

Why are you important (why do we need to know about/study you)? Provide details. _____

_____

Figure 6.10   *Continued.*

The Odyssey Postcard Project

Assignment Guidelines

<u>Supplies Needed:</u>

- 10 *5′ x 8′* note cards, lined on one side
- Colored pencils or crayons
- Pencil
- Copy of <u>The Odyssey</u>

<u>Directions:</u>

1. <u>Pre-write:</u> On a scrap sheet of paper, brainstorm a timeline of the important events and characters for the episode.
2. Choose (1) who your letter will be addressed to and (2) who it will be from. You do NOT have to choose main characters; however, the person "writing" the letter MUST be present in the current episode.
3. <u>Compose:</u> Using the first-person point of view ("I"), write a letter that summarizes what happened to "you" in this episode. Your voice and perspective should sound like the real character. Do not just list events; also, describe how you felt about them.
4. <u>Evaluate & Revise:</u> Re-read your letter. Did you include all the important events? Did you include anything that doesn't belong? Did you express yourself clearly? Is your letter creative? Do you sound like the character? Use the rubric to evaluate your work; then, improve it based on the rubric's guidelines.
5. <u>Edit:</u> Proofread your letter for spelling, grammar, and punctuation errors. Make sure your letter is formatted correctly with a salutation (ex. "Dear...") and a closing (ex. "Sincerely...").
6. <u>Publish:</u> On the unlined side of your 5′ x 8′ note card, draw an illustration depicting a key scene from your episode. Sketch your art with pencil before coloring to prevent mistakes. Your artwork should be neat and colorful. Postcards often say where they are from. Advertise the setting somewhere in your art.
7. On the lined side of your note card, write the final draft of your postcard letter. Print neatly. Do not skip lines. Your note should be located on the left-side of the card and cover ¾ of the card. Draw a line at the ¾ mark to ensure a neat margin to your letter.
8. To the right of the ¾ mark, you will address your letter. Your address must include the (1) person's name, (2) a creative epithet to describe him or her, and (3) a creative, made-up address that tells where the recipient of the letter would live. This address should be centered between the top of the card and the bottom.
9. Write your FULL name and block number in the lower right-hand corner of your card.
10. Optional: Draw a stamp in the upper-right hand corner. SUBMIT on TIME!

You will create a postcard for each of the following episodes in Odysseus' epic adventure. Check off each episode as your complete it. Then graph your data when you get your grade.

1.__ Calypso's Island (Bk. 5)   6. __   the Land of the Laestrogynians (Bk.10)
2.__ Coast of the Cicones (Bk. 9)   7. __   the Abode of Circe (Bk.10)
3.__ The Lotus Eaters (Bk. 9)   8. __   the Land of the Dead (Bk.11)
4.__ The Cyclops (Bk.9)   9. __   the Sirens, Scylla and Charybdis (Bk.12)
5.__ the Island of Aeolia (Bk.10)   10. __ the Island of the Sun God (Bk.12)

Bonus Cards: 11. __ Nausicaa (Bk.6)   12. __   the Palace of Alcinous (Bk.7)   13. __ the Phaeclan Games (Bk.8)

Figure 6.11   Teressa's *Odyssey* postcard project.

Name: Date: Block: SCORE=

The Odyssey Postcard Project Rubric

Episode of Card: _____

	Outstanding A (20-18)	Good B (17-16)	Satisfactory C (15-14)	Needs Work D/F (13-0)
Summary of Events _____ / 20	The note sums up all the important events and details in the episode. The card does not include any irrelevant details.	The note sums up the important events and details in the episode but one. The card may include one detail is irrelevant.	The note sums the episode, but may be missing more than two important events and details. The card may include a few irrelevant details.	The note does not sum up the episode. It is missing important events and details. The card may include several irrelevant details.
Point of View (Voice) _____ / 20	The writer sounds like the real character. Through consistent word choice and by including certain events and details, the author establishes a believable persona.	The writer sometimes sounds like the real character. Through word choice and by including certain events and details, the author establishes a persona.	The writer relates events from the point of view of the character but does not establish a clear persona.	The writer includes events from the episode but does not relate them from the character's point of view OR the point of view may be inconsistent.
Presentation & Format _____ / 20	The card is colored vibrantly and presented neatly using the proper format. The creator invested time and effort into this card.	The card is colored and presented neatly, meeting all the format criteria except one. Time and effort is apparent.	The card is colored, but it lacks neatness. It meets all of the format criteria except two. Time and effort are lacking.	The card is only partially colored, or it is not colored at all. It fails to meet more than two criteria. It is clear the creator invested little or no time into this card.
Address _____ / 20	The postcard is clearly addressed to another character and includes the name, an original epithet, and location.	The postcard is addressed to another character and includes the name, epithet, and location.	The postcard is addressed to another character and includes the name, an unsatisfactory epithet, and location. (The author has attempted to include an epithet, but it is not correct.)	The postcard is addressed to another character, but fails to include the necessary components of name, epithet, and/or location. OR No address is present on the card.
Mechanics _____ / 20	There are no incomplete sentences. Standard English punctuation, capitalization, and spelling are used appropriately for this grade level.	There may be no more than one incomplete sentence. Standard English punctuation, capitalization, and spelling are used appropriately for this grade level with a few problems.	There may be no more than two incomplete sentences. Inconsistent use of Standard English punctuation, capitalization, and spelling disrupts the reader's comprehension.	Incomplete sentences, errors in capitalization, punctuation, and spelling severely detract from the card's content.

Additional comments:

Figure 6.11 *Continued.*

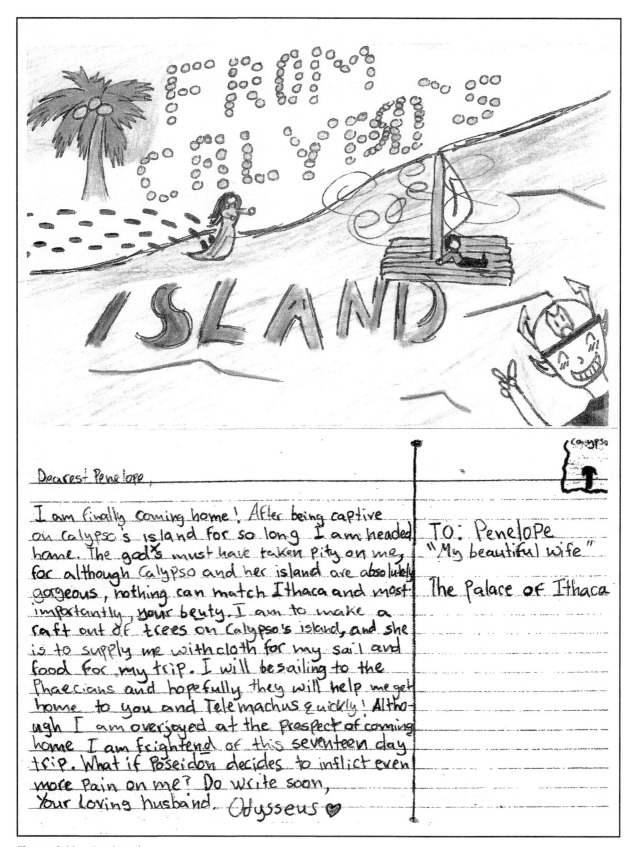

Dearest Penelope,

I am finally coming home! After being captive on Calypso's island for so long I am headed home. The god's must have taken pity on me, for although Calypso and her island are absolutely gorgeous, nothing can match Ithaca and most importantly, your beuty. I am to make a raft out of trees on Calypso's island, and she is to supply me with cloth for my sail and food for my trip. I will be sailing to the Phaecians and hopefully they will help me get home to you and Telemachus quickly! Although I am overjoyed at the prospect of coming home I am frightend of this seventeen day trip. What if Poseidon decides to inflict even more pain on me? Do write soon,
Your loving husband. Odysseus ♥

TO: Penelope
"My beautiful wife"

The Palace of Ithaca

Figure 6.11 *Continued.*

Imagine coming to work every day and not being recognized for your hard work. (Perhaps you've experienced this.) It's true that receiving some recognition for your efforts is directly related to the amount of effort you're able and willing to sustain over time. The same holds true for students—all of them.

Your reward and recognition (R/R) system must be aligned to the desired outcomes of the class. To illustrate this point, lets assume for a minute that you believe that school should model the *real world* and teach students the *harsh lesson* that not everyone is capable of getting an "A." If this is your philosophy, then you've probably created a system around the sports model, you know— winners and losers. (We actually know—and no doubt you do too—some teachers who brag about how few students can get an "A" in their class. They view this as a badge of honor and evidence of their excellent teaching. Really? It sounds like their paradigm is that of *teacher* and not *facilitator of learning* doesn't it?)

The R/R system of the teachers described above likely includes something like this: tickets to the "winners" ("A" students) to enter into a drawing, or allowing the "best" students (winners) a chance to pick a "toy" out of the magic box, or free homework passes for anyone who gets an "A." If this describes your system, have you considered how this approach impacts the other students and their motivation or enthusiasm for learning? If a certain few students seem always to be the *"chosen"* ones, can you imagine how it feels to be one of the others? The teacher in this system may be thinking along these lines: *"It is a mistake to allow every student to think s/he will be successful."* Or, *"We shouldn't reward everyone because that's not how it is in the real world. And, we have to teach students this lesson."* We can understand this mentality because for years our schools have functioned on the sports model of winners and losers. Consequently, traditional teachers set their expectations accordingly. If your belief is as described above, then you *will treat some students differently and you will get results that mirror your belief system.* This is because you will have created a system where only some students can be successful. Further, it once again proves Dr. Deming's point about your system yielding exactly the results you planned for.

This book challenges you to change the frame of your thinking, and provides you with specific steps to take to create a student-focused, learning-centered classroom. In this way, you've learned to align your classroom system around the two principles and have facilitated a strategic planning process for the class aimed at success for all. You've set class goals and put processes into place so more students can learn more. This is a very different approach. We hope you will go back and review—check out key classroom systems to assure they are aligned with the class vision, mission, and goals. If not, stop now and take time to consider how to align things. One of the most challenging steps for teachers is to align their classroom management techniques and processes with the desire to have a student/learner-centered classroom. If you are used to creating class rules, for example, your system will automatically be out of alignment. BBQ classrooms honor and respect the fact that every student is a worker in the system, and as Dr. Deming said (near the end of his life), "Over 90% of all problems within an organization are due to systems and processes and *not* people." Empower the workers to help solve problems!

If the system is aligned, then doesn't it make sense to let the students—workers—have a voice in deciding appropriate rewards and recognition? If you have class goals (not to say students can not also have personal goals) that everyone has agreed on, then how will you determine appropriate recognition? In this case, if everyone in the class meets the goal, how will the class be recognized and rewarded? First, let's share our bias with you. Only under the rarest of circumstances do we feel food is an appropriate reward. Given the childhood obesity rates in this country, we simply feel there are many other options available. So many children view *edible treats* as the only acceptable way to celebrate, but we know there are innumerable alternatives. We've witnessed students asking for five minutes to skip around the room, ten minutes to listen to music, five extra minutes on the playground, a few minutes just to talk to friends. Some other students desire—as a class—to eat lunch with their teacher, in their classroom. Others want to have the principal come and sit in a special place in the cafeteria. One class wanted to play ball with their teacher. Imagine her surprise! Each of these approaches delighted the students and acted as additional motivation for future work.

Beyond that, we always strongly recommend that the school administrator be alerted whenever a class meets a goal or target and announce it on the PA or on closed-circuit "school news." This is cause for celebration throughout the school, and during the day any adult who interfaces with that class ought to give each student a "high five" and pat on the back. After all, isn't the purpose of school *learning?* No matter our age, we always appreciate having others recognize our hard work.

A steady diet of external rewards doesn't work to motivate students over time. In fact, it is a major demotivator. Stickers, candy, cookies, pencils—they are all external rewards. Perhaps a class celebration and party at the end of the year with stickers, food, and so on, is fine. But please do not use these as the only acceptable way to reward students.

A process that works well is to establish a celebration immediately upon setting any class goal. Ask the students, *"How will we celebrate when we've met the target or goal?"* Then, have the students brainstorm ideas. Once all ideas are exhausted, then you can go back through the list and explain if there are any ideas that are prohibited by your school or district. (You have an obligation to explain these before taking them off the list, and practice restraint about making judgments without checking first. Perhaps no one has ever asked before. You may be pleasantly surprised at the response from your administrator.) The next step would be to have your students multi-vote on the three ideas they like best. Each time there's cause for celebration you can take the top vote-getting idea. In this way, eventually, the ideas of all your students will be part of the class's recognition and reward system.

IN SUMMARY

We have purposefully hit "extra hard" in this chapter by encouraging you to take bold steps to include the student as worker and partner with you, the teacher. Unless your school and district have already embraced Baldrige-based quality, there are doubtless many aspects of the classroom system that will change from the traditional model. Most common are the rules and consequences we set forth at the beginning of the year. Trust us when we say (over and over, we know), when students are allowed to be part of the process and their feedback is used, student motivation, positive behavior, and engagement increase beyond your expectation! We see this in every BBQ school.

This chapter has focused on students taking responsibility for owning and charting their individual progress. We have also expanded on the principle of being "response-able to the success of the class." Students are introduced to quality factors and quality features by learning the difference between the two and applying QFs to their work. These are tied to important life skills as well.

At the close of this chapter, if you are taking a step-by-step chapter approach, you have achieved (or are working to achieve) all of the observables in level 2 (see page 287, Chapter 8). Don't worry if your learning style dictates another approach. Our wish is that while you may still view yourself as a BBQ teacher "work in progress," you can relax a bit and be confident that your efforts will pay off in increased student learning. As your ability to be a "systems thinker" is reflected in your classroom, you will be gaining time formerly lost to classroom disruptions, reteaching, and disengaged students. Stay the course.

TOOLBOX

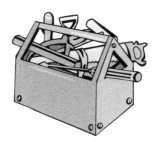

FORCE FIELD ANALYSIS

What

A *force field analysis* is a planning tool that encourages team or group discussion about the driving and restraining forces that impact goal attainment. The object is to reduce or eliminate the restraining forces rather than focus on the driving forces.

How

1. Draw a horizontal line about four inches from the top of a piece of flip-chart paper. Write the "goal" statement in this area.

2. In the center of the paper, just under the goal statement, draw a vertical line to the bottom of the paper.

3. Draw a horizontal line approximately three inches down. In the rectangle on the upper left, draw a large "+" sign. These are the "driving" forces.

4. Draw a large "–" sign in the space to the right of the vertical line. These are the "restraining" forces.

5. Explain that the object of this is to identify all the positive and negative forces that will affect goal attainment.

6. Ask the question "What are the things that might make it easier to reach the goal?" Write these in the "+" column and draw an arrow from each to the center line.

7. Next, ask the question "What are the things that might make it more difficult to reach the goal?" These might be distractions or actual impediments such as lack of knowledge. Write the responses in the "–" column with an arrow drawn to the center line.

When

Use this tool:

- If the class, an individual, or a team is having difficulty

- In an individual counseling session or student/parent conference setting

- Prior to beginning a major project

- If the focus is lost and the team, class, or individuals are not making progress

Example: Presentation Capabilities

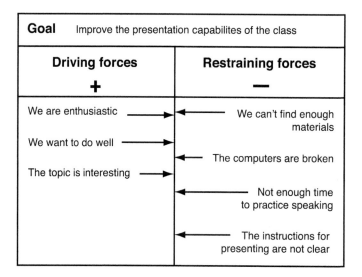

Example: Counseling

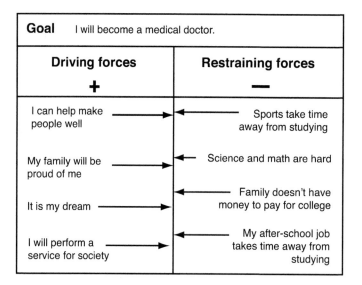

FORCE FIELD ANALYSIS TEMPLATE

1. Identify the desired change.

2. Brainstorm the driving forces and restraining forces.

3. Prioritize the driving forces and restraining forces (identify the critical few and rank-order the top three).

4. List actions to be taken (focusing on the critical few driving and restraining forces).

Desired change or goal:	
Driving forces Those that currently exist and support or drive the desired change.	**Restraining forces** Forces that may inhibit the implementation of the desired change.

Action plans:

PLAN–DO–STUDY–ACT—SECONDARY
(When student is failing—or nearly failing)

Class _____   Period _____   Date _____

Plan

- Define the problem.

  The problem is: _____

  The goal is: _*I will be successful in this class.*_____

- Assess the current situation.

  The average of all my tests and quizzes this marking period is _____

  I have not turned in _____ homework assignments out of a total of _____ homework assignments.

  When I look at my assignments I notice: _____

- Analyze causes (Check all that apply)

  ❏ I don't understand the material.

  ❏ I can not understand the teacher.

  ❏ I don't ask questions when I don't understand.

  ❏ I don't learn well when a teacher lectures.

  ❏ I don't like this class.

  ❏ I don't write dates for tests and quizzes in my agenda.

  ❏ I don't have my notes organized.

  ❏ I have to babysit/go to lessons/work after school and don't have time to study.

  ❏ I don't take my books home to study for tests and quizzes.

  ❏ Other. _____

- Write an improvement theory

  To improve my grade in this class I will _____

  _____

Do

- I will chart the data in my data notebook.

Study the Results

- Because of my improvement theory and doing things differently, my situation has ❏ changed ❏ not changed.

- I know this because _____

Act

- To continue improving I will _____

Signed _____   _____
        Student   *Parent*

PLAN–DO–STUDY–ACT—SECONDARY
(When student has a history of being tardy to class)

Class _____   Period _____   Date _____

Plan

- Define the problem.

  The problem is: *I am often tardy to class, which is disrespectful to my classmates and teacher.*

  The goal is: *I will come to class on time and ready to learn with all my materials.*

- Assess the current situation.

  In the past _____ weeks of school I have failed to turn in _____ assignments (out of _____ assignments) on time.

- Analyze causes (Check all that apply)

  ❑ My previous class is too far away to get to class in the given amount of time.

  ❑ The halls are too crowded to pass through easily and in a timely manner.

  ❑ I have too many books to carry them to every class. My locker is in a different hall.

  ❑ I often have to go to the bathroom in between classes.

  ❑ I meet my friends and we lose track of time.

  ❑ The hall clocks are not synchronized so I don't know much time I have.

  ❑ Nothing important happens the first five minutes of class, so it doesn't matter if I'm on time.

  ❑ Other. _____

- Write an improvement theory

  To improve my grade in this class I will _____
  _____

Do

- I will chart the data in my data notebook.

Study the Results

- Because of my improvement theory and doing things differently, my situation has ❑ changed ❑ not changed.
- I know this because _____

Act

- To continue improving I will _____

Signed _____   _____
        Student   *Parent*

PLAN–DO–STUDY–ACT—SECONDARY OR ELEMENTARY
(When student has a history of not completing work on time)

Class _____   Date _____

Plan

- Define the problem.

   The problem is: _I don't get my work done on time._ _____

   The goal is: _To complete and turn in all assignments on time._ _____

- Assess the current situation.

   In the past _____ weeks of school I have failed to turn in _____ assignments (out of _____ assignments) on time.

- Analyze causes (Check all that apply)

   ❏ I don't write my assignments in my agenda.

   ❏ I have lessons (or babysit or work) every day after school.

   ❏ No one at home looks at my homework.

   ❏ I wait until the last minute to do my work.

   ❏ I don't use my time wisely at school when I could start working on my assignments.

   ❏ I don't always understand the assignment and requirements.

   ❏ I don't always remember to take my agenda and books home.

   ❏ Other. _____

- Write an improvement theory

   To complete my assignments on time I will

   1. _____

   2. _____

   3. _____

Do

- I will chart the days that I follow my plan in my data notebook.

Study the Results

- After _____ days of trying my improvement theory, my situation has ❏ changed ❏ not changed.

- I know this because _____

Act

- To continue improving I will _____

Signed _____   _____
                 Student   *Parent*

PERSONAL IMPROVEMENT PLAN
(SUITABLE FOR GRADES 2 AND UP)

Class goal: _____

_____

_____

My goal: _____

_____

To accomplish my goal I will (*plan*): _____

_____

_____

This week my data tell me (assess the current situation): _____

❑ I reached my goal

❑ I did my personal best

❑ I didn't reach my goal

❑ I didn't do my personal best

This is because (analyze root cause): _____

_____

_____

_____

I plan to do my personal best and reach my goal next week by (improvement theory): _____

_____

_____

_____

To stay on track I will remember to: _____

_____

I will ask _____ to help by: _____

_____

Signature _____

7

BBQ and Twenty-First Century Skills

CONVERSATION WITH THE TEACHER

It isn't easy to organize a series of learning activities that capture the imagination of all students while pushing their abilities to learn more and more to meet the challenges of their adult life. It's complicated because of the range and type of variation in learning styles and comprehension rates of the students. At the same time, this is one of the root causes of why students begin—as early as third grade—to "opt-out" of school well before they are of age to drop out of school. For these students, the school experience is painful, and after a while who would willingly engage in an activity that "hurts"? This realization is not news, but this is about the future of every student and really defines the obligation of teachers to become facilitators of learning who embrace the two principles, who diligently listen and learn from students, who are committed to continuous improvement, and who break out of their own comfort zone to make change happen for the betterment of all.

It is a fact that we (adults/educators) have no concrete conception of all the skills this generation and the ones that follow will need to possess in order to be successful. Aside from academic skills, futurists emphasize that successful graduates must be able to work with diverse groups of people to achieve complex tasks or projects. This concept goes beyond cooperative learning activities. It requires teachers to think about how students can be organized in different ways and learn how to self-organize and self-manage, and how to lead or participate on teams to address real-life problems in their school, community, or the nation. It requires a holistic approach to learning. We hope that the silos of secondary education can be broken so students have an opportunity to experience true learning and not only "school" learning.

Sadly, about seven years ago we had the opportunity to listen to a group of high school Social Studies teachers explain an effort to increase the number of ninth-graders passing Social Studies. They explained that during the previous five years, nearly 40% of all ninth-graders failed Social Studies, regardless of the teacher. To address the situation, the

227

teachers brainstormed the causes of students' not learning and came up with "don't do homework" and "are disorganized" as the major causes. Then they surveyed students to find their perspective. Overwhelmingly, the students said "class is boring." The teachers came up with a list of approaches they thought might work so more students would pass, and asked students to prioritize the list. Students said they wanted to work in teams, and put as a very low priority a homework hotline. The teachers then agreed to allow students to work once a semester in teams. They also instituted a homework hotline, gave students a short course on time management, and provided them with daily planners. At the end of the semester, failure rate dropped from 40% to less than 15%. Students also rated the effectiveness of the interventions. Working in teams was the approach that all students felt helped them the most. Meanwhile, no one ever called the homework hotline although it was manned by teachers every day. Would you believe that this group of teachers dropped the team project work and continued the homework hotline? (No kidding, this is a true story. Go figure!) What lesson do you think the students learned from this experience?

In this chapter you will learn:

- What to do when or if an informal PDSA model doesn't work

- About student-led conferences

- Ways to get feedback from parents about their satisfaction

- A model for team projects—twenty-first century skills and BBQ

WHEN MORE THAN AN INFORMAL PDSA IS REQUIRED

Thus far we've focused on changing classroom processes based on what we would call an *informal* PDSA. But, what if more is required? What if the situation is drastic and the problem is not easily understood? These situations call for a more formal use of PDSA, with greater depth of analysis of the problem. The following case study is designed to help you learn to do just that. This is not something a BBQ teacher would use every day, but there is a "need to know" how to go through the steps and learn more tools that are available to you. The directions for the tools are in the Toolbox section at the end of the chapter. They're not difficult to learn, and we urge you to practice using your own classroom data. In fact, we strongly recommend it to anchor your learning. This brings BBQ into focus.

Case Study

Mrs. Ann Oying, an experienced seventh grade math teacher, was at her wits' end. In February she realized that her classes weren't on track to meet the year-end requirements. Her anxiety was growing, and she was especially worried about fourth period because it is a split class—that is, lunch period comes in the middle of the class. Methods that Mrs. Oying had successfully used in the past seemed to work fine for most of the students in her other classes, but not for this group.

Last fall, Mrs. Oying had the opportunity to attend professional development for the block schedule and BBQ but didn't go because she had planned an international vacation and didn't learn about the PD offering until after paying for the trip.

A few days ago she chatted with the department chair, Mr. Fixit, and shared her concerns. She shared some data with him on homework, attendance, quiz grades, and unit grades. See her grade book in Figure 7.1. Immediately, Mr. Fixit gave Mrs. Oying some tools suggestions and asked her to put these data into chart form, reflect on it, then arrange a meeting with him. Mr. Fixit agreed that he would observe the class and mentor her in some of the new approaches learned during the PD workshop, and the BBQ principles and techniques he had been learning about.

Student	Quizzes			Homework										Unit 1	Unit 2	Unit 3	3rd qtr	4th qtr	Sem	Final exam	Final grade
1 (F)	7	6	5	✓	✓	✓	✓	✓	✓	✓	✓	✓	✓	12							
2 (F, N)	4	3	4	✓			✓							6							
3 (F, S)	2	6	5	✓	✓		✓		✓	✓			✓	12							
4 (F)	8	8	6	✓		✓	✓			✓	✓			18							
5	5	4	4	✓	✓	✓	✓	✓	✓	✓	✓		✓	14							
6 (F)	2	6	5	✓			✓		✓		✓	✓	✓	12							
7 (F, N)	2	2	3	✓		✓			✓					8							
8	6	7	8	✓	✓				✓	✓		✓	✓	22							
9	3	9	7	✓	✓									24							
10	8	5	9				✓		✓	✓	✓		✓	12							
11 (S)	5	7	5		✓				✓					8							
12 (F)	4	6	7	✓	✓	✓	✓		✓		✓			24							
13	2	6	8	✓	✓	✓	✓	✓	✓	✓	✓	✓	✓	7							
14 (N)	2	6	3	✓						✓				7							
15 (F, S)	5	4	4	✓			✓						✓	9							
16 (F)	5	9	7	✓		✓			✓		✓			24							
17 (F)	8	8	5	✓		✓	✓		✓	✓	✓		✓	18							
18	9	9	9				✓		✓				✓	27							
19 (F, N)	2	6	3		✓		✓	✓		✓				14							
20	8	4	6	✓		✓	✓		✓	✓				14							
21 (F, N)	3	2	2		✓								✓	10							
22 (F)	2	6	4	✓	✓	✓	✓	✓	✓	✓	✓	✓	✓	15							
23 (N)	1	2	4	✓										5							
24 (S)	3	6	6		✓		✓			✓		✓		12							

(F = F/R Lunch, S = SPED, N = ELL)

Figure 7.1 Mrs. Oying's grade book.

When Mrs. Oying heard that she was going to have to put these data into graph form, she was annoyed. "What is the need of that? I can tell at a glance from my grade book that things are not going well." Mr. Fixit replied that she might be surprised by what she learns once she makes the charts.

Assess the Current Situation

Mr. Fixit suggested that Mrs. Oying use a *line graph* (using method #2, Figure 7.2) for the quiz data so she could see at a glance what was happening with her fourth period class. The directions for the line graph are in the Toolbox section at the end of this chapter. (Method #2, line graph allows you to see the spread of variation in the class. Over time you can easily see if the bandwidth of variation is narrowing [a good thing], and where the bulk of the results are.)

He recommended a bar graph for the homework assignments. Figure 7.3 shows the class's homework data. She was curious about the fifth and ninth assignments.

Mrs. Oying's next and final task was to put the unit test data into a histogram. (Directions for histograms are in the Toolbox section at the end of this chapter.) The "footprint" of Mrs. Oying's fourth-period class more resembles an L shape than a J shape (Figure 7.4). While she knew that the results were dismal, she had no real sense of how bad things really were just by looking in the grade book. Things didn't bode well for Mrs. Ann Oying! She was getting nervous, but vowed to learn all that she could in hopes of vastly improving student learning results by the end of the school year.

After doing the graphing, she arranged a meeting with Mr. Fixit. He asked her what she thought was the main problem in the classroom. She quickly said, "Well, it's that darn break during lunch. By the time they return to class, whatever little energy there was in the class is lost. If only we hadn't gone to the block schedule, things would be fine!" Mr. Fixit smiled and asked her again to reflect on issues that were within her circle of concern, things that she could control. This time he

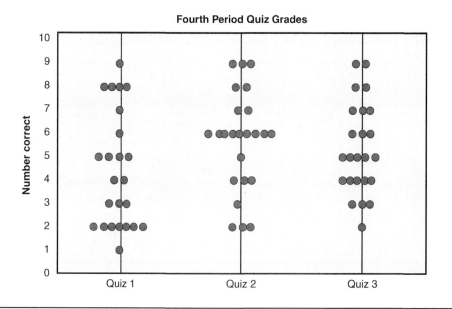

Figure 7.2 Line graph of fourth period quiz grades.

Fourth Period Homework Turned In

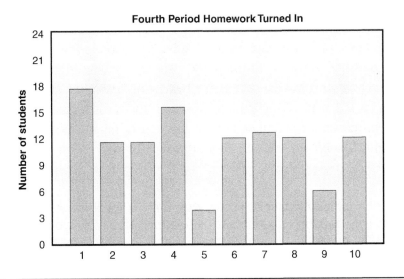

Figure 7.3   Bar graph of fourth period homework turned in.

Fourth Period Unit Test #4

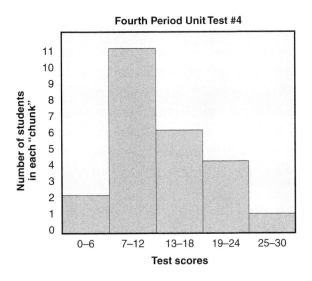

Figure 7.4   Histogram of fourth period unit test #4.

expressed curiosity about the homework graph and asked what was different, if anything, about the fifth and ninth assignments. The question took Mrs. Oying aback, but she went back to her files and discovered that both assignments required students to solve complex, multi-step word problems. She also noticed that the fifth assignment was to be returned on a Monday, and the ninth assignment was given on the night of the boys' basketball game. It was the final home game of the season. Realizing these were issues she should have been aware of, Mrs. Oying began to think about the many non–English speakers and SPED students in the class. Had she done enough prework to prepare them for this type of assignment?

In general, she didn't have many students returning homework anyway. She assumed it was because the students were unmotivated and didn't care. While this thought raced through her brain, she was also vaguely aware that many more students in her other classes turned in homework, and the assignments were the same for each period. That had her wondering.

Mr. Fixit then asked her to reflect on the quiz results. The line graph showed some positive movement after the second quiz, but the gains were nearly all lost on the third quiz. Mr. Fixit asked about the quizzes and if she was asking students to recall the most recently learned material only, or if they were also tested on a random sample of previously taught math operations. She hadn't thought about that until Mr. Fixit explained about the 70:30 rule.

The 70:30 rule: Administer a weekly quiz with 70% of the items from the most recently taught material and the remaining 30% from a random sample of all previously taught material. Set the expectation that students will be held accountable for everything that is taught (according to grade-level expectations) and that by using the 70:30 rule you are helping assure they have mastered the material.

That thought had never occurred to her. In fact, she'd never before had anyone suggest it. It made perfect sense, so she vowed to take time over the weekend to make a list and write some sample questions covering all the previously learned math concepts and operations for the seventh grade.

Mr. Fixit asked her what type of errors her students were making on the quizzes. This, too, was not anything she'd thought about investigating. As she graded the papers she knew that there were many errors related to basic math facts, but she never dug deeper to see if she could better understand what type of help her students needed. Mr. Fixit gave her the directions for a Pareto chart and sent her off to look at the third quiz results by error type. They arranged to meet on Monday after school.

The third quiz mostly focused on decimals and fractions. This required Mrs. Oying to chart the number of errors (by type) made by each student. The class results for this quiz were very poor, and multiple errors were made by every student. What a shock it was to learn that her 24 students made a total of 475 errors on this one quiz. Most students made multiple errors on each question. Figure 7.5 shows the Pareto chart for Mrs. Oying's class. (Instructions for the Pareto Chart are in the Toolbox section at the end of this chapter.)

Mr. Fixit explained the valuable information yielded by a Pareto chart. He explained that if she focused her efforts on the most significant problems, then more students would learn the math operations needed to be successful at year's end. Looking at the Pareto chart, we can see that the top four error types accounted for over 80% of all errors. These represent the significant few error types. It was clear that a lot of remediation (rework) had to be done. Mrs. Oying wondered how she could help her students learn these concepts beyond the methods she'd been using. She was skeptical because so many seemed to lack basic math facts, but at the same time she was determined to find an answer. Now she was getting eager to learn more.

For the next two days Mr. Fixit came and observed the class. He noticed she didn't have the two principles posted (remember, Mrs. Oying didn't attend the professional development workshops to create a BBQ classroom), nor did she have a vision or mission. The students were seated at

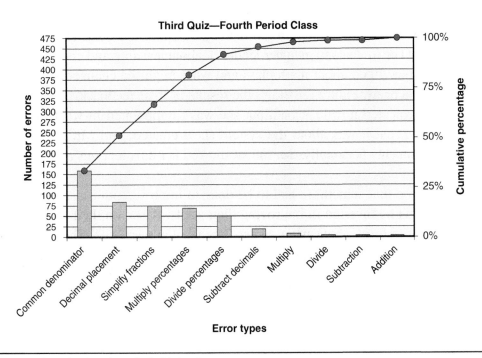

Figure 7.5   Pareto chart for fourth period, third quiz.

individual desks, facing the front, and it looked like a traditional classroom. Mrs. Oying was pleasant to the students, and her primary teaching method was to work problems from the book. Her explanations seemed fine. Some students were engaged and asking questions. Most of the students didn't ask any questions. She then gave them an opportunity to practice, and followed it by having some students put selected problems on the board. Homework for the next day was assigned and class ended.

Plan

Mr. Fixit asked Mrs. Oying if what he had observed was typical, and she replied in the affirmative. Because it was February, he didn't recommend she work with students to create a vision, but he did suggest she spend part of the next day engaging them in a discussion about the importance of learning math, its application to real life. He then recommended she share the data charts with the class, not in a shame and blame mode, but rather, "I realize that my approaches to teaching you math are not working as well as they should. I want to become a better teacher and am learning some new ways to work, but I need your help. Are you willing to work with me so that we can all learn more (yes, I need to learn too) and be more successful?" Mrs. Oying had already made some posters with the two principles (I am responsible . . . I am response-able) and hung them at the front of the room. When the students affirmed their willingness to help her become a better teacher, she led them in a reflection on the two principles.

After lunch that day, she asked Mr. Fixit to lead the class to develop a mission statement. By observing him, she learned how to do this for all her other classes. When the mission was agreed on and signed by all, Mrs. Oying posted it next to the two principles. The class set two goals and signed each, committing to doing everything possible to achieve the goals (Figure 7.6). The next day, Mrs. Oying asked her students to give her feedback about learning and enthusiasm, and to give specifics about what they liked about math class and what might be changed so they could learn more using a plus/delta chart. Figure 7.7 shows the results of their feedback.

Mrs. Oying had expected it to look bad, but she was disappointed in what the students said. Still, she was learning that it was about the system she'd created, and Mr. Fixit told her not to take the students' comments personally. So, she swallowed her hurt feelings and thanked them for their honesty.

The teacher realized that something had to be done to improve enthusiasm for learning math; otherwise they wouldn't be invested in improving their skills. Based on their feedback, she gave a homework assignment to think about what career they wanted to pursue. She also asked the students how they wanted to celebrate improvement toward reaching the class goals, with the caveat that it not include food. After two minutes to brainstorm, the students multi-voted on how they wanted to celebrate. They agreed that every week the class improved on their basic math facts quiz, the teacher would give them five minutes to talk with their friends.

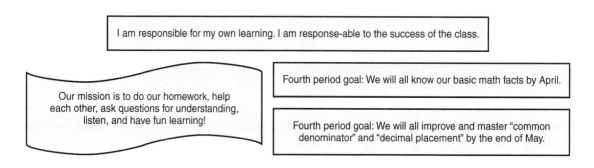

I am responsible for my own learning. I am response-able to the success of the class.

Our mission is to do our homework, help each other, ask questions for understanding, listen, and have fun learning!

Fourth period goal: We will all know our basic math facts by April.

Fourth period goal: We will all improve and master "common denominator" and "decimal placement" by the end of May.

Figure 7.6   Class mission and goals.

Learned a lot!				●	
Learned some			●	●	
		●	● ●	●	
Learned a little	●	● ●	● ●	●	
	●		● ●	●	
Didn't learn much	●	● ●			
		Didn't like it at all	It was okay	Liked some of it	Loved it!

+	Δ
We can sit with friends	Don't know the English words
I liked that one time we played a math game	Afraid to ask questions
	Always hated math
	It's not interesting
	You only pay attention to the same students
	No one can help when I don't "get it"
	Too much homework
	You go too fast
	Get nervous before a test

Figure 7.7   Fourth period E/L and plus/delta charts—current situation.

Do: Carry Out the Improvement Plan

Mrs. Oying told the class that from now on they would follow the 70:30 rule for quizzes (graded) and all would include questions related to "common denominator" and "decimal placement." Personal best scores would be noted, and if the class improved, they would get to have lunch in the classroom the next day. The students groaned about the 70:30 thing, but thought having lunch in the room could be fun.

The next night Mrs. Oying spent time researching various ways people use math in each of the career fields the students mentioned. She made a list and gave each student a copy to put in their organizers. Then, she went over her weekly lesson plans and incorporated some specific problems related to several careers. She'd already decided to differentiate and give the students a choice about which of those problems to work on in class. She worked hard to assure that the math operations were similar, but changed the context.

With so many students deficient in basic math facts, the next day she asked the students to brainstorm ways they would like to learn the facts (for example, games, song, flash cards) She asked her students to prioritize the way they wanted to learn, and discovered that the class was evenly split between four different ways. She told them that each day right after the lunch break they would spend 15 minutes working on math facts in small groups, and that each week she'd give them a nongraded quiz on the basic facts. She and the class spent the rest of that day working collectively on the math facts that would be quizzed. Each student left the class with a list of expected math facts to master. These would be the ones they'd practice for 15 minutes a day. Mrs. Oying made certain that the students all understood the basic operations of each of the facts while they were making this list.

In addition to that, Mrs. Oying used the Pareto chart information and determined that she had to do some whole-class instruction to address common denominator and decimal placement issues the students were having. She reviewed her lesson plans from the past few months and realized that she had been in a rut. Even though students weren't learning, she continued teaching the way she had for the past several years. Once again, she went to the students and shared her findings, and then asked them for help about *how* they would like to learn these operations. At first, students were shy, but once she gave a couple suggestions, they became more engaged. She also decided to call the directors of special education and English language learners and ask for their help. Then, she put her plans into action.

Mr. Fixit taught Mrs. Oying how to chart the nongraded quiz (method #1 line graph directions are on page 274.) He also suggested using method #2 for the graded quiz. It was important for Mrs. Oying to watch the spread of variation and for the class to see how it was progressing.

Study

Figure 7.8 shows the results of the next two graded quizzes. The class could readily see how much they were improving, and this motivated them even more. She charted the number of students who did their personal best, and it helped, too. The noise level in the classroom was that of excited, engaged learners. Mrs. Oying was feeling much better even though there was a long way to go.

She was pleased to see how well the students were adapting to her new strategies. The results of the non-graded quiz on basic math facts looked like Figure 7.9.

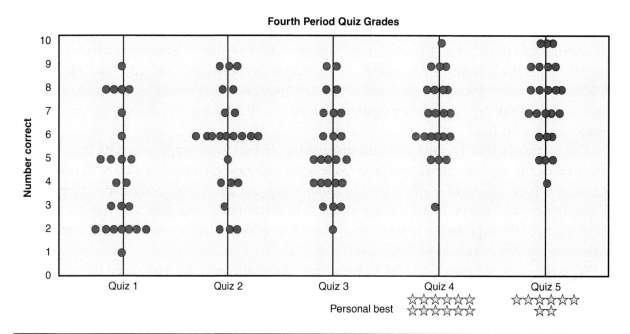

Figure 7.8 Fourth period quiz grades.

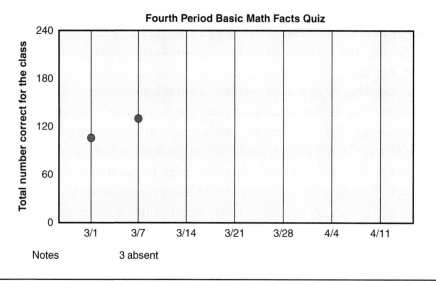

Figure 7.9 Fourth period basic math facts quiz grades.

The class period before the unit test, Mrs. Oying wanted to know how confident her students were about taking the test. She had a poster laminated with a Confidence-O-Gram (Figure 7.10) and asked her students to place a dot in the space that best described their feelings.

She asked the class what questions they still had, and then was able to directly address their concerns. By the end of the class period everyone had a good idea what would be covered on the test.

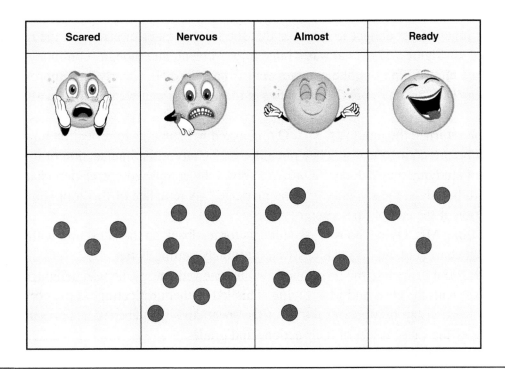

Figure 7.10 Fourth period Confidence-O-Gram.

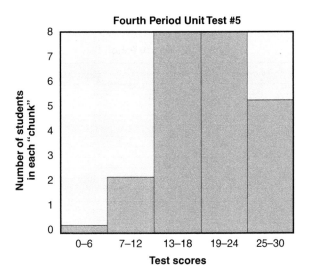

Figure 7.11 Fourth period histogram for unit test #5.

The unit test results pleased Mrs. Oying very much. She was delighted to show her class how the shape (footprint) of the histogram had moved in the direction of a J shape (Figure 7.11). Clearly, things were getting better, and even though there was a long way to go, she felt much better just to be certain her strategies were working. She took the fifth quiz home and once again counted the errors by type.

Can you imagine her delight to discover that the total number of errors on the quiz had gone from 475 to 230 (Figure 7.12)? That was a huge improvement, and though "common denominator" was still in the number one slot, the number went from 180 to 50. Clearly, her improved strategies were working. The students were delighted to see these results and were highly motivated to work even harder.

When she returned the unit tests, Mrs. Oying asked her students to reflect on how much effort they'd put in before taking the test. They put a dot on a chart at the intersection of their grade and the amount of studying they'd done. Figure 7.13 shows the completed correlation chart. Analyzing the chart with her class, the students "got the message." (A template of this tool is included in the Toolbox section at the end of this chapter.)

One last thing Mrs. Oying did was ask students for feedback on the latest unit with an E/L chart and plus/delta chart (Figure 7.14). Things were definitely getting better.

When Mr. Fixit came into the room and saw the renewed energy, he was delighted, and shared his enthusiasm with the class and Mrs. Oying. This led to them reflecting on the correlation chart showing the relationship between results and time spent studying. The students became aware for the first time of the cause/effect of their actions and grades.

The students were intrigued to see what was in the box that Mr. Fixit brought. It was filled with student data notebooks—one for each. As he passed them out, he had the students fill in the two principles, class mission and goals, and their career aspirations. Earlier, Mrs. Oying had completed

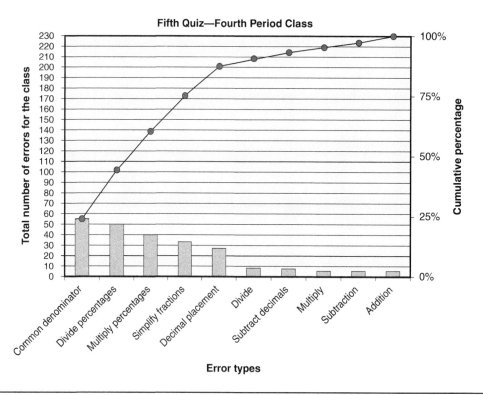

Figure 7.12   Fourth period Pareto chart for fifth quiz errors.

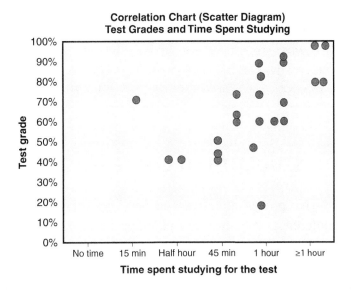

Figure 7.13   Fourth period correlation chart—test grades and time spent studying.

	Didn't like it at all	It was okay	Liked some of it	Loved it!
Learned a lot!			● ● ● ●	●
Learned some	●	● ●	● ● ●	● ●
Learned a little		●	● ●	
Didn't learn much		●		

+	Δ
We can sit with friends	You could challenge us more
Liked the 15 minutes to work on math facts	We can work harder
Thanks for asking us how confident we were before the test and then helping us	Still hate math but not quite so much
	Need more help with the English words
Liked learning how math is used for different jobs	Please review homework before we leave class

Figure 7.14   Fourth period enthusiasm and learning chart and plus/delta chart post-intervention.

a bar graph for each student's previous quiz and unit test grades. She asked them to fill in their own data for this unit test.

Act

Mrs. Ann Oying was aware that way too many of her students had a long way to go to master the seventh grade competencies. At the same time, she realized how much improvement there had been in a short amount of time. She learned a lot from Mr. Fixit, and committed to keeping her data wall up to date and making improvements based on data and feedback from her students.

Reflection: Take some time to compare and contrast your approach to similar situations. In the past, what steps have you taken to eliminate the barriers to student learning? Have you empowered the students to help you understand the problem(s)? What are the key things you learned from this case study? The paradigm shift to BBQ?

STUDENT-LED CONFERENCES

Student-led conferences have proven effective and very powerful in the school districts where they are used. These conferences require more planning because teachers need to help students know how to organize their portfolios, and how to present test or quiz information. The approach empowers students and verifies the message, *"I am responsible for my own learning."* Imagine how proud the children are when they share what they've learned with their parents, show them charts where they've tracked their own progress, can identify strengths and areas for improvement, and share their goals for the next marking period.

Beyond the obvious benefits to students, there are vast benefits for parents. These conferences give them the opportunity to have focused time with their child to hear and see accomplishments and concerns. Parents who've had this experience often leave school with a renewed sense of pride in their children. It is definitely a win–win for everyone.

Student-led conferences require planning on the part of the teacher to "set the stage" with parents. They (teachers) advocate for the students and at the same time set clear expectations for parents when they arrive. As you can see from the materials in the Appendix (and adopted from Leander ISD, Leander, Texas), teachers guide parents and students through the process. In addition to preplanning, teachers are available to spend time with any parent who so desires it, but primarily this is a time for parent and child to communicate. Teachers will want to stay in the background and avoid the temptation to "rescue" or "tell it like it is." Obviously, this concept truly requires teachers to trust students and parents. With adequate and careful mentoring, you'll be amazed at the results. Try it, as the benefits far outweigh the risks and effort involved.

Begin preparing students for this event early in the school year. Let them know that they'll be sharing their data folder and a portfolio of "quality work" with parents/guardians later in the year. Set the expectation immediately when introducing data folders, goal setting, and the appropriate tools, such as line graph, radar chart, run chart, quality factors, and so on.

At the same time, begin preparing parents/guardians for the new approach in the beginning of the school year. Obviously, the best way to begin this conversation is with information sent home introducing the BBQ approach through a letter, your class newsletter, the school newsletter, during PTA meetings, and at open house. The principal is responsible for creating the anticipation of student-led conferencing and takes a personal hand in setting the ground rules for all parents. Of course, parents can also request one-on-one conferences with teachers if they deem it important. These would not replace the student-led approach, if that is the agreed-on schoolwide or grade-level approach.

Students from all grades can participate in this approach, yet the expectations vary with the grade level. There are two major aspects of this conference for which students must be coached in order to have a successful experience. First, students will have to keep track of their own data on learning progress and behavior. These would be tracked in a data notebook, as described in Chapter 6, using charts and graphs. Second is a portfolio of the student's highest-quality work. The portfolio would include growth in items like writing samples, project work, science labs, and so on. This requires students to discriminate about the *meaning of quality* and reflect on the ways they've improved. Finally, students are asked to write action plans to address skills most in need of improvement. This, too, requires commitment on the part of the teacher to help students learn to discriminate and be able to explain why one piece of work is superior to another. The reflection activity helps develop, from an early age, critical thinking skills required in the twenty-first century.

We strongly recommend that the school staff and principal work together to establish the types of information and data each student will share at the conference. Goal setting for the next nine-week period is one of the most valuable parts of this approach, as each student identifies areas that represent significant opportunities for improvement and sets personal goals.

The success of student-led conferences hinges almost entirely on each teacher's ability to establish a process and follow through on each of the steps. The steps include:

- Early in the school year, explain to the class that during the year they'll be expected to share their learning with their parents/guardians during a student-led conference. (I am responsible for my own learning.)

- Set up student data notebooks, and begin right away to have students start charting their own data. Set up the notebooks to include things like class vision, mission, and goals; personal vision, mission, goals, and action plans; student QFs, learning styles inventory, physical education data, behavioral assessments (elementary), weekly quiz results and unit test grades, use of PDSA for personal improvement based on data, and so on.

- Establish basic quality factors for writing, and provide students with a checklist for self and peer assessment (as described in Chapter 6).

- Regularly have students select the "best" example of quality writing and keep it in a portfolio. Use something like the My Best Quality Work template (see Appendix). Other areas that could be included are science, social studies, art, music, technology, and so on. Every month have the students look at more recent work samples to see if there has been growth. Keep the two or three that show the most growth over time as a motivator for even the most struggling students and also for their parents.

- About six weeks before the conference:

  - Send a note home to parents asking them to prioritize the best time to schedule their conference. When these are returned, plug in the names on a master schedule.

- Have students decorate an invitation for their parents/guardians. (You will insert a notice with the assigned time, date, and place.)

• About two weeks before the conference, start having students organize their data notebook and be certain it is up to date. Find a checklist template in the Appendix.

• Check portfolios for "best quality" work samples and reflective analysis:

- Help students organize their papers. We recommend the inclusion of "best examples" of work across at least the four core subject areas. Students can and should be able to explain why these samples are "quality" work. If you have established QFs, then this is quite simple. Ask the students to make sure they have their *best* work included. (It's better to keep it simple and not have an overwhelming number of papers— possibly the best two that clearly show learning growth. Too many papers can quickly confuse the students and frustrate them.)

• A week prior to the conference, help students get ready to answer some possible questions parents may ask:

- What is one of your strengths?

- What area do you need to improve?

- What have you enjoyed most this year?

- How has your reading changed from the beginning of the year to this point?

• A week before the conference, send information home to parents about what to expect and also what is expected of them. See the templates on pages 303 and 304 in the Appendix.

• You may want to spend a little time in class, especially just before the conferences, role-playing with the class. It will help improve students' confidence and help reduce any anxiety the students may be feeling.

For readability, we have bundled all the templates in the Appendix. Following is a list. These have been successfully used by other teachers; however, we encourage you to modify any or all to suit your needs. Our recommendation is that you work together as a whole faculty, department PLC, or grade-level PLC to determine your approach. The templates are:

1. Learning styles inventory

2. My best quality work

3. Examples (2) of student prompts for the conference

4. Pre-conference responsibilities—students

5. Checklist for midyear parent conference

6. Preparation for midyear student-led conference

7. Informative letter to parents

8. Conference time notice to include in the invitation

9. Homework for parents before the conference

10. Parent/guardian responsibilities before the conference

11. Parent/guardian responsibilities after the conference

12. Parent/guardian feedback survey

PARENT SATISFACTION—RELATIONSHIP MANAGEMENT

In Chapter 2 we addressed the need to capture feedback from parents about their needs and expectations and to begin to engage them as partners. While that is a good start, it is not sufficient to manage and sustain relationships. We "hear" you: *There's not enough time in the day* to deal with the complexities of the job, let alone worry about parents." That's true, but the greater challenge comes when dissatisfied parents complain to the principal, superintendent, or board members that their child is being singled out and treated unfairly, and so on. Take a proactive approach and learn how to engage parents differently to mitigate problems before they start. Relationships, in general, are complex, and sometimes things go off the rails. Have you thought about what a good relationship boils down to? Three things: communication (two-way), respect, and forgiveness. You can control the first two of these by taking action to engage parents of all students (yes, even those who are resistant). Take a proactive approach, build stronger parental partnerships, and you may be surprised at the outcome.

Today there are many more opportunities for parents to gain information about how well their child is doing in school. Many schools have technology that allows parents with a password to access their child's grades and attendance. There are newsletters, e-mail, and class websites too. These keep parents informed and allow parents to alert teachers if a problem arises. These are all excellent approaches, and in a day when everyone is busier than ever, it's important to have ways for teachers to access information at all hours of the day and night. Seldom, however, do we see evidence of teachers systematically seeking feedback from parents about their satisfaction with the education the child is receiving. We're not talking about the end-of-year survey sent out by the district (or school) because that information doesn't allow for making any midcourse corrections. Notice that we continue to talk about making midcourse corrections. That's because you have an opportunity to get actionable feedback, which allows you to make changes and/or remove barriers keeping the *current set of students* from being successful. If you wait until the end of the year, you've lost the chance to improve things for that set of students. Figures 7.15, 7.16, and 7.17 are all examples of tools used to measure parent satisfaction.

Upon review of these surveys you'll discover that each provides teachers with information that can be put into action. Personally, we believe anonymous surveys are better, simply because your biases may prevent you from seeing an important *truth*. At any rate, when you receive the surveys,

---

Parent Feedback on Flexible Math Grouping—Intermediate Grades

---

Please take the time to fill out this survey on the Flexible Math program your child has participated in this year. We appreciate your time.

1. My child has benefited academically from this program.

____ Yes

____ No

Comments: _____

2. My child's self-esteem has improved regarding his/her math skills this year.

____ Yes

____ No

Comments: _____

3. My child has reacted positively to the transition made moving from group to group or teacher to teacher.

____ Yes

____ No

Comments: _____

4. I would like to see this program continue in the future.

____ Yes

____ No

Comments: _____

Additional comments: _____

Circle one: Grade 3   Grade 4   Grade 5

Name (optional) _____

Figure 7.15   Example of parent feedback form for intermediate grades.

---

look at each question and chart the responses. You are looking for patterns, and unless a comment relates to safety, you're not going to *tinker* with the system and make big changes based on one or even a handful of responses. Instead, you'll want to note what those are and monitor processes that lead to any particular response. In that way you can proactively use PDSA to improve a process if it deteriorates further.

That being said, if you see a pattern develop across the surveys, you're going to want to take careful note of the issue. Of course, you're going to inform all (yes, all—even if you didn't get a good response rate) parents about the results. Thank them for their feedback and provide the data. For those patterns mentioned above, seek the help of parents if more information is needed. This can be accomplished when you share the data by simply asking for four or five volunteers to help you understand the issue and make improvement suggestions.

Once you've made any decisions about what you will change, inform all parents, and then after four to six weeks pass, re-survey just on the process that you've been improving. This approach will certainly make parents feel that (1) you care about their child(ren), (2) you listen to parents,

Parent Satisfaction with Teacher—Elementary Grades

Dear parents/guardians,

In my efforts to show continuous progress I have developed this Parent Satisfaction Form. I will use these results to help improve my teaching skills. Your input is very valuable to me, so please take what I hope is just a few minutes to fill out this form and return it to school with your student. There will be a box out on the hall table, outside my room, for students to drop off these evaluations. I'll summarize the results and make copies available to you. Thank you very much for filling this out and returning it to me as I feel we must always move forward!

Sincerely,
Valerie Stowell-Hart

Please return this assessment with your son/daughter as soon as possible. Results will be summarized and available should you like a copy.

In the *priority* scoring column, please tell me *how important each of these items is to you.* Regardless of how you think I am doing at the present time on the item, give each a rank from 1 to 5, with 5 being the most important and 1 being the least important.

In the *evaluation* scoring column, please tell me *how you think I am doing at the present time* on each item. Give a rank of 1 to 5, with 5 being excellent and 1 being unacceptable.

Overall outcomes	Priority	Evaluation
High expectations		
Effective learning environment		
Amount of assigned work		
Classroom management		
Parental communication		
Grading and assessment		
Teacher availability		
Academic outcomes	**Priority**	**Evaluation**
The curriculum includes experiences that:		
Provide opportunities for creative expression		
Provide for a variety of learning styles		
Provide for real-life learning		
Provide for experiences in goal setting and decision making		
Meet goals of courses of study as reflected on our new report cards		
Develop an interest in lifelong learning		
Develop citizenship skills		

Please use the reverse side for additional comments.

Signature _____ Date _____

Figure 7.16   Example of parent feedback form for elementary grades.

Parent Satisfaction with Teacher—Middle School or High School—Social Studies

Please return this evaluation form with your son/daughter as soon as possible. Results will be summarized and available should you like a copy.

In the *priority* scoring column, please tell me how important each of these items is to you. *Regardless of how you think i am doing at the present time on the item*, give a rank of 1 to 5, with 5 being the most important and 1 being the least important. In the *evaluation* scoring column, please tell me *how you think I am doing at the present time* on the item. Give a rank of 1 to 5, with 5 being excellent and 1 being unacceptable.

Overall outcomes	Priority	Evaluation
High expectations		
Effective learning environment		
Relevant curriculum		
Amount of assigned work		
Type of assigned work		
Multi-age environment		
Classroom management		
Parental communication		
Grading and assessment		
Teacher availability		
Academic outcomes	**Priority**	**Evaluation**
Curriculum includes experiences that provide for the study:		
Of the ways humans view themselves over time		
Of people within a given place, time, and environment		
Of social identity		
Of interactions among people and institutions of the time		
Of how people have created and change structures of power and governance		
Of how people deal with scarcity, choice, and costs in a given society		
Of relationships between technology and society		
Of global and cultural connections and interdependence		
Of ideals, principles, and practices of citizenship in a democracy		
Nonacademic outcomes	**Priority**	**Evaluation**
Adult life skills		
Thinking and decision-making skills		
Interest in lifelong learning		
Citizenship knowledge and skills		

Please use the reverse side for additional comments.

Your child's name _____ Grade _____ Period _____

Your signature _____ Date _____

Figure 7.17   Example of parent feedback form for middle or high schools.

and (3) you are committed to improvement. All this will lead to increased parent satisfaction, and cooperation if any problems should arise or if you need volunteers.

If you work in an area where most parents are technology savvy and have access to computers, you can save some time by subscribing to Survey Monkey. This allows you to create surveys, and even scores them for you. We find it a very useful tool, and it is pretty cost-effective when you consider the services provided. A side benefit for secondary teachers would be surveying your students several times a semester. Here's the link: http://www.surveymonkey.com/.

Reflection: In what ways do you build and sustain relationships with parents or guardians?

TEAM PROJECTS: RIGOR, RELEVANCE, AND TWENTY-FIRST CENTURY SKILLS

Sputnik shocked America (back in 1957) into the realization that the industrial revolution had ended, and the United States government realized we were not poised to remain the world's greatest power. In response, President Kennedy stated his vision *to land a man on the moon within a decade.* He provided resources, gathered together the best/brightest people to create NASA, provided additional money to improve K–16 math and science instruction, and encouraged students to pursue scientific and engineering careers. He challenged NASA to achieve his vision. It was the nation's largest peacetime team effort ever, and national pride soared as we watched Neil Armstrong walk on the moon in 1969.

The road to NASA's success, however, was not smooth. It required *constant evaluation of problems, teamwork at many different levels,* a *willingness of leadership to listen to others, a way to measure effectiveness and efficiency of all systems, and astronaut selection and training.* All this had to be planned and executed to precise specifications in order to achieve the goal. Lessons learned by analyzing data to discover root cause of problems seemed to be the critical piece. This required the collective thinking of many scientists, computer analysts, and engineers; equally important was their ability to work together, to communicate effectively with each other, and work well under highly stressful conditions.

The implications for education go beyond those just mentioned as so many skilled and unskilled American jobs have been relocated to other countries. Despite claims by some, the reason for outsourcing jobs is only partly due to lower wages. In the '80s, when manufacturing jobs began to be lost to low-wage nations, American entrepreneurs invented new technologies, which spawned Silicon Valley and the Technology Age.

Today, our nation is faced with a similar situation largely because there are fewer engineers and scientists graduating from our nation's universities. Many are concerned that we will lose our entrepreneurial edge unless our K–12 system vastly improves and many more students enroll in the most rigorous high school programs. They must be prepared to successfully enter and graduate from technical schools, colleges, and universities. Entrepreneurs stem from the most curious of us all! This is why it is critical that K–12 teachers, curriculum coordinators, and policy makers put innovation on the "fast track" from "thinking about it" to "doing and evaluating the results." Indeed, teachers should be rewarded for taking calculated risks to work with cross–subject matter peers to put together team project–based learning relevant to the real world.

Tony Wagner, Codirector of the Change Leadership Group (a collaborative with the Graduate School of Education, Business School, and Kennedy School of Government at Harvard University) has written about the skills students will need in the twenty-first century (*The Global Achievement Gap*). The emphasis on interdependencies, teamwork, and solving real-life problems with a diverse group of people is something that is incongruous with the "silo" departmentalized approach of traditional American high schools. You can learn more about the twenty-first century schools movement and the work that is being done by accessing http://www.21stcenturyschools.com/What_is_21st_Century_Education.htm.

UNESCO identified the years of 2005–2014 as the Decade for Sustainability in Education. At an international conference in Gothenburg, Sweden, educators, scientists, government representatives, and people from nongovernmental organizations met to discuss global issues and to make recommendations to assure a better quality of life for all people. The central sustainability issues of access to education and healthcare, eradication of HIV/AIDS and other diseases, clean air/water, adequate sewage facilities, dependence on nonrenewable energy sources, violence, and an appreciation for diversity were constant themes of the conference.

These are global issues that will require teams of diverse individuals to communicate and work together to solve them. These are the challenges of the second decade of the twenty-first century and the foreseeable future. As an example, the Arab Spring that began in 2011 brought hope as well as concerns about the stability of the region. As human rights violations increase, so does violence. In every region of the world the needs are so great that it is mind-boggling. It will take courageous governmental leaders, entrepreneurs, and great communicators/problem solvers many years to make a difference for the millions of people now trapped in very inhumane conditions. With this as a backdrop, how can K–12 educators change the system and in so doing ensure that American students have opportunities to work with others to resolve real-world problems and make a difference?

Beginning with one's circle of concern, projects could improve the school or local community, and then expand through the grades into high school, where because of technology, students can form teams with peers from other schools, other states, even other nations to effect change on a larger stage. The ThinkQuest International Team Project sponsored by the Oracle Education Foundation is an example of this. Dr. Deming, the father of modern quality theory, realized the power of teams to solve problems and emphasized the necessity of engaging those involved in the process to lead the way in finding solutions to the problems of business, industry, healthcare, government, and education.

Perhaps a step in the right direction is to begin with a simple team project, then design a team cross-curricular project. This approach is not new to indigenous peoples, as they learned from their forefathers the importance of working together. However, it is infrequently used in American public high schools. A good example comes from Mt. Edgecumbe High School, in Sitka, Alaska. This school made a remarkable turnaround with mostly Alaska natives through connecting all learning to the real world. One of the major benefits of a cross-curricular team project is that students are required to produce one significant piece of work that is graded by each of the content teachers for their expertise. In other words, writing would be graded by the English teacher and based on the division/state writing rubric, the use of data and graphs could be graded by a math or science teacher depending on expertise, and so on.

Brain Research and Teaming

Building on the concepts above, lessons from brain research teach us that the use of real-life, complex tasks anchors the new knowledge into one's long-term memory. Students must use the information and apply the skills they learn. This is especially true if those tasks resemble those that will be encountered in the real world. When real-life, complex tasks are combined with a team approach, students can learn the interpersonal skills and team responsibilities useful in most careers. In fact, in his book *The Global Achievement Gap*, Tony Wagner (2008) interviewed corporate and business leaders and discovered the need to have employees be able to work with diverse groups of people, many scattered in far-reaching parts of the world. It is through experiential learning that we're going to prepare students who become problem solvers. In fact, when business leaders charter teams, they are expected to write a mission statement, define roles and responsibilities, and set expectations. Does all this sound familiar? It is because the BBQ model is applicable and used widely across sectors.

Aside from the benefits of having students learn to work in teams and develop significant interpersonal skills, students become more energized, motivated, and demonstrate an increase in self-esteem and pride when their team's work helps make their community a better place to live. In many schools, this is referenced as "service learning."

Beginning in early elementary, teachers can and must "hook" the state standards and learning objectives to real-life situations so that students begin to realize that school is not something that "happens" separately from the real world. School has to be connected! Students have to see how it connects!

Today, perhaps more than ever, it is particularly important for students to become better communicators and more tolerant of diversity. Cultural, socioeconomic, gender, and racial differences are four obvious influencers of communication styles. Less obvious may be differences of religion, sexual identity, and physical size (extremes of height or weight). Effective teachers seek out learning opportunities (hooked and aligned always with the standards) that capitalize on broadening students' views and abilities to work with others—a key twenty-first century skill.

Much has already been written about learning styles. We would simply remind you that learning activities that capitalize on several intelligences at once are the most powerful in advancing student long-term learning.

Team projects designed with quality factors that include creativity and that require a product at the end (service project, game, multimedia, music, presentation, newspaper, and so on) include many of the intelligences and address all the twenty-first century skills.

Stages of Team Development

To obtain the desired results, you must understand how this fits into the Baldrige framework. Team projects are a result of action plans developed during strategic planning. Figure 7.18 shows the Work Core and the direct relationship to results. Results improve when teachers provide students opportunities to work together and learn the standards within the framework of real-life application.

Team projects represent a change in student work systems (how they are organized to complete their work), and this requires the teacher to front-load the process very carefully to avoid losing valuable instructional time. During team projects (in a BBQ classroom) students are empowered to self-manage and monitor their own progress following the agreed-on expectations and product specifications. They work collaboratively with the teacher to establish quality factors and a time frame for completion before deciding on the nature of the product they will produce (within a broad topic decided by the teacher). (Later in this section you'll find a process for team projects suitable for use in elementary and secondary schools.)

Reflection: Take three minutes to think about these questions. Have you ever experienced a time when you were part of a high-performing team? How did it feel to belong to the group? Are you able to compare that experience with another one where you were a member of a dysfunctional team, or a team without a passion or clear goal? What were the differences in (1) your energy level and your eagerness to participate and complete your tasks, (2) the feelings you had for the rest of the team, (3) the feelings you had when the task was completed?

One theme we repeatedly hear from teachers is that team projects are too time-consuming, and frequently a few students do all the work while others do little or nothing. They claim that it is an inefficient way to get "through the curriculum" because so few students know how to work together

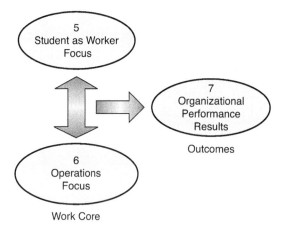

Figure 7.18 Work core leads to results.

as a team. Isn't this ironic? We know what students need, yet don't have the *time* (or is it the *will*) to coach students to work together. It's really no different than what occurs whenever any group of people come together to form a new team. It is important to note that simply putting people together and giving them a task rarely results in a high-performing team. This is true of teachers within a school, administrators within a district, and students within any classroom.

In 1965 Bruce Tuckman from the Naval Medical Research Institute wrote a research paper that is relevant today about the stages of team development. The stages are "fixed," and every team goes through all four stages. The trick for educators is to find a way to shorten the cycle of the first three stages so that students can develop into high-performing teams quickly to maximize their learning. Figure 7.19 depicts the stages of team development. Proper planning assures greater success, and you will see how the team project model we recommend can help students move beyond the *storming* phase. Also note how the interpersonal skills required by employers can be learned as students participate in team projects. Above all, do not assume that students have the skills necessary to become a high-performing team without appropriate guidance and instruction.

Reflection: Review the stages of classroom or team development by yourself. Think about your class. Read the "observables" for each stage. Make a preliminary judgment of the stage you think your class is at now, or how they ended the school year. How much time was spent in rework because of the stage your class is/was in? What could you have done (hint: review the group and individual behaviors) to improve the situation and move the entire class to the high-performing stage earlier in the school year?

We believe students as young as kindergarten or first grade can successfully complete simple team projects. Imagine the pride in workmanship students feel when they model the two principles of a BBQ classroom: "I am responsible for my own learning" and "I am response-able to the success of the class." (Go to page 260 to see a modified team project process for early elementary students.)

Develop a Cross-Curricular Team Project

Before embarking on any team project, the teacher has important responsibilities for its success. Naturally, before introducing the class to team projects some prework is necessary. We have outlined these responsibilities below. The team project model we recommend follows the PDSA process, which means students have a structured approach within which to operate. At the same time, they learn self-organization and how to use PDSA and tools to produce a high-quality product.

Front-Load the First Project—Prework

1. Determine the purpose or "aim" of the assignment. Outline what skills will be developed during the project, what cross-curricular standards are included, and so on.

Stage 1: Forming individual	Group	Observables
Why am I here?	What's the purpose of this class?	Sporadic and uneven participation
What's expected of me?	What are we supposed to accomplish?	Strong personalities may try to take over
How much influence will I have?	What methods/procedures can we use?	Testing and false starts
How much am I willing to give?	What should the class's code of conduct be?	First agreements

Stage 2: Storming individual	Group	Observables
Do I agree with the class purpose and am I committed to it?	How should the class deal with code of conduct violations?	Personal power struggles and clashes
How do I feel about the power structure (teacher and/or student leaders) in the class and its effect on my personal freedom?	How should the class handle conflict when two or more persons can't get along?	Negative emotions and body language
		Lack of consensus-seeking behavior
	How can conflicts of purpose or methods be resolved?	Confusion/loss of interest/opting out
What are the benefits and risks of sharing information and asking questions in this class?		Lack of progress
	How is student leadership decided?	Attack the student leaders and/or teacher

Stage 3: Norming individual	Group	Observables
I have a sense of belonging to the class.	A unified mission/purpose	Consistently setting and achieving task milestones
I have a sense of personal accomplishment.	A healthy balance of power among student leaders	Students acknowledge and solicit the unique contributions of other students
I understand my role(s) and contribute effectively.	Effective group procedures are practiced	Class attacks problems, not each other
I have freedom to be myself and express my ideas.	Sincere attempt to achieve consensus decisions	Use of we, us, our; not I, me, you, mine
I feel I can trust the class members and they can trust me.	Students and the teacher honor the code of conduct	Good communications
	A "class" identity emerges	Free participation
	High productivity	Steady progress

Stage 4: Performing individual	Group	Observables
Fun and exciting	Creative use of existing resources	Humor
High feeling of trust and friendship with class members	True consensus decision making	Smooth task and process flow within the class
	Very high level of mutual support	
High personal commitment to the class	Sense of pride in being part of the class and with classmates that extends beyond the class	Flexibility and versatility
Involvement with the class inspires my best		Excited and animated participation
	Internalized purpose and mission become a basis for action	Enthusiastic commitment to class decisions
		Lots of volunteering
	Optimal communication and exchange with "outside world"	Pride in class accomplishments
		Open expressions of appreciation, recognition, and caring

Figure 7.19 Stages of classroom or team development.

Source: Thanks to Hewlett-Packard for the four stages of team building in operational terms.

2. Decide on the quality factors (essential elements) that must be included in the final product. (Example: Will the teams be required to write a research paper, make charts and graphs, invent something, create a multimedia presentation, and so on?)

3. Coordinate with English teachers and teachers from other academic disciplines to ensure that expectations for writing, math, and other disciplines are included if possible. This helps students realize the continuity of all subjects and expectations.

4. With the class, operationally define each quality factor to eliminate variation in the final products, allow for innovation, and improve each student and team's ability to succeed. Note: Final products may vary for each team, but the requirements (QFs) remain the same for all.

5. Determine the parameters within which the students will be allowed to operate. (Will they be able to have unlimited access to the computer lab? Media center? Where and when can they work?)

6. Determine the project time frame for completion and process checkpoints along the way.

7. Develop a list of potential resources to include Internet sites, media materials, experts, and so on, available to teams.

8. Make a decision about how students will be divided into teams.

9. When the teams are determined, facilitate all teams writing a mission statement and assigning roles and responsibilities. Teams will use the tools and complete the work necessary to produce the result described at each step.

Plan—Team Organization

Step 1—Purpose: What is the team's purpose for this project?

> *Product of this step:* A written statement, signed by all members of the team, stating the team purpose.

Step 2—Mission: How are you (as a small team) going to accomplish this purpose?

Define the way you will work together as a team. What social skills will the team identify as critical to success? (Think about action verbs such as *accept responsibility, help, respect, come on time,* and so on.) (The template for a social/team skills matrix is in the Toolbox section at the end of this chapter.) Figure 7.20 shows an example of what this step looks like.

> *Product of this step:* A written mission statement signed by all members of the team that describes the way the team is committed to working together to achieve the purpose of the project.
>
> A *social/team skills matrix* using the verbs from the mission statement (QFs for teamwork) and a matrix with operational definitions for each QF.

Step 3—Set expectations: What are the quality factors for the project? What will the team need to learn about and what will the team's final product "look like" when the project is completed?

The team will need to gain a clear understanding of what will be expected of them. Quality factors with clear and specific operational definitions allow students to achieve at higher rates.

Team name: _Sharks_

Project: _Ecosystems of the Ocean_

Coach: _Celia_

Date: _November 15_

Team mission: We will *participate* every day, *cooperate with* each other, take full *responsibility* for completing our work on time, *contribute* by helping each other and offering information, and take our *leadership* roles seriously. We'll maintain a good sense of humor.

Quality factors

Name	Participation	Cooperation	Responsibility	Contribution	Leadership	Coaching tips
	Each day we will come to class on time and take an active role in learning and team decision making.	We will get along with each other, and willingly help each other by answering questions and assisting with any and all tasks.	We will take full responsibility for all assigned tasks and complete them on time. If there are problems or questions, we will ask for help early enough to get the job done on time.	We will make suggestions, bring materials, add to the discussions, and challenge each other to think more clearly about the project.	We will take charge of the assigned tasks we have and get whatever supplies are necessary, arrange for meetings, and speak for the team when it is our turn to lead a portion of the project.	
Norma	NY	NY	NY	Y	NY	Please try to be happy and come ready to listen. I like you, and the team needs your help.
Celia	Y	NY	NY	NY	Y	I need to be happier and more willing to listen to other suggestions
Shari	NY	NY	Y	NY	Y	Please talk more in team meetings and offer more suggestions.
Thomas	Y	Y	NY	Y	NY	Please come to class with your assignments finished. If you need help, just ask us.

Has the QF as stated in the operational definition been met? *Yes*

Has the QF as stated in the operational definition not been met? *Not yet*

Figure 7.20 Social/team skills matrix.

Products of this step: A completely filled out QFs for learning matrix

A brainstormed list and determination of the final product (for example, multimedia presentation, newspaper, or game)

An example of a partially filled-out QFs for learning is shown in Figure 7.21. You'll find a template on page 265.

Once again, we strongly recommend that the project be front-loaded for excellence by carefully identifying (at first by the teacher and then operationally defined with the students) the expectations for the completed project. When the class has agreed and understood, and each student is

Quality factors		Q?	
Written reports	**Operational definitions**	**Not yet**	**Coaching tips**
Grammar (no errors)	Spelling		
	Subject–verb agreement		
	Punctuation		
	Capitalization		
	Parts of speech		
	No sentence fragments		
	No run-on sentences		
Paragraphs	Each—Topic sentence		
	All—At least three supporting details that all relate to the introduction or topic sentence		
Data collection and charts			
Sources	Data from three different sources		
Accurate	No errors in data		
Charts	No errors on charts		
	At least three different types of charts or graphs		
	Proper labeling of all charts with titles		
Creativity			
Color	Use at least two or more colors		
3-Dimensional Audio Video Interactive	Select one or more of these modes for your presentation.		
Neatness (polish)			
	No wrinkles		
	No erasures		
	Use a word processor		
	No smudges		

Figure 7.21 Team project quality factors for learning matrix.

given a copy of the QFs, then they will be ready to proceed and begin their project work. Some may think this is "overkill" or that it will take too long. It is a matter of philosophy. Think about how important it is to you to create a system in which all students have equal opportunity to do excellent work, turn it in on time, and work successfully with their peers.

At the same time, you're going to need to distinguish between QFs and quality features when the projects are completed. Your assessment must be based solely on the QFs (stated expectations). It simply isn't fair to anyone to assess on quality features. To address issues of what the "real world" is like, for example, not everyone can "win," you will need to think about ways in which you might recognize any team who has gone way above and beyond expectations. Recognition does not have to equate to a "grade."

This is a philosophical argument we've heard from educators for a long time. Some say, "If it meets my expectations, then it deserves a 'C' grade. It means it is average." Isn't this interesting? Why would teachers set the expectation for "average" when we know without a shadow of a doubt that employers today don't want to hire "average" workers. They want and expect above-average employees. The truth is that nearly all jobs (decent-paying ones anyway) will require more than a high school diploma. Students will be expected to attend postsecondary schools, for example, technical, two-year college, or four-year university and beyond. Team projects and QFs are a way to propel your students into the twenty-first century, allow them opportunities to gain important social and academic skills, and have fun at the same time.

Obviously, the projects that are suitable for the early grades are going to be much less complex than those of middle or high school students. Properly done, it will require teachers to work together differently too. No longer will teachers be able to work in silos. The twenty-first century requires teachers of all disciplines to seek out ways to create real-life, service-oriented projects that will be graded by teams of teachers, each taking responsibility for his/her content area, but with a designated project manager who oversees the work of student teams.

We can hardly think of any schools or communities in this country that are problem-free, where it would take an immense stretch to "find" some useful project for students to work on while mastering the academic standards. If this is your situation, then work together with peers to create an entrepreneurial opportunity for students. Learning can take many, many forms—who said it had to happen within the four walls of one classroom at a time, with disjointed skills being taught? Why not take the opportunity to create a system that engages students and forces them to "sit up and take notice"? They will discover that school really isn't disconnected to their future.

Step 4—Responsibilities: Who is responsible for taking charge of specific tasks related to the project?

In this step, the team will brainstorm using a lotus diagram to determine all the tasks required to complete the project. Reference the QFs for learning matrix to make certain every aspect of the project has been carefully considered. Brainstorm a list of responsibilities. (Remember, if a task isn't assigned to a specific person, there is a good chance it will not get done, causing the team problems in completing the project on time.)

Decide who will assume the role of overall project manager and which team member(s) will take responsibility for *coordinating* each role. In addition, determine what needs to be done to ensure that the entire project will come together on time and meet all QFs. Identify another team member to become the *quality inspector*, who has responsibility for assessing the project at each process checkpoint. The team may decide to share this role, with several members taking responsibility at different checkpoints. This will assure that team members receive adequate editing/coaching so project deadlines and QF specifications are met. Although there are shared responsibilities, one person should be assigned as project coordinator for each role.

We recommend that team members be provided the option to select the area in which they are most interested in working. Naturally, everyone on the team will be held accountable for meeting each of the core competencies assigned to this project and for learning the standards. (There is a test covering all standards embedded in the project given at the completion of all projects.)

> *Product of this step:* A list of specific tasks for which each student will be responsible. Note who will coordinate each task.

Step 5—Resources: What resources are available in the community and/or school to assist in the completion of the project? (Example: library, Internet, businesses, computer, and so on)

The teacher provides a list of potential resources, but teams are encouraged to add others for which the team will need to get appropriate approval.

> *Product of this step:* Teams members will have signed off on *a list of resources* to use for their project.

Step 6—Manage the team process: How will work flow to meet the project deadlines and specifications?

The teacher provides the deadline for project completion and dates for critical process checks along the way. The team will determine how work will flow to meet all process checks and the final deadline for a quality project. There are several online project management tools that can be used by students. Check out the Helpful Websites in the Recommended Resources section at the end of this book.

> *Product of this step:* A *flowchart* or *Gantt chart* with tasks, responsibilities, start and finish times, and process checkpoint dates.

Do—Learning

Step 7—Process information: Team members conduct research and/or experiments to accomplish the necessary learning, achieve the aim of the project, and construct and complete the final product.

Teams move through the process, completing their responsibilities, and periodically asking the quality inspector to check their work to be sure all QFs for learning are achieved. Figure 7.22 shows an example. Teachers use this information to guide their instruction. If many students are making the same errors, it signals that time has to be given for some whole-group instruction. Likewise, the teacher may work with small groups on a mini-lesson to alleviate specific error types. Using this approach, the teacher keeps abreast of learning advances for the class and for each student.

Name: _Norman_   Project title: _Ecosystems of the Ocean_   Date: _November 15_

Fill in the box opposite the QF indicating the errors.

Process checkpoints

Quality factor	1 Nov 1	2 Nov 7	3 Nov 15	4
Example: QF—Correct spelling	20 errors	10	3	3
Subject–verb agreement	6	5	3	1
Punctuation	23	15	15	5
Capitalization	0	0	0	1
Parts of speech	6	4	4	2
No sentence fragments	3	3	1	0
No run-on sentences	0	1	0	0

Figure 7.22   Quality Inspector Form—QFs for learning.

Product of this step: When the project is turned in, the *Student Error Chart* with an assessment of each QF from the team's quality inspector will be filled out and given to the teacher. *The final product is presented.*

Study—Assessment As Part of the Project

Projects may be assessed in at least four different ways:

1. All students are given an opportunity to evaluate and score the products of all (or some of) the other teams. (If the class is large and there are many teams, you may want to randomly select and assign two different teams to evaluate each project. Using this method, each team would receive feedback from two student teams and one or more teachers.) The entire class will collaborate and reach consensus on a fair, equitable approach to grading. Some classes determine a percentage of the total QFs that must be met and turn that into a grade. Others weight the QFs by assigning a number (5 points for the most critical, 3 points for important QFs, and 1 point for those of lesser importance to the project) to each and reaching a score based on the total number of points awarded the project. When students are empowered to collaborate on the decision of how the projects will be graded, there will be more student buy-in to the process.

   Teams of students are required to justify their score, citing evidence based on QFs and the product. You can readily see how this type of assessment increases students' critical thinking skills and capacity to work together to reach consensus. The value added far exceeds the time spent.

2. Each teacher(s) assesses the *product* of all projects using the same scoring guide. In addition, each teacher is responsible for evaluating the specific QFs related to his/her subject area.

3. At the end of the project, each team member will summarize his/her experience of being a member of the team. We suggest asking them to write a one-page summary, "*What I learned from doing this project and being a part of this team.*"

4. Last, but certainly not least, students will be given a typical "school-type" assessment in each subject area covering the specific skills and knowledge students were expected to learn during the project.

After the Project—Study the Results

Upon completion of each team project and the test, use a line graph or histogram to chart the class results. You might also want to analyze the test results by level of learning in order to better understand the success (or not) of students' ability to advance their learning. Post all results in the classroom for all to see, but be sure results are anonymous.

Seek feedback from the students about what kept them from being successful and/or what contributed to their success and the overall success of the team. Use a plus/delta chart, and on the *delta* side solicit suggestions for improving the next team project. It's equally important to capture student feedback on an E/L chart, and by using "How Helpful were These Resources?" The latter is found on page 143.

Armed with all this feedback, and looking at the hard data results, you and your fellow teachers can plan the next projects using "lessons learned" from each previous one. This is called *cycles of improvement*. Be sure to keep the data and feedback for historical purposes and for reflection with peers and administrators at the end of the year.

The goal of the teacher—as the facilitator of learning—is to embrace the two quality principles and take whatever action is necessary to eliminate any and all barriers to student and class success.

I am responsible for my own learning.

I am response-able to the success of the group.

Do not forget: *If students report satisfaction with the team projects, but haven't met the content standards, it signals a process problem that must be analyzed.*

A Modified Team Project Process for Elementary Grades

If you think this approach is too cumbersome for elementary students, you're right. Figures 7.23 and 7.24 clarify how the process can be modified to accommodate younger children. We suggest you use these as starting points, then modify the process as needed after the projects have been evaluated and student knowledge tested, and taking into account the E/L chart and plus/delta responses.

Your students have already learned how to write mission statements and have used a lotus diagram, so these things won't be new to them. We've witnessed teams of pre-K students work

	Task	Product for this step
Plan team organization		
Step 1	**Mission** How will your team accomplish its purpose?	A mission statement signed by all students and the teacher that states how the team expects to behave and work together to accomplish the purpose.
Step 2	**Decide on quality factors for the project** What will the project look like when it is finished?	A completed lotus diagram with pictures and/or words describing what the expectations of the project are.
Step 3	**Responsibilities** Who is responsible for specific tasks related to the project?	Student assignments (volunteers) for parts of the project. Everyone is expected to assume responsibility for leadership for some part of the project. Everyone does research.
Step 4	**Resources** What resources are available to be used for this project?	A list of resources students can use to complete the project.
Do the project		
Study the results		
Step 6	**Assessment** How well did the team meet the quality factors for the project? How smoothly did the teams work together to accomplish the task?	Student test scores covering the skills and knowledge to be learned. Student response—plus/delta and E/L charts
Act (Teacher)	Use student results, feedback, and suggestions to make improvements in the next team project.	

Figure 7.23   Team projects for grades K–2.

amazingly well together to "rehab" their classroom to meet everyone's needs. It was fun, and they were totally committed to the process and making a difference. One amazing kindergarten project had to do with healthy bodies. The students did research on nutrition and counted fat grams and sugar content in fast food. They were able to plant a garden (with the harvest being shared among families), learned to prepare healthy meals (students as dietitians, chefs, and servers), and were required to make an oral presentation to the class and their families explaining what they learned and the importance of eating healthy. The next project their teacher planned was related to improving physical fitness. Amazing!

You see, "no shame, no blame" if you're not "there" yet, but it can be done and is being done in some schools to the great benefit of the students. Our mantra for you is "Be a learner, be brave, and be a coach to your peers to begin planning a team project at your grade level." If we engage young children in team projects, and it becomes a normal way of learning, then by the time they go to high school there will be no stopping their learning or joy of learning! Isn't that the ultimate goal?

Help Is a Click Away

There are some great free websites aimed at project-based or problem-based learning (PBL). This one offers a framework for creating project-based learning opportunities: http://www.pbl-online. org/. Signing on to the site means you can access other teachers' projects, copy them, use them, and so on. It also means that if you put a project up there, other subscribers will have access to it.

	Task	Product for this step
Plan team organization		
Step 1	**Mission** How will your team accomplish its purpose? What social skills will the team identify as critical to success?	• A written mission statement signed by all members of the team that describes the way the team is committed to working together to achieve the purpose of the project. • A team skills matrix listing the quality factors (verbs) from the mission statement and operational definitions for each.
Step 2	**Determine quality factors for the project** What will the team need to learn about? What will the project look like when it is finished?	• A completely filled-out QF matrix
Step 3	**Responsibilities** Who is responsible for taking charge of specific tasks related to the project?	A tool that shows who is responsible for specific tasks, signed by all team members. Everyone is expected to assume responsibility for leadership for some part of the project. Everyone does research.
Step 4	**Resources** What resources are available to students (in school and/or the community) to complete this project?	• Team members will have signed off on a list of resources students can use to complete the project.
Do—Learning		
Step 5	**Process information** Team members conduct research and/or experiments to accomplish the necessary learning and achieve the aim of the project.	• A completed QF matrix with a peer and self-assessment of each QF for learning is required.
Study		
Step 6	**Team effectiveness and efficiency** How well does this team function together?	• Each person will complete a team skills assessment for each team member. • A personal summary statement from each student: "What did you learn from doing this project and being part of a team."
Step 7	**Peer and facilitator evaluation** When all the projects are completed, review the QFs and assess the projects of other teams.	• A completed QFs for learning matrix with an assessment of each QF and coaching tips for assigned team projects. • Plus/delta and E/L charts.

Figure 7.24   Team projects for grades 3–5.

There's also a way to evaluate the projects, which is an interesting and exciting way to improve your own projects. You can even work collaboratively with other teachers to develop team projects. George Lucas of Edutopia, the Buck Institute for Education, and the U.S. Department of Education have contributed funding to the PBL site. The site is housed in the Department of Educational Technology at Boise State University.

The Buck Institute for Education website, www.bie.org, is another great site for project-based learning. There are many video examples on the site.

Edmodo is another free web tool with far-ranging possibilities for teachers to share with other teachers from around the world. Check it out at http://www.edmodo.com. With this safe and secure tool (likely as safe as any web tool can be) you can share things with students, other teachers, and parents.

Another resource is the International Center for Leadership in Education. It has developed a series of Gold Seal Lessons designed to add rigor and relevance to any content. Lessons are cross-curricular for the most part, and might stimulate your thinking. You can go online to their website at http://www.leadered.com, select "resources," find the Gold Seal Lessons for Rigor and Relevance—9–12, and download an excerpt for free. Not all the lessons are geared for team projects, but with a little creativity you can adapt any of them.

SUMMARY

This chapter has stressed four significant steps to assure that your BBQ system is effective and one where students are living the two principles. First, you learned through a case study (Mrs. Ann Oying and Mr. Fixit) how a BBQ classroom functions as a system. Second, you learned about the empowerment of having student-led conferences, where each child really demonstrates the principle "I am responsible for my own learning." Next, we walked you through a discussion of seeking systematic satisfaction feedback from parents and provided a few tools.

Finally, you learned the importance of helping your students learn to work in diverse team situations as well as tying your curriculum to real-life situations. The payoff for you, the teacher-leader, is the shift to "student as worker" that is occurring in your BBQ classroom. Yes, the students will make mistakes, and yes, teamwork is often "messier" than the traditional model of "teacher at the front doing most of the explaining." When you think about it, this is what school learning should encompass. When students work together to produce quality products that frequently solve real-life problems, it teaches them important life lessons that can not be learned through books and typical schoolwork.

Team projects can address every one of the Common Core Standards and every one of the twenty-first century skills. The topics are limitless, and we can almost guarantee that if you follow the model provided, your students will not forget what they have learned. Hooking the standards to the real world and providing all students with meaningful work greatly increases motivation and enthusiasm for learning.

This approach will instill a sense of individual and group pride while providing opportunities for students to reach higher standards in a nonthreatening classroom climate. Yes, your classroom system is changing. Your BBQ classroom has been launched.

TOOLBOX

SOCIAL/TEAM SKILLS MATRIX

Team name: _____

Project: _____   Coach: _____

Team mission: _____   Date: _____

Quality factors →

Names						

Has the QF as stated in the operational definition been met?

Has the QF as stated in the operational definition not been met?

TEAM PROJECT QUALITY FACTORS FOR LEARNING MATRIX

State standards included: _____   Project due date: _____

_____   Team members: _____

Quality factors	Operational definitions	Q? Not yet	Coaching tips
Written reports			
Oral presentations			
Data collection and charts			
Creativity			
Neatness (polish)			

QUALITY INSPECTOR FORM
Individual Student Error Chart—QFs for Learning

Name: _____ Project title: _____ Date: _____

Fill in the box opposite the QF indicating the errors. (To be given to the teacher.)

Process checkpoints

Quality factor	1 Date	2 Date	3 Date	4 Date

TEAM PROJECT—PROCESS CHECKPOINT COACHING TIPS

For team member _____

Deadline for completion _____ Process checkpoint # _____ Date _____   Quality inspector _____

Quality factor	Operational definition	Quality or not yet	Coaching tips

CONFIDENCE-O-GRAM

Mark the box that reflects how you feel about taking the test/quiz tomorrow.

Scared	Nervous	Almost	Ready

GANTT CHART

What

A *Gantt chart* is a picture of the timeline for completing a project. It shows the flow of the work and provides information about the start time and completion times for tasks within the project. A Gantt chart can also show who is responsible for seeing that each task is completed.

How

1. Make a list of all activities that must be accomplished to complete the project.

2. Review each activity to determine whether or not it requires some previous action or is otherwise integral to another activity.

3. Note where one activity is dependent on another and list them in sequential order.

4. Determine the project completion date.

5. Determine the approximate amount of time it will take to complete each task.

6. Make certain that tasks that must be done in sequential order are properly planned with time allowed to complete all tasks. Individuals with responsibility for each task may need to negotiate shorter completion times and/or there may need to be an adjustment to the date for project completion.

7. Avoid assigning to the same individual the tasks that are overlapping in time.

8. Draw the chart. Determine how time will be displayed: days, weeks, months, and so on. Place the allotted time frame across the top of the chart. Along the left-hand side, list the activities in sequential order. On the far right-hand side of the chart, list the individual responsible for each task and ensuring that the activity is completed.

9. Post the chart so it is visible to everyone working on the project. Provide everyone on the team with a copy of the chart. Refer to the Gantt chart at every project update meeting. As situations arise that prevent certain activities from being completed on time, note what the problem is (this is an opportunity for process improvement) and, if necessary, adjust the time frames for subsequent activities.

When

Use this tool:

- When it is desirable for all team members to see the project scope and sequence

- As a means of keeping team members on task

- To teach students how to develop and use timelines

Example: Team Project—Charity Spook House

Task (What?)	Date (When?) October										Who?
	15	16	17	18	19	22	23	24	25	26	
Research other spook houses	X	X									Sue, José, and Josh
Research place for spook house	X	X									Tim, Tabetha, and Maria
Team meeting reports and decisions			X								Team
Plan the scary events in spook house and choose roles to play				X	X						Team
Process check					X						Teacher
Get materials for "events"						X	X				Tim, Tabetha, Josh
Do artwork to set the atmosphere						X	X	X			Maria, Sue, José
Use technology to make advertising posters and tickets						X					Tim, Josh
Sell tickets							X	X	X		Team
Set up spook house									X		Team
Open spook house									X	X	Team

Example: Class Poetry Journal Project

Task	Date School year 2004–05						Who?
	Jan	Feb	Mar	Apr	May	June	
Establish guidelines for submission	▓						Class
Submit poems to committee	▓	▓					All tenth-graders
Select poems for submission			▓				Journal team
Proofread selected poems				▓			Proofing team
Design cover			▓	▓			Cover team
Journal layout and design				▓			L & D team
Develop marketing/sales plan		▓					Marketing team
Take copy to print shop					▓		Mr. Harry
Take journal orders				▓			Sales team
Distribute finished product						▓	Class

HISTOGRAM

What

A *histogram* is a snapshot, in bar graph form, of the distribution of data. In other words, the data are lined up according to frequency. It is a useful tool for helping groups see how powerful data in picture form can be, and is often used in the popular press to make a point.

How

1. Determine the process or system to be studied.

2. Select the "classes" or subdivisions to display the data (for example, grading scale— 93–100, weight—75–90 lbs, 91–116 lbs, stanine scores on a standardized test, and so on).

3. Using data from a check sheet or other quality tool, arrange it into the aforementioned class.

4. Draw the graph with an *x*-axis (horizontal) and a *y*-axis (vertical). Each axis will be the same length.

5. Divide the *x*-axis into the number of classes and label each.

6. Scale the *y*-axis from zero to the total number of data points in the class with the most frequency. (Example: 10 students weigh 75–90 lbs. That is the most of any weight group. Scale the *y*-axis from 0–10.)

7. Draw the graph.

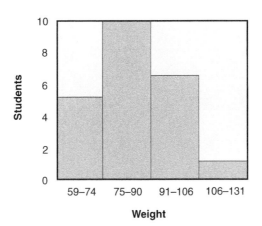

When

Use this tool when:

*   It is important to see the frequency of distribution of the data

*   The group is studying statistics

*   There is a need to understand the amount of variation in any set of data

Example:

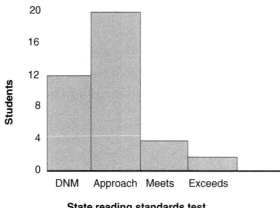

Chart Interpretation

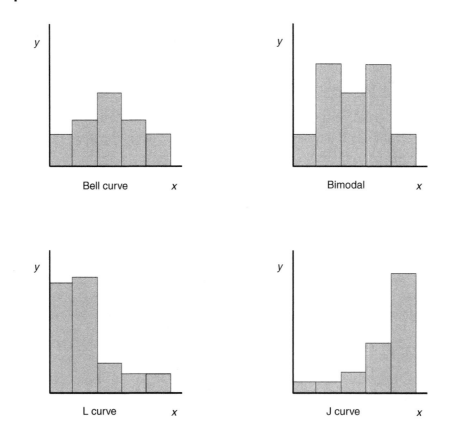

The ideal shape for learning results is a J curve. Repeat a histogram to show progress over time and look for the results to shift from an L curve or bell curve to a J curve.

LINE GRAPH

What

A *line graph* gives a vertical picture of the bandwidth of variation in any process. There are several types of line graphs. We will share the two most frequently used methods. Method one depicts the total score for the class on any measure. Method two displays individual scores along a line and shows the spread of variation.

How

1. State what is to be measured at the top of the page.

2. Draw a vertical axis to accommodate the amount of data.

3. Draw a horizontal axis extending from the bottom of the vertical axis and off to the right, long enough to accommodate at least nine data points.

4. Draw evenly spaced vertical lines up from the horizontal axis all across the page. (There should be one line for each data point you intend to collect.)

5. Label the horizontal axis "time." Each vertical line coming up from it will be labeled with a date. (It is best to use one chart per marking period or for one semester. Each vertical line would represent a week.)

6. Label the vertical axis as follows: Method 1—Total number correct for the *class*. Method 2—Correct responses per *student*.

7. Scale the vertical axis as follows: Method 1—The number of items tested per week times the number of students in the class (Example: 10 items per week × 20 students enrolled in the class = 200. The vertical axis would be scaled from 0–200.)

Method 1—Line Graph—Class Progress

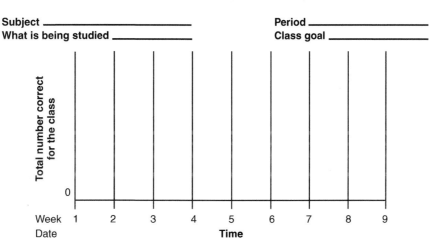

When

Use this tool when you want to watch class progress on any critical indicator (process measure) toward mastery of any content. Method 2 provides you with the bandwidth of variation within the class and allows you to share with parents and students how they are doing relative to the class as a whole.

Examples:

Method 1—Class Progress

Subject _____*Math*_____ Number of students ___*20*___
What is being studied _*Timed multiplication facts*_ Class goal for year ___*90%*___

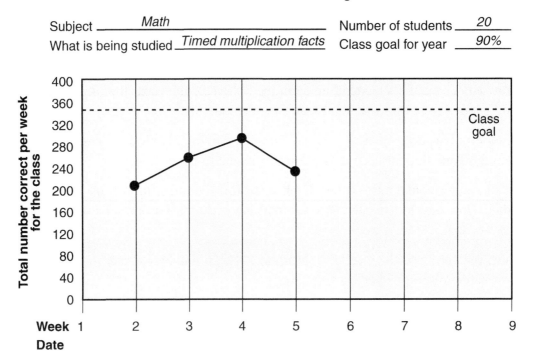

Method 2—Individual Scores—Class Progress

Subject _____ *Math* _____   Students enrolled __*22*__

What is being studied __*Algebra problem solving*__   Class goal _____ *80%* _____

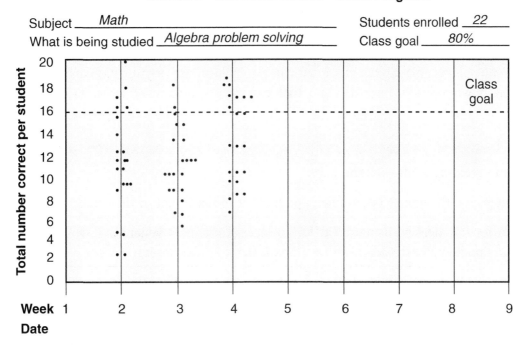

LOTUS DIAGRAM

What

The *lotus diagram* is an analytical tool that can also be used for organization and brainstorming. It helps break down topics or information, which can then be prioritized for additional study.

How

The steps to creating a lotus diagram are:

1. Determine the topic to be studied and place it in the center of the center box.

2. Brainstorm ideas by using the affinity process (or simply generating ideas through a more traditional approach) and prioritize the ideas into major topics

3. Create a lotus diagram by folding a large piece of paper into thirds lengthwise and creasing the folds. Open the paper and fold it again into thirds in the opposite direction and crease the folds. This yields nine (9) smaller squares. Outline the center box with a marker. Fold the paper again into thirds lengthwise, then fold it into thirds one more time, making sure to crease the folds. Open the paper and fold it back into thirds horizontally, and then fold the paper again into thirds. Crease all folds. Open the paper and you should have 81 squares.

4. Use a dark marker to draw lines on each of the folds.

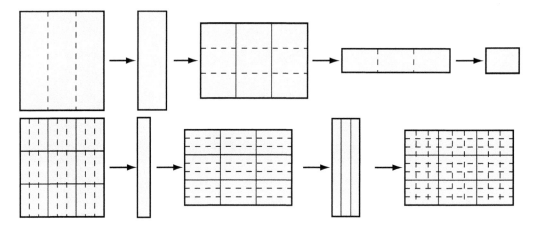

5. Place the main topic in the center rectangle of the lotus diagram. Beginning at the diagonal right outer rectangle, number each around the center from 1 to 8. (See the example on the next page.)

6. Take each of the "headers" from the affinity diagram and place each in a numbered rectangle around the center. These are the subtopics to study. Each one is then carried over to the corresponding center box of one of the outer rectangles. Number 1 moves to the upper-right rectangle, 2 to the center-right rectangle, and so forth, clockwise around the center set of boxes.

7. Brainstorm information about each of the subtopics to study. Students can then research each of the ideas.

When

Use this tool:

- To promote logical and creative thinking

- As a spatial and interactive activity

- When it is important to engage all the students in analysis and brainstorming

- As a means to study for an upcoming unit test

- As a break from more traditional learning approaches

- As a means to address all learning styles

Example: Georgia History

Students used the affinity process to brainstorm what they wanted to learn about.

7 Events	Other 8 famous people	1 Civil war
6 Religion	**Georgia History**	2 Famous politicians
5 Customs	4 Pirates	3 Trade

At this point, students determined what aspect of Georgia history they wanted to research. These became the work teams for the unit. Each team took one section and created a second lotus diagram for their research and made a presentation to the class. See the next page for a completed lotus diagram.

Example: Elementary

7 Orange	8 Red	1 Purple
6 Yellow	**Colors**	2 Green
5 Black	4 Brown	3 Blue

7 Trees	8 Jell-O	1 Peas
6 Chalk-board	**Green**	2 Limes
5 Grass	4 Eyes	3 Broccoli

Example: What Will Be Studied About Transportation

Car	Wagon	Motorcycle	Donkey	(Picture)	Thoroughbred racehorse	Swimming	Aircraft carrier	Cruise ship
Farm tractor	**Wheels** (1)	School bus	Bull riding	**Hoof** (8)	Horse-drawn carriage	Pontoon boat	**Water** (7)	Steamer
Truck	Train	In-line skates	Oxen	Horse	Horse-drawn sleigh	Tubing	Speed boat	Surfing
WWII pigeon	Biplane	Propeller airplanes	**Wheels** (1)	**Hoof** (8)	**Water** (7)	Interplanetary cars	Personal aircraft	Jet shoes
Jet airplane	**Wings** (2)	Birds/insects	**Wings** (2)	**Transportation** (4)	**Future** (6)	Space bus	**Future** (6)	Cars that drive themselves
Skydiver	Jet fighter	Angels/fairies	**Paddle** (3)	**Space** (4)	**Feet** (5)	Intergalactic spaceships	Speed-of-light trains	Highway people-mover belts
Canoe	Duck	Racing skiff	Spaceship	Space walk	Mars rover	Walking	(Picture)	Hopping
Kayak	**Paddle** (3)	Scuba diver flipper	Hot air balloon	**Space** (4)	Rocket	Running	**Feet** (5)	Sliding
Paddle-wheeler	Paddle boat	Row boat	Lunar lander	Lunar module	Space shuttle	Jumping	Leaping	Skipping

PARETO CHART

What

A *Pareto chart* is a bar graph that displays the data from "most" to "least." It separates the vital few items or activities that contribute to a problem from the useful many. It provides a starting point for continuous improvement projects.

How

Steps to creating a Pareto chart are:

1. Determine the data to be collected, taking into account the significance of things such as time of day, place of occurrence, gender, and so on. Operationally define the data to be collected.

2. Determine what period of time the data are to be collected over.

3. Determine who is in the best position to collect the data.

4. Use a check sheet, and collect the data for the specified length of time.

5. Organize the data categories in descending order.

6. Draw the chart by drawing three equal lines to form a "U" shape.

7. Scale the chart by adding up the total of all data combined. On the left vertical axis, scale the chart from zero at the bottom to the total number of data points (for example, total errors of all types) at the top.

8. On the right vertical axis, scale the chart in percentages, noting 25, 50, 75, and 100%.

9. Divide the horizontal axis into equal parts to match the number of categories of data collected.

10. Look at the data for each category and label the chart *in descending order* from *left to right*, the categories along the horizontal axis.

11. Draw the bar for each category.

12. Place a dot at the upper right-hand corner of the bar for the first category. Imagine you will stack the next "bar" on top and total both to calculate the cumulative percentage. Place a dot at the "imagined" right-hand corner where the second category would extend.

13. Continue to do this for all categories of data. Connect the dots (which will add up to 100%).

14. Interpret the chart by looking for causes that add up to approximately 70–80% of the total. (The Pareto principle says that 80% of the effects come from 20% of the causes.)

15. Begin the improvement plan by focusing on one of the most significant problems.

Example: Tardy to First Period

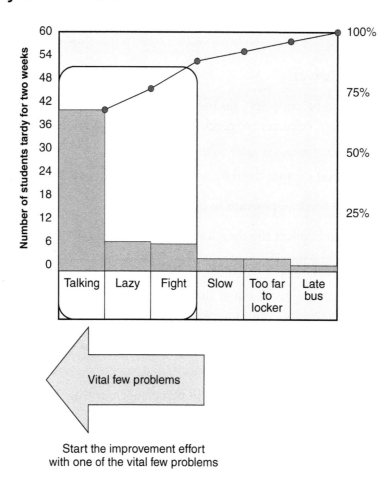

Start the improvement effort
with one of the vital few problems

When

Use this tool when:

- It is important to determine the most significant cause of a problem

- It is important to approach the problem in a focused way, getting the biggest improvement with your efforts

- You want to observe how the improvement efforts have affected the issue

Example: Classroom Math

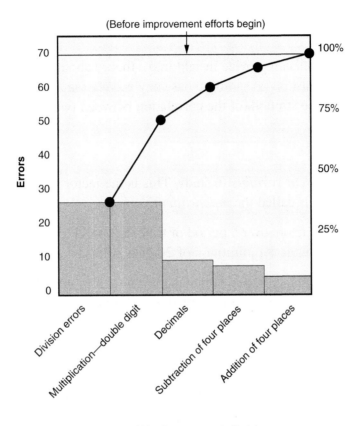

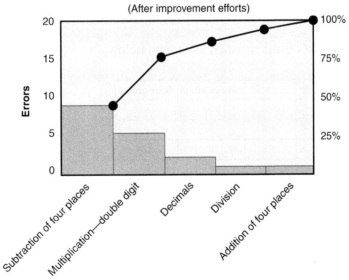

SCATTER DIAGRAM

What

A *scatter diagram* is a tool that can provide insight into a theory about whether a relationship exists between two factors. Care must be taken not to base any correlation as absolute fact; however, one can draw inferences about the strength of the correlation between two different pieces of data.

How

1. Determine the *dependent variable* to study. This is the factor believed to be affected by another factor, which is called the *independent variable.*

2. Collect data on both factors over a period of time that provides enough data points to show a pattern. (We suggest a minimum of 20 data points.)

3. Both sets of data must be collected simultaneously, such as attendance and weekly quiz grades, or the number of laps swam in practice and timed swims.

4. Draw the diagram using a vertical and horizontal axis of the same length.

5. Place the dependent variable on the vertical axis. Scale the chart appropriately.

6. Place the independent variable on the horizontal axis and scale it appropriately.

7. Using the two sets of data points, enter each point at the intersection of the dependent and independent variables.

8. Continue entering data until finished as shown below.

Student	Attendance	Quiz grade	Student	Attendance	Quiz grade
1	4	7	11	3	5
2	3	5	12	2	8
3	5	9	13	5	10
4	2	3	14	5	7
5	5	8	15	4	9
6	2	2	16	3	6
7	3	5	17	5	8
8	5	9	18	4	10
9	5	10	19	4	7
10	4	10	20	3	8

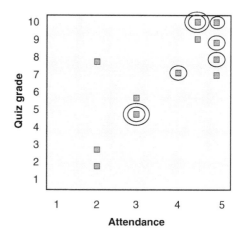

When

Use this tool whenever you need to determine if there is a relationship between two factors.

Chart Interpretation

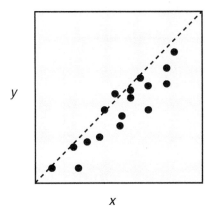

Positive correlation—An increase in *y* may depend on an increase in *x*. If *x* is controlled, *y* might be controlled. Note how close the data are to the line of central tendency.

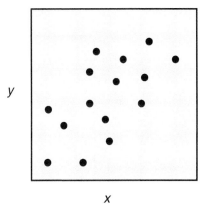

Possible positive correlation—If *x* is increased, *y* may also increase somewhat. It is not possible to make strong inferences from these data.

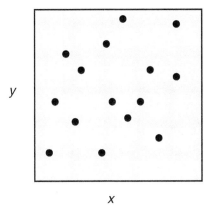

No correlation—*y* may be dependent on another variable.

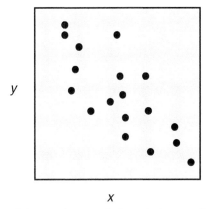

Possible negative correlation—An increase in *x* may cause a tendency for a decrease in *y*.

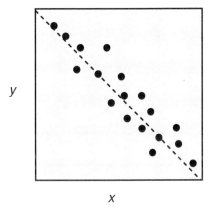

Negative correlation—An increase in *x* may cause a decrease in *y*. As with the positive correlation, *x* may be controlled instead of *y*. Note how close the data are to the line of central tendency.

SCATTER DIAGRAM (CORRELATION CHART—TIME SPENT STUDYING AND TEST GRADE) TEMPLATE

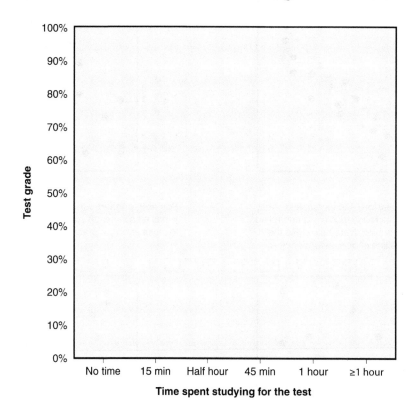

8

BBQ Observables and Final Thoughts

OBSERVABLES: LEVELS 1, 2, AND 3

Congratulations! You have begun your BBQ journey, one of the most challenging steps for any educator. At the beginning of this book we told you there would be BBQ observables provided. These are organized into levels 1, 2, and 3. These provide you with a quick and easy way to monitor your progress and the depth of your knowledge. We strongly recommend you go through each chapter and check off the observables that you learned in each.

We've organized the observables pretty much in the order in which you'll want to build and develop your BBQ classroom. Level 1 observables relate to the *beginning of alignment*. Whether you're building a house, a family, or a classroom, the necessity to align key processes with aim and vision are critical to your future success. Once the system is aligned, you have an opportunity to learn ways to integrate all aspects of the system. Level 2, *beginning a systematic approach to improvement* means that you've begun to evaluate the effectiveness and efficiency of key processes. The central theme is to use cycles of improvement regularly and systematically to improve effectiveness and efficiency.

Level 3 expands on levels 1 and 2, and is described as *the system is fully aligned and integrated; process improvement is a routine way of life*. Included here are expanded approaches to getting actionable feedback from parents, expanding students' leadership through student-led conferences, and addressing twenty-first century skills through meaningful, real-life team projects.

The observables are shown in Tables 8.1, 8.2, and 8.3.

Table 8.1   Baldrige level 1 observables.

Level	#	Outcomes	Heard about it	Intellectually understand its use	Used in my classroom	It is part of our class culture	Can teach it to others
BBQ (Baldrige level 1) Beginning of alignment	1.a	Posts *school vision, mission* in the classroom					
	1.b	Uses *quality tools* (e.g.: run chart, bar graph, etc.) to *analyze results data* from previous year(s) and uses information gleaned to make changes to classroom organization, learning activities, instruction, assessment, etc., prior to the start of the school year					
	1.c	Posts the *two quality principles*: (I am responsible . . . and I am response-able . . .) prominently in the classroom					
	1.d	Seeks *feedback from students* (e.g., surveys, True Colors, etc.) to get to know needs/expectations					
	1.e	Uses at least one tool to get *feedback from parents* to get to know needs/expectations (e.g., surveys, focus groups, etc.)					
	1.f	Seeks feedback from the next teacher in line about *"essential skills"* students will need to succeed					
	1.g	Facilitates the creation of a *class vision statement* signed by all and displayed in the classroom					
	1.h	Facilitates the creation of a *class mission statement* signed by all and displayed in the classroom					
	1.i	Involves students in defining a *quality student*, signed by all and displayed in the classroom					
	1.j	Involves students in defining a *quality teacher*, signed by all and displayed in the classroom					
	1.k	Establishes *class academic goals* that are aligned with the vision and displays them in the classroom					
	1.l	Creates *action plans* for each academic goal and set *targets* for achieving each					
	1.m	[Teachers of grades 5–12] Facilitates each *student's creation of personal vision, mission, individual goals, and action plans* (works with colleagues as appropriate)					
	1.n	Standardizes at least one key noninstructional process with a *flowchart* (e.g: daily routine, homework, transitions)					
	1.o	Uses several *quality tools* (Examples: brainstorming, affinity diagram, multi-voting, flowcharting) with students					
	1.p	Facilitates with all students creation of a *data notebook* with class (or personal) vision, mission, goals, and student QFs					

Table 8.2 Baldrige level 2 observables.

Level	#	Outcomes	BBQ classroom					
			Heard about it	Intellectually understand its use	Used in my classroom	It is part of our class culture	Can teach it to others	
BBQ (Baldrige) level 2 — Beginning of a systematic approach to improvement	2.a	All level 1 outcomes are part of the class culture and routines						
	2.b	Establishes a *measurement plan* with leading and lagging indicators and sets an alert trigger system on a *dashboard* to signal when improvement is necessary						
	2.c	Establishes a *class data wall*—dashboard indicators (includes class vision, mission, goals, action plans, targets, student QFs, and graphic displays of progress toward class goals)						
	2.d	Students help define *"quality work"* and *operationally define* each factor to reduce variation for all assignments. For work that is best assessed through rubrics, students assist with creating, then improving the rubric.						
	2.e	Facilitates the class assessment of mission specificity using a *radar chart*; display on class data wall with evidence of action plans for improvement						
	2.f	Provides time for students to assess themselves (*student QFs*), filling out a chart in their data notebook, and follows up with reflections about ways to improve						
	2.g	Regularly uses *enthusiasm and learning* and plus/delta charts with students—uses data to drive improvement—display on data wall						
	2.h	Regularly has students *monitor their own academic and behavioral progress* using student data notebooks; facilitates students' keeping track of their own learning						
	2.i	Regularly *collects data* that measure progress (in-process) toward class goals; display on data wall using two or more different *quality tools* (Examples: run chart, histogram, line graph, etc.)						
	2.j	Uses *informal PDSA* with student to drive improvement for instruction on a routine basis. (Incorporates some quality tools such as: plus/delta, brainstorming, affinity diagram, etc.)						
	2.k	Has the class regularly assess teacher effectiveness using the *QFs for teacher.*						
	2.l	[Teachers of grades 2–4] Facilitates the process of students *creating their own individual academic goals*						
	2.m	Actively engages students in determining appropriate, regular *celebrations for accomplishment of targets and class goals*						
	2.n	Uses *fast feedback and/or how helpful were these resources* regularly and systematically and uses the feedback to improve the instructional process						

Table 8.3 Baldrige level 3 observables.

Level	#	BBQ classroom — Outcomes	Heard about it	Intellectually understand its use	Used in my classroom	It is part of our class culture	Can teach it to others
BBQ (Baldrige) level 3 — The system is fully aligned and integrated; Process improvement is a routine way of life.	3.a	All Level 2 outcomes are part of the class culture and routines					
	3.b	Regularly and systematically uses a variety of *different tools to display data toward achievement of class goals* (e.g., line graph, run chart, histogram, Pareto chart, scatter diagram)					
	3.c	Regularly seeks *feedback from students* about their *readiness to take a test* (e.g., confidence-o-gram, affinity diagram, lotus diagram, etc.) and uses it					
	3.d	Regularly asks *students* to assess the effectiveness of their study habits in relation to test results using a *correlation chart*, and uses this to reflect and set new plans for improvement					
	3.e	Presents data from *students at risk of not meeting the class goals*, and works with peers and administration to analyze root cause and use PDSA to improve. Weekly updates indicate success/failure to understand root cause. Team meetings reflect these discussions; information is sent weekly to administration.					
	3.f	The *class data wall is regularly analyzed* by students and teacher; *action plans are changed to reflect improvements*. Students are able to interpret individual and class data and are fully engaged as partners in suggesting and implementing changes. (PDSA)					
	3.g	Facilitates the improvement of any/all *noninstructional processes* that are inefficient or ineffective (e.g. cause lost instructional time, jeopardize safety, etc.) by engaging students in *PDSA*					
	3.h	[Elementary Teachers] Engages *students to facilitate weekly class meetings* for purposes of reflecting on the week (mission, dashboard review, and other issues of the week); seeks suggestions for improvement and uses them					
	3.i	Systematically seeks feedback from parents at least twice yearly about their satisfaction with their child's education; collates data, uses feedback to improve (e.g., survey), and shares improvement plans with parents					
	3.j	Demonstrates a dedication to continuous improvement of self and *all* students; embraces the two principles of a BBQ classroom in all interactions with students, parents, peers, and administration					

Continued

Table 8.3 *Continued.*

Level	#	BBQ classroom					
		Outcomes	Heard about it	Intellectually understand its use	Used in my classroom	It is part of our class culture	Can teach it to others
BBQ (Baldrige) level 3	3.k	Regularly engages students in team projects to meet skills of the 21st century; works with students to establish the QFs for the project and operational definitions. Students create a mission and goals for the project. Assessment includes the product and an assessment of skills learned; a formal evaluation of the project is completed by students for cycles of improvement.					
	3.l	Implements *student-led conferences*					
	3.m	When faced with evidence that key processes are not capable of yielding the desired results, takes action: *benchmarks "best practice" within the district, state, region or nationally, or innovates and designs a new process.*					

POINT–COUNTERPOINT

Over the years of training thousands of teachers around the country, we have accumulated a list of the most frequent reasons teachers give us for why this approach would not be feasible for them. No kidding! Here they are.

Top Ten Reasons Why Teachers Can't Create BBQ Classrooms:

10. I've got to cover the curriculum.

9. The district requires me to teach to the state standards.

8. I teach special needs students. This won't work with them.

7. Parents won't like it if I ask their kids to help others.

6. My students aren't capable of knowing how they want to learn.

5. You don't understand my students—they are apathetic and undisciplined.

4. The reading (or) math program my district uses is scripted. I can not deviate.

3. The district won't let me hang anything on the walls of my classroom.

2. Business models don't work with students—we don't make widgets.

And the *number one reason* why teachers can't create a BBQ classroom is

1. *I'm held accountable for students passing the state test.*

In response to these reasons, we consulted with teachers who *have* been successful in creating a BBQ classroom and came up with these reasons why you must change your system.

Top Ten Reasons Why Teachers Can't Afford *Not* to Create BBQ Classrooms

10. There's a lot the students are required to learn and know.

9. My students have to take the state standards test, and to be successful they need to learn the basics and critical thinking.

8. Students in my class(es) come with a large range of abilities and interests.

7. Parent communication and cooperation need to improve.

6. My students are apathetic, bored, or disenfranchised.

5. I am tired, frustrated, and feel unappreciated by the district, parents, and students.

4. We have a new curriculum, but I know it isn't working for all my students.

3. The district is holding me accountable for student learning results.

2. We don't produce widgets.

And the *number one reason* why teachers can't afford *not* create a BBQ classroom is

1. *I take great pride in my teaching, am stressed out, and need to learn how to help all the students and myself, too.*

LESSONS LEARNED

We'll share our lessons learned in the hope that they will help you in your journey:

- There is never one "right" way to do something, but by standardizing key processes after making changes using a "management by fact" approach you have a greater chance of success. Repeated cycles of improvement allow you to predict improved results.

- If you don't evaluate satisfaction and results on a regular and frequent basis—in-process—you can never be sure of your effectiveness.

- Enthusiasm for learning is vital, and when you listen and act on suggestions from your students, motivation and desire to learn increases.

- Every time I am *certain* that I am right, I realize I am not. The antidote for this is to ask for feedback and make changes accordingly.

- You have to identify and know what your customers need and expect.

- Individuals who are angry have most likely been "hurt" by the system and feel disenfranchised. Look for ways to empower them to help fix the system.

- Many problems are more complex than can be described in a book. We encourage you to work with your PLC (and other peers) to build the bridges between these concepts and your own circumstances.

- Although critics may challenge your thinking, you need to remain open to what they say. It follows that you will be led to a better way to approach issues, and design lessons that engage and excite all students.

- Students who do not "fit in" with a traditional approach are the most likely to become missionaries and champions for BBQ over time. Conversely, students who have been highly successful with the traditional approach may be the most resistant to change. This is why the *two principles* and *building the culture of success for all* are so crucial to your success.

- Be very clear about your purpose. It frames everything you do.

- The school board, PTA, and administrators are more likely to support a BBQ approach if students share their enthusiasm and improved learning results with these groups. It is hard for board members and other adults to ignore children and youth.

- If students are not learning more, no matter how enthusiastic they are, there are significant classroom system problems that must be addressed.

- The more regularly and systematically you ask for feedback, share the results, and make improvements, the more buy-in and cooperation you'll receive from students, and vice versa.

- Make and take time to regularly renew yourself so you have energy to continue over time. We encourage you to find a trusted peer who is willing to embark on the journey with you for support, feedback, and encouragement.

- Never, ever give up.

Good luck! Enjoy your journey and let us know through our website, www.qualityeducationassociates.com, your thoughts, questions, and comments.

Appendix

Templates for Student-Led Conferences

LEARNING STYLE INVENTORY

Name _____ Grade _____

Make a check on the line next to the statement that describes how you do your best learning.

1. My best time of the day to learn is:

   _____ morning (8:00–11:00)   _____ afternoon (1:00–3:00)

2. The best way for me to really learn something is:

   _____ using manipulatives

   _____ having the teacher tell me about it

   _____ having the teacher show it on the board or overhead

3. I learn best:

   _____ by myself

   _____ with a partner

   _____ in a small group (3–5 students)

4. I know my strengths in learning:

   _____ not at all

   _____ maybe one or two strengths

   _____ not sure

5. I know my weaknesses in learning:

   _____ not at all

   _____ maybe one or two weaknesses

   _____ not sure

6. I can concentrate for a long time when I:

   _____ take breaks often and move around

   _____ move around a few times

   _____ I don't need many breaks. I can sit still for a long time.

7. I ask questions:

   _____ never, it's too embarrassing

   _____ not very often—I don't know what to ask

   _____ only when I'm confused.

   _____ when I understand, but I want to learn more

8. When taking tests (like math and language arts):

   _____ I get very nervous and can't do my best work

   _____ I am easily districted by noise and movement

   _____ I don't worry much

9. Often I:

   _____ don't care about working hard at school

   _____ need to be reminded by my teacher and parents to study and work hard

   _____ like learning but only when it's made fun for me

   _____ am excited to learn and take responsibility for my own learning

MY BEST QUALITY WORK

Name_____ Date_____

Subject _____ Assignment _____

I believe this is an example of my best work because:

_____ I followed all the directions.

_____ It is neat.

_____ I met all the quality factors for this assignment.

_____ I reflected on my work and made improvements before turning it in to my teacher.

(Other comments) _____

_____

_____

_____

This sample is better than my earlier work in this subject because _____

_____

_____

_____

To improve even more, I will _____

_____

_____

_____

_____

Student

SAMPLE A—STUDENT PROMPTS FOR THE CONFERENCE

Name_____ Date_____

What is my purpose for coming to school? _____

_____

These are some things I think I am good at: _____

_____

These are some areas I need to improve: _____

_____

By the end of _____ grade, I want to be able to _____

_____

_____

In order to reach my goals, I will _____

_____

_____

I will need your help with _____

_____

_____

SAMPLE B—STUDENT PROMPTS FOR THE CONFERENCE

Name_____ Date_____

I am proud of _____

_____

I am good at

    1. _____

    2. _____

    3. _____

I need to work on

    1. _____

    2. _____

    3. _____

My goals are

    1. _____

    2. _____

    3. _____

To reach my goals, I will

    1. _____

    2. _____

    3. _____

Mom and Dad, to help me reach my goals you can

    1. _____

    2. _____

    3. _____

PRE-CONFERENCE RESPONSIBILITIES AND CHECKLIST
(For the Student to Complete)

Does the data folder have the following:

_____ Your learning inventory

_____ Weekly math timed quiz graphs

_____ Weekly spelling quiz graphs

_____ Portfolio of *best* examples of quality work for these subjects

     _____ Science

     _____ Social Studies

     _____ Writing

     _____ Art

     _____ Computer

     _____ Other

_____ Radar chart for quality student (or mission criteria)

_____ The paper listing your strengths, areas for improvement, and goals

CHECKLIST FOR MIDYEAR PARENT CONFERENCE— STUDENT AND TEACHER

(S = Student, T = Teacher)

T   S

_____   _____   *Subject matter notebooks* (no loose or torn papers, all papers are filed correctly)

_____   _____   *Data folder* (no loose or torn papers, everything is filed correctly, matrices marked neatly, productivity charts colored neatly)

Favorite book selected from reading list _____

_____   _____   Filled out portfolio note on why you selected the book

_____   _____   Locate documentation of your reading on your productivity chart

_____   _____   Made arrangements to have the book at the conference

_____   _____   Selected a Social Studies item for your portfolio

_____   _____   Filled out a portfolio note on why you chose this item for your portfolio

_____   _____   Make a list of needed materials for your science demonstration

_____   _____   Make sure there is a lab sheet or booklet that accompanies the demonstration

_____   _____   Select a hands-on math activity

_____   _____   List the materials needed for the math activity

_____   _____   Show the teacher that your math journal states what you learned from the activity

_____   _____   Have your Language Arts results charted to show results from the beginning of the year to now

_____   _____   Have your Math results charted to show results from the beginning of the year to now

_____   _____   Write your personal vision and mission, and list your short-term goals.

_____   _____   Have your writing log displayed

_____   _____   Have the class mission statement displayed

Do you need any music?   Do you need anything else?

Homeroom teacher (advisor) signature: _____

Math teacher signature: _____

Language Arts teacher signature: _____

Social Studies teacher signature: _____

Science teacher signature: _____

Encore teacher signature: _____

Encore teacher signature: _____

Encore teacher signature: _____

PREPARATION FOR MIDYEAR STUDENT-LED CONFERENCE
Math Profile Reflections

Name_____ Date_____

Number of problems I missed: _____

Reasons I missed them:

(Types of careless mistakes)

_____

_____

_____

(Specific skills that caused you to miss the items you did not know)

_____

_____

_____

Here are my plans for correcting the problems I missed:

_____

_____

_____

_____

_____

_____

_____   _____
Student signature   Teacher signature

INFORMATIVE LETTER TO PARENTS

Dear (name),

I am happy to share something new we're trying at our school this year. Instead of the traditional teacher-led parent conferences, we've asked our students to take responsibility for sharing their learning progress with you.

During this conference, your child will be sharing his/her portfolio of *quality* work, charts showing progress in all his/her core subjects, and a learning inventory with you. The students will also be sharing their strengths and areas for improvement, goals they've set, and special interests they have. Although I will be in the room, this will be a *student-led conference.*

In preparation for this conference, the students have had to think about their purpose for attending school, their progress, and their plans for improvement. Each student has written a personal vision and mission, and set short-term goals. Please ask your child about this. Your child is getting ready to teach you what each has learned about him/herself.

We've been given the opportunity to schedule conferences during the day on _____ , _____ . In order for me to plan a smooth day and give everyone the opportunity to participate, *please check the most convenient time for you* and your child and *return this sheet to me no later than* _____ .

_____ Morning (8:00–11:45)   _____ Afternoon (12:15–3:00)

_____ After school (3:00–4:30)   _____ Evening (6:30–9:00)

I will be as flexible as I can. If you are unable to attend on our scheduled day, please let me know a better time and day for you. You can reach me by e-mail at _____ or by phone at _____ . I am looking forward to seeing you. Your child is really excited about sharing with you.

Sincerely,
(Signature)

NOTICE OF CONFERENCE TIME

Fill out this form and insert it into each student's invitation.

Dear _____ ,

Your student-led conference will be at (time) on (day). Please check the appropriate response and return this no later than (date).

_____ *Yes*, I will be able to come.

_____ *No*, I will not be able to come to the conference. A better time would be (time) on (day).

The conference is scheduled for room _____ . Please arrive two minutes before your scheduled time.

_____

Signature

HOMEWORK FOR PARENTS *BEFORE* A CONFERENCE

Parent _____   Student _____

Please answer the questions below to help me prepare for our upcoming conference. If you require more space, please use the back of this sheet. Return this form to school no later than _____ . Thank you for your comments and questions.

1. How does your child currently feel about school?

2. How often do you and your child discuss school, and what do you discuss?

3. What school subject does your child enjoy the most?

4. What are your feelings about your child's homework assignments?

5. Where and when does your child usually do his/her homework? What kind of homework assistance do you give?

6. What, if any, schoolwork has your child expressed concern about?

7. What concerns, if any, do you have about your child's interactions with teachers and/or other students?

8. In what ways can we help you and your child?

9. What questions would you like to have answered at our conference?

PARENT/GUARDIAN RESPONSIBILITIES— BEFORE THE CONFERENCE

Beginning the conference and a timetable:

- Come in and find your child's table. Wait there for your child to get his/her portfolio.

- To make this a private time for you and your child, conferences have been scheduled for 15 minutes. This is a student-led conference, and the purpose is for your child to share his/her progress thus far this year.

- If you are not finished at the end of 15 minutes, please feel free to continue the conference in the hall.

Question Prompts

Please use these questions prompts to assist your child in leading the conference:

- What is one of your strengths?

- What is one area you need to improve on and what can you do to improve?

- Ask about the reading goal

- What have you enjoyed *most* this year?

- How has your reading changed from the beginning of the year to this point?

- How has your math changed from the beginning of the year to this point?

PARENT/GUARDIAN RESPONSIBILITIES— AFTER THE CONFERENCE

1. *Write a note to your child.* When the conference is over, please take a few minutes and write your child a quick note. Tell them how proud you are of them and how you felt when they were explaining their work. You will be given a "note" form before the conference begins.

Dear _____ ,

_____

_____

_____

_____

I love you!

_____

---

2. *Complete the feedback survey (next page).* Please take a few minutes and give me some feedback on the conference. No names are needed. Surveys will be given to you before the conference begins. You can leave the completed survey in the box near the door. Thank you.

PARENT FEEDBACK SURVEY

Please help me improve on our conferences by taking a few minutes to complete this form. You do not need to put your name on it, so please be honest. Your input will be used to make the next conference even better!

Thank you.

1. Please rate the student-led conference.

   _____ Great   _____ Good   _____ Fair   _____ Poor

   Please explain your choice: _____

   _____

   _____

2. What did you learn from this experience with your child? _____

   _____

   _____

   _____

3. Was the time allotted long enough? _____ Yes _____ No

   If not, how long would be better? _____

4. Would you recommend we have student-led conferences again next year?

   _____ Yes _____ No

   Please explain: _____

   _____

   _____

   _____

   _____

   _____

Glossary

action plans—Refer to specific actions that respond to short- and long-term strategic objectives. Action plans include details of resource commitments and time horizons for accomplishment; they are a critical stage in planning when strategic objectives and goals are made specific. An example of a strategic objective might be to achieve student performance in the top quartile of the state's annual assessment. Action plans could entail determining in which subjects students have the lowest scores, understanding skill deficiencies in those subjects, and developing curricula that enable students to master those skills.

active learning—Students involved in active learning often organize their work, research information, discuss and explain ideas, observe demonstrations or phenomena, solve problems, and formulate questions of their own. Active learning engages students in higher-order thinking tasks such as analysis, synthesis, and evaluation, and multiple intelligences. It promotes interdependence and individual accountability to accomplish a common goal. This term can also relate to leadership, faculty, and staff learning through the use of PDSA cycles.

alignment—Refers to consistency of plans, processes, information, resource decisions, actions, results, and analysis to support key organization-wide goals. Effective alignment requires a common understanding of purposes and goals. It also requires the use of complementary measures and information for planning, analysis, and improvement at three levels: the organizational level, the key process level, and the program (school, class, or individual) level.

anecdotal versus systematic—*Anecdotal* evidence to support one's point of view relies on one or two observations, or gaining feedback from one or two sources. The danger is that you can not generalize about success or failure of any process or program based on anecdotal information. *Systematic*, however, refers to regularly scheduled collection of data from a random sample or the whole group to understand the effectiveness of a process or approach.

approach—Methods used address the requirements of each of the categories of the Baldrige criteria. The approach answers these questions: what do you do about this or that, how often it is done, and who is involved.) For details about the exact criteria requirements, refer to the Baldrige National Quality Program: Education Criteria for Performance Excellence. Check the Baldrige website to order a free copy.

Baldrige Criteria for Performance Excellence—The Baldrige Program was signed into U.S. law in 1987 and is named after deceased Secretary of Commerce Malcolm Baldrige for his managerial excellence. A framework for excellence includes seven interdependent categories of criteria that when aligned and integrated yield excellent results. The framework and criteria are now recognized as the best approach to system improvement in the world. The Baldrige award is given to role-model organizations with proven effective and efficient processes and excellent results in all aspects important to the organization. Awards can be given for large or small business, manufacturing, healthcare, and education. In 2001, the first education winners were announced. They were Chugach School District in Alaska, Pearl River School District in New York, and the University of Wisconsin–Stout. Thus far there have been six K–12 winners. For more information see the website information provided in the Recommended Resources section.

bandwidth of variation—Every process has variation. The bandwidth is understood as the top and bottom score, or range of data points, for any series of data. For example, in any class, five students score 100%, and three students score 5%, while all others are in between; we would say the bandwidth of variation on that test was 95%. In a BBQ classroom, the goal is to continuously work to reduce the bandwidth of variation for every process—pushing the mean higher for learning and other things you wish to improve, and pushing the mean lower to extinguish negative behaviors or errors. For more information, see *variation*.

bell curve—A normal distribution of data points more or less evenly split on each side of the average (mean). Generally, we speak about data falling about +/– three standard deviations from the mean. A bell curve represents a traditional model of "winners and losers." Many educators and policy makers who embrace traditional school models consider the bell curve to be about how the data will be distributed from any group of students. If your class results reflect a bell curve, you will never reach excellence. These results demonstrate that the system is not working for all students. The goal is to have the results resemble a J curve with a higher mean and many more students on the plus (+) side of the mean.

benchmark process—Refers to processes and results that represent "best practices and performance" for similar activities, inside or outside the education community. Organizations engage in benchmarking as an approach to understand the current dimensions of world-class performance and to achieve breakthrough improvement. Benchmarking is the approach to use if it becomes evident that current processes are not capable of yielding the desired results, and/or the process has not changed for a period of seven or more years.

brainstorming—An active process for gaining many ideas around a topic from a group of people. Formal brainstorming requires systematically asking team members for ideas. Brainstorming rules include (1) all ideas are included, (2) no discussion until all ideas are "on the table," (3) everyone is given equal opportunity to provide suggestions, and (4) no "yeah, buts" are allowed. (A *yeah, but* is a naysaying comment referring to a perception that a particular idea had been tried and failed in the past.)

cohort group—A single group of students from the same grade; used to compare how well a particular group of students performs over the course of time. For example, you want to compare the performance of a specific group of students in third grade in 2009 through fourth, fifth, or sixth grades on a normed test, to measure value added each year of enrollment. This constitutes a cohort group from—2009–2012. True cohort groups identify students by name and follow only those students over the years.

constancy of purpose—Focus on the *aim* of the organization. What is it designed to do?

continuous process improvement—The quality improvement process known as PDSA, or plan–do–study–act. It is a systematic, scientific approach to problem solving.

customer—The primary customers of a classroom system are the students and the next teacher in line. Other internal customers of a classroom system are the school and district. External customers include parents, postsecondary institutions, and world of work for those leaving high school.

cycle time—The amount of time required from the planning phase until roll-out of any new process and/or to complete a task. Examples include time required to repair computers, time to align curriculum with standards, and so on.

dashboard—A series of measures that allow the teacher to monitor the health of the classroom system. It provides the teacher with a "dashboard of vital signs."

data—*Hard data*—things that can be counted or measured; factual data. *Soft data*—satisfaction and perception data—or feedback. Both types are important to collect, chart, and analyze. Data are the basis for decision making in a Baldrige-based quality school and classroom.

data collection plan—This is a systematic approach to the collection of data to inform the organization. The decision about what data to collect is important and must be aligned with all schoolwide and districtwide strategic goals. The data collection plan addresses questions of what, how, where, when, and an explanation of how the data are to be used to improve.

data-driven decision making—Decisions about what to change in any process are based on data collection, and a root cause analysis.

Dr. W. Edwards Deming—The father of modern quality. A statistician (1900–1993) who taught the Japanese his quality management theory that focused on involving the workers to improve processes and systems. Born in Iowa, he lived most of his adult life in Washington, D.C. He received an MS degree from the University of Colorado, and a PhD from Yale. Deming believed that 95% of all problems within organizations were due to faulty systems and not people. His teachings and theory have kept many U.S. businesses profitable and are the basis for the Malcolm Baldrige National Quality Criteria for Performance Excellence.

deployment—Deployment answers the "how and when" question. It refers to how often, how many, where, when, and so on, something is done, for example, how widely applied the approach is. Full deployment means that an approach is used widely throughout the school with no groups or grade levels not participating. For example, a fully deployed anti-bullying program would mean that all students in all grades receive the instruction and activities, and that every adult in the building is addressing this problem. A fully deployed process for sharing the vision and values may mean that the information is affixed to all communication sent to faculty, staff, parents, and all other stakeholders; that the leader and leadership team refer to it at all faculty and staff meetings, PTA meetings, and when addressing outside groups; and so on.

differentiated instruction—This is an approach that requires teachers to use different modalities and resources to meet the needs of a diverse student body within any class.

effectiveness measures—Measures such as learning gains, improved attendance, student joy of learning, and graduation rates are measures of an educational system's effectiveness. They answer the question of whether a process yields the desired results (quality by fact).

efficiency measures—Timeliness of data made available to teachers for making midcourse corrections, time to make repairs, up-time of district server, and so on, are examples of efficiency measures of an educational system. They answer the question of whether a process yields the desired results within a specified amount of time. Reteaching, time away from learning, and drop-out rates are examples of system inefficiency.

feedback—Feedback is information about the system or any process provided by faculty and staff, customers, stakeholders, and partners. Systematic feedback implies collecting data (perception—soft data) on a regular basis either using a random sample or by surveying the whole group, or holding regularly scheduled focus groups. Informal feedback is usually anecdotal, and consequently one should not have a lot of confidence in its reliability; therefore, making changes based on anecdotal feedback carries some risks to avoid.

feedback instruments—There are many feedback instruments, including satisfaction surveys, needs assessments, focus groups, affinity process, plus/delta charts, fast feedback, how helpful were these resources, enthusiasm and learning chart, and many others.

feedback plan—A well thought-out approach that uses a variety of feedback tools and approaches on a regular and systematic basis so that the information can be analyzed and midcourse improvements made to improve the chances for achieving the goals and ultimately delighting the customer.

focus on innovation—Innovation refers to making meaningful change to improve instruction and services, and create new value for customers, students, and all stakeholders. Innovation is a multi-step process that involves development and knowledge sharing, a decision to implement, implementation, evaluation, and learning. Leaders of BBQ schools seek knowledge from a variety of sources, and then use it to change the leadership system and/or processes, resulting in greater student learning and performance excellence throughout the school.

formative assessment—Refers to frequent or ongoing evaluation during courses, programs, or learning experiences that gives an early indication of whether the current approach is likely to yield the desired results. Formative assessment is often used as a diagnostic tool for students, providing information with which to make real-time improvements in instructional methods, activities, or approaches.

goals—Refers to a future condition or performance level that one intends to attain. Goals can be both short-term and longer-term; they are the ends that guide the actions. *Quantitative goals*, frequently referred to as *targets*, include a numerical point or range. Targets might be projections based on comparative and/or competitive data. The term *stretch goals* refers to desired major or breakthrough improvements.

governance—Refers to the organizational reporting structure. Schools that are part of a larger district are governed by a superintendent and board of education. Independent, private, parochial, and charter schools often report to a board. Governance also refers to outside organizations with laws and policies that the school must adhere to, such as the health, fire, and other state or federal requirements.

hard data—Factual data that can be counted or measured. In addition to student learning results, examples include student or staff accidents, number of grievances, absences, tardies, books taken out of library, and so on.

high-performance work—Refers to ever increasing levels of individual performance. For example, instituting a new work system for students, designed to improve work performance, would show up in an increase in individual and/or team learning results. You would also expect to see the class as a whole becoming more efficient and with far fewer discipline issues, and so on.

hold the gains—Each process demonstrates normal variation and over time, unless specific process checks are made, will deteriorate. To "hold the gains" means a decision has been made to periodically and systematically gather data and analyze it at specific key process points after an improvement project has been completed. In this way, if the data start to exhibit a downward trend, targeted interventions can be taken immediately.

if/then improvement theory—A theory the team comes up with after identifying the root cause of any problem. The theory is written after a brainstorming session to determine actions to eliminate the root cause of a problem. It is the last step in the *plan* phase of PDSA.

innovation—Taking an "out of the box" approach to solve a persistent system problem; sometimes this involves benchmarking an organization in or outside of education. Other times, an innovation can be suggested as a result of a brainstorming process by faculty, staff, students, or other stakeholders. Action research in the form of PDSA is used to validate the effectiveness of the innovative approach.

inputs—People, policies, and resources that flow into the system and impact it in some way.

integration—Refers to how all aspects of the organization work in concert with each other to support the aim of the organization and the strategic objectives. For example, after all aspects of the classroom system are aligned (vision and goals and action plans, then mission and QFs for teacher and students), everyone who interacts with the class has to be committed to working together to achieve the purpose and goals. This includes the media specialists, counseling, and so on.

key value-creation processes—Processes that produce benefit for students and stakeholders of the organization. These are the processes most important to "running" the school and those that produce positive organizational results for students and the next teacher in line. See the classroom system diagram on page 9.

knowledge assets—These include current knowledge and skills, as well as new learning that individuals within the organization possess. To optimize the capability of each class and grade-level or content PLCs it is important to keep historical information on cycles of improvement to key processes. This information, aka "knowledge assets," is valuable for ongoing improvement and affects the overall effectiveness and efficiency of the school. It is important to the whole organization to capture this information (and to make it a habit to refer to it prior to making major decisions to change any process) and make it easily accessible (such as a school or district intranet, or within the classroom, a class website). This is a key part of the Baldrige framework.

learning-centered education—This is a strategic concept and one of the Baldrige core values that demands constant sensitivity to changing and emerging student, stakeholder, and market requirements and to the factors that drive student learning, satisfaction, and persistence.

measurement system—This is a systematic approach to collecting data with mission and vision specificity. The system includes measures for vision, mission, and class goals, and is used to inform teacher, students, and stakeholders about progress, and for improving the classroom system.

measures and indicators—Refers to numerical information that quantifies input, output, and performance dimensions of programs; they might be simple (derived from one measurement) or composite. Baldrige criteria do not make a distinction between measures and indicators. Some users, however, prefer the term *indicator* (1) when the measurement relates to performance, but is not a direct measure of such performance, or (2) when the measurement is a predictor or "leading indicator" of some more significant performance. For example, a gain in student performance or satisfaction might be a leading indicator of student persistence.

multiple intelligences—Howard Gardner has identified eight different ways people learn. They are logical/mathematical, verbal/linguistic, visual/spatial, body/kinesthetic, musical/rhythmic, interpersonal, intrapersonal, and naturalist. Too often, educators rely heavily on verbal/linguistic and logical/mathematical and do not provide enough opportunities for students to learn through the other intelligences. It is the responsibility of the teacher to discover how students learn (by asking and observing) and then provide learning activities that utilize more of the intelligences. It is the combination of verbal/linguistic, body/kinesthetic, and musical/rhythmic that advances literacy skills rapidly.

operational definitions—Operational definitions allow people to understand their jobs with less confusion. They are short, precise, detailed definitions of a measure. A good operational definition yields either a "yes" or "no" response. Operational definitions provide clear communication to everyone about how something is to be measured. Applied to student work, operational definitions reduce the variation in the quality of work the teacher receives.

output measures—These are results measures. They are used to inform policy makers and administrators about how well students achieve and to measure satisfaction at the end of the year. Results measures must be considered by the leadership team during strategic planning in terms of making system improvements for the following year.

outputs—The results of classroom processes. In education, the outputs include student learning results, student, stakeholder, and partner satisfaction and dissatisfaction results, and student enthusiasm for learning results. Outputs are what comes out of the system. If the teacher is not satisfied with these results, significant questions are raised: Is the system aligned and are processes designed to meet customer requirements? If not, PDSA must be applied and improvement must be made to the key processes. It is the only way to predict better results.

PDSA cycle—The seven-step quality improvement process that eliminates problems provided the true root cause is understood. P = *plan* (four steps: identify the opportunity for improvement, assess the current situation, analyze root cause, write an improvement theiory), D = *do* (put the improvement theory into practice), S = *study* (analyze the results from the improvement theory), A = *act* (make decisions about expanding the improvement to the whole system, or go back and understand the root cause). Repeated cycles of improvement (PDSA) lead to ever increasing results.

performance excellence—Refers to an integrated approach to organizational performance management that results in (1) delivery of ever improving value to students and stakeholders, contributing to improved education quality, (2) improvement of overall organizational effectiveness and capabilities, and (3) organizational and personal learning. The Baldrige Education Criteria for Peformance Excellence provide a framework and an assessment tool for understanding organizational strengths and opportunities for improvement, and thus for guiding planning efforts.

process—A series of steps taken to achieve a task.

process measures—These are predictors of future success and allow the teacher to make midcourse corrections leading to improved success at the end of the year. Data collected in-process ought to be the most critical predictors. These data, collected and analyzed regularly throughout the year, provide great insight for leaders, teachers (PLCs), and staff in making adjustments to key processes to improve the chances of achieving the strategic objectives. In the classroom it is the teacher and students who are most actively involved in analyzing in-process measures.

process measures for literacy—The five in-process measures and best predictors of future success in reading, writing, and speaking are phonemic awareness, phonics, vocabulary, fluency, and comprehension. These are the important things teachers ought to regularly and systematically collect data on to assure that more students reach the grade-level expectations for reading.

quality by fact—The product of the system actually functions as promised. An example in education is that students leave the grade or school with the required skills and have the ability to apply them to other situations.

quality by perception—Perception is reality in the eyes of the customer and stakeholders. This measures whether or not customers believe the product is of high quality. When newspapers report the results of state standards tests, perception about the quality of instruction and education at each school is formed.

quality by process—This measures effectiveness and efficiency of the processes making up the system. Graduation rates would be an example of the effectiveness and efficiency of the instructional process.

quality factors—The absolute essential characteristics or elements that must be present to meet any standard, and to cause someone to say, "*Wow,* that was excellent." Quality factors (QFs) set expectations. The customer determines quality factors, and they constantly raise the bar on expectations. We advocate for QFs for teachers and students. Some schools also establish QFs for PLCs and the administration. QFs, if measured regularly, provide information to individuals and groups for improvement.

quality features—Additional elements that delight the customer. These are not essential to the overall working of any product, but make it nicer, brighter, more "alive," and so on. Quality features often become quality factors over time. An example may be the expectation that students are required to use word processing to write essays.

segment—Segmentation of data refers to disaggregating by subgroup. There are numerous ways to segment the data in a class, such as by gender, ethnicity, free/reduced lunch, SPED, ELL, and so on. A high school teacher might find it interesting to also segment class data by student career cluster choice. Likewise, school or district leaders would be wise to segment data on faculty/staff, for example. They might look at the groups by education levels attained, years of service, grade level or courses taught, and so on. Segmenting data generally provides the leaders with a better perspective of the situation. Another example is parent satisfaction, which can be segmented by the child's grade level, SPED, ESOL, gifted, free/reduced lunch—or those who volunteer, are active in PTA, or by their educational level, and so on.

seventy:thirty rule—A way to assess student progress toward mastery of content. Seventy percent of the assessment is made up of the most recently taught material and thirty percent is randomly selected from all previously learned material in the course. This requires students to demonstrate that they have learned (no permission to forget by just testing recently taught material and then moving on) and not just memorized for the sake of passing a test.

soft data—Perceptual data that reflect a person's feelings about something. Examples include satisfaction and enthusiasm.

strategic goals and/or strategic objectives—These address the most important challenges to success that the organization faces. During the strategic planning process, after the environmental scan is conducted, strategic challenges are identified. For each one of these, one or more corresponding strategic goals or objectives is identified. Action plans are developed and resource allocation follows according to the priority of each.

student as customer—Students are the direct customer of teachers. They receive instruction, instructional support, and climate for learning from teachers.

student as worker—Students are workers in a system traditionally created by the teacher. Students are expected to "fit into" the system, and if they won't or can't, they are viewed as difficult students and often cause disruptions to the instructional process. Students are in the best position to identify the barriers to their success, and it is up to the teacher to change the system. Unless teachers empower students to provide feedback and make suggestions for improvement, the barriers will remain and the results will be the same.

summative assessment—Refers to analysis of the learning and performance of students at the end of the semester or year. Summative assessments are formal and comprehensive and include state standards tests, or end-of-course exams. Such assessments may be conducted at the conclusion of a course or program and could be compared to the results of pretesting to determine gains and to clarify the causal connections between educational practices and student learning. In practical terms, a unit test becomes a summative assessment of the recently studied material in that there is no way to "build in quality" and make midcourse corrections to the instructional process so that more students can learn and master the material. It is too late. Hence, the need for in-process assessments of leading indicators.

system—A series of processes linked together to achieve the *aim, vision,* and *mission* of an organization.

system alignment—Alignment refers to consistency of plans, processes, information, resource decisions, actions, results, analysis, and learning to support the organization's key goals. In this case, the classroom is a subsystem of the school, and, therefore, it's mission must align with the school and district vision and mission. Class goals will be aligned with school and district goals and expectations.

system integration—Effective integration is achieved when the individual components of a performance management system operate as a fully interconnected unit. That is, plans, processes, information, resource decisions, actions, results, analysis, and learning all support the key organization-wide goals.

teacher as leader—Teachers are leaders in the classroom, and as such they are responsible for removing barriers to student success. Most barriers are due to faulty systems and ineffective or inefficient processes. A teacher-leader empowers students to help identify system and process barriers and participate in finding solutions. Teacher-leaders are competent, of high character, value all students, seek and engage in partnerships with students and parents, and view data as a friend that allows them to learn and to engage in continuous improvement of self and the system.

teacher as service provider—Teachers provide instruction and support, and create the learning climate. These are all services. Students provide feedback in terms of achievement, satisfaction, and dissatisfaction manifested by behaviors, attendance, and attitudes. Teachers need to be customer-focused to make changes based on student and stakeholder needs and expectations.

team projects—Within a BBQ context, team projects engage students in problem solving and real-life application of the content standards through self-directed teams. This is a twenty-first century skill and central to every student's future success. The systematic approach to organizing students in teams, and the responsibilities they each assume, allows everyone to gain important social, academic, and workforce skills. Effective, high-performing (Stage 4—see page 252) teams demonstrate interdependence, as illustrated by Stephen R. Covey's *maturity continuum.*

trends—A minimum of three cycles of data points comprise a trend. The number of data points is dependent on the length of the cycle to accomplish any task. For example, the results of any normed test happen annually. Therefore, a trend would cover at least three years. Absenteeism might be trended by month, yielding 9–12 data points for the school year, depending on the length of the school year.

value—A perception of what anything is worth. For example, each year a student is enrolled they will learn more as measured by some instrument (preferably a normed one). If this happens, we can say that each grade was "value-added" to the education of that child. Another example might be about a particular professional development program. In this case, pre/post-learning results would indicate the value-added of the program. If students in classrooms where the approach was fully deployed did better than previously, we could say the professional development program was "value-added."

variation—Every process exhibits some variation whether in manufacturing or education. The idea of a quality organization is to minimize the bandwidth of variation and move the average higher for things like learning, attendance, and enthusiasm, and lower for things like tardiness, absenteeism, failure, and acting-out behavior. The way to reduce variation is to provide precise operational definitions and expectations, then measure effectiveness and follow the PDSA cycle for improvement.

work system—Refers to how students are organized to get work done and to accomplish the vision, mission, and goals. An effective work system is designed to align the components with the vision, mission, and goals, and enables and encourages students to contribute effectively and to the best of their ability.

Recommended Resources

Blazey, Mark L. *Insights to Performance Excellence 2011–2012: Understanding the Integrated Management System and Baldrige.* Milwaukee: ASQ Quality Press, 2011.

Byrnes, Margaret A., with Jeanne C. Baxter. *The Principal's Leadership Counts! Launch a Baldrige-Based Quality School.* Milwaukee: ASQ Quality Press, 2005.

Campbell, Linda, Bruce Campbell, and Dee Dickinson. *Teaching and Learning Through Multiple Intelligences*, 3rd ed. Boston: Allyn and Bacon, 2003.

Chen, Milton. *Education Nation: Six Leading Edges of Innovation in Our Schools.* San Francisco: Jossey-Bass, 2012.

Conyers, John G., and Robert Ewy. *Charting Your Course: Lessons Learned During the Journey toward Performance Excellence.* Milwaukee: ASQ Quality Press, 2004.

Covey, Stephen R. *The 7 Habits of Highly Effective People.* New York: Simon & Shuster, 2004.

Deming, W. Edwards. *The New Economics: For Industry, Government, Education*, 2nd ed. Cambridge, MA: Massachusetts Institute of Technology Center for Advanced Engineering Study, 1994.

Gardner, Howard. *Frame of the Mind: The Theory of Multiple Intelligences.* New York: Basic Books, 2011.

———. *Five Minds for the Future.* Boston: Harvard Business School Publishing, 2006.

Glasser, William. *The Quality School: Managing Students without Coercion*, rev. ed. New York: HarperCollins, 1998.

Hjalmarson, Fran. *Differentiated Parent Support: Engaging Parents in Unique Ways to Increase Their Involvement in School.* Ramona, CA: TurnAround Schools, 2011.

Jacobs, Heidi Hayes. *Curriculum 21: Essential Education for a Changing World.* Alexandria, VA: ASCD, 2010.

Jenkins, Lee. *From Systems Thinking to Systemic Action: 48 Key Questions to Guide the Journey.* Lanham, MD: Rowman & Littlefield Education, 2008.

———. *Permission to Forget.* Milwaukee: ASQ Quality Press, 2004.

Jensen, Eric. *Brain-Based Learning: The New Paradigm of Teaching.* Thousand Oaks, CA: Corwin Press, 2008.

Johnson, Lou Anne. *Teaching Outside the Box: How to Grab Your Students by Their Brains,* 2nd ed. San Francisco: Jossey-Bass, 2011.

Lemov, Douglas. *Teach Like a Champion: 49 Techniques That Put Students on the Path to College.* San Francisco: Jossey-Bass, 2010.

Marino, Jay, and Jan Polderman. *Leading Continuous Improvement: Inspiring Quality Worldwide.* Amersfoort, Netherlands: Magistrum, 2011.

Marzano, Robert J. *What Works in Schools: Translating Research into Action.* Alexandria, VA: ASCD, 2003.

Robles del Melendez, Wilma, and Vera Beck. *Teaching Young Children in Multi-Cultural Classrooms: Issues, Concepts, and Strategies,* 3rd ed. New York: Albert Whitman, 2009.

Tokuhama-Espinosa, Tracey. *Mind, Brain, and Education Science: A Complete Guide to the New Brain-Based Teaching.* New York: W.W. Norton & Co., 2010.

Trilling, Bernie, and Charles Fadel. *21st Century Skills: Learning for Life in Our Times.* San Francisco: Jossey-Bass, 2009.

Wagner, Tony. *The Global Achievement Gap.* San Carlos Park, FL: Civitas Books, 2008.

Ziskovsky, Betty, and Joe Ziskovsky. *Optimizing Student Learning: A Lean Systems Approach to Improving K–12 Education.* Milwaukee: ASQ Quality Press, 2011.

HELPFUL WEBSITES FOR MORE INFORMATION

George Lucas's Edutopia—www.edutopia.org. A cornucopia of real-life examples from teachers, many free downloads, and video examples.

Kahn Academy—www.KahnAcademy.org. Short, to-the-point lessons on a multitude of topics suitable for secondary students struggling to learn certain concepts.

Moodle—www.Moodle.org. Provides open source community-based tools for learning and sharing.

Project-Based Learning—www.pbl-online.org. Offers many free examples and opportunities to access other teachers' projects, including ways to evaluate projects and collaborate with others.

Zoho—www.zoho.com/projects/. Free project management software.

STUDENT DATA NOTEBOOKS

Cedar Rapids Community Schools—http://quality.cr.k12.ia.us/Tutorials/data_folders/data_folder_index.html.

Montgomery County, MD—http://www.montgomeryschoolsmd.org/info/baldrige/staff/addresources.shtm.

TRUE COLORS SOURCES

True Colors—www.truecolors.com. Learn your communication style and insights into your students' learning styles; based on Myers-Briggs personality inventory; some may be accessed free. The following publications are also available:

Kalil, Carolyn. *Follow Your True Colors to the Work You Love*, new ed. Pacific Palisades, CA: Dreammakers, 2011.

Kalil, Carolyn, and Don Lowry. *Follow Your True Colors to the Work You Love: The Workbook*. Santa Ana, CA: True Colors, 1999.

MEMORY JOGGERS MINI-TOOLS RESOURCE BOOKS

Call toll free: 800-643-4316 or 603-1944

Boehringer, Robert D. *The Process Manager Memory Jogger: Building Cross-Functional Excellence*. Salem, NH: GOAL/QPC, 2008.

Brassard, Michael, and Diane Ritter. *The Memory Jogger 2: Tools for Continuous Improvement and Effective Planning*. Salem, NH: GOAL/QPC, 2010.

Brassard, Michael, et al. *The Problem Solving Memory Jogger: Seven Steps to Improved Processes*. Salem, NH: GOAL/QPC, 2000.

Martin, Paula, and Karen Tate. *Project Management Memory Jogger: A Pocket Guide for Project Teams*. Salem, NH: GOAL/QPC, 1997.

WEBSITES OF BALDRIGE NATIONAL QUALITY AWARD EDUCATION WINNERS (K–12)

2010—Montgomery County Schools, Maryland. www.montgomeryschoolsmd.org/.

2008—Iredell-Statesville Schools, North Carolina. www.iss.k12.nc.us.

2005—Jenks Public Schools, Oklahoma. www.jenksps.org/.

2003—Community Consolidated School District 15, Palatine, Illinois. www.ccsd15.net/.

2001—Pearl River School District, New York. www.pearlriver.org.

2001—Chugach Schools, Anchorage, Alaska. www.chugachschools.com.

BALDRIGE PERFORMANCE EXCELLENCE PROGRAM

www.nist.gov\baldrige

Index

The Knowledge Center
www.asq.org/knowledge-center

Learn about quality. Apply it. Share it.

ASQ's online Knowledge Center is the place to:

- Stay on top of the latest in quality with Editor's Picks and Hot Topics.

- Search ASQ's collection of articles, books, tools, training, and more.

- Connect with ASQ staff for personalized help hunting down the knowledge you need, the networking opportunities that will keep your career and organization moving forward, and the publishing opportunities that are the best fit for you.

Use the Knowledge Center Search to quickly sort through hundreds of books, articles, and other software-related publications.

www.asq.org/knowledge-center

Ask a Librarian

Did you know?

- The ASQ Quality Information Center contains a wealth of knowledge and information available to ASQ members and non-members

- A librarian is available to answer research requests using ASQ's ever-expanding library of relevant, credible quality resources, including journals, conference proceedings, case studies and Quality Press publications

- ASQ members receive free internal information searches and reduced rates for article purchases

- You can also contact the Quality Information Center to request permission to reuse or reprint ASQ copyrighted material, including journal articles and book excerpts

- For more information or to submit a question, visit **http://asq.org/knowledge-center/ask-a-librarian-index**

Visit www.asq.org/qic for more information.

TRAINING   CERTIFICATION   CONFERENCES   MEMBERSHIP   **PUBLICATIONS**

ASQ
The Global Voice of Quality™

Belong to the Quality Community!

Established in 1946, ASQ is a global community of quality experts in all fields and industries. ASQ is dedicated to the promotion and advancement of quality tools, principles, and practices in the workplace and in the community.

The Society also serves as an advocate for quality. Its members have informed and advised the U.S. Congress, government agencies, state legislatures, and other groups and individuals worldwide on quality-related topics.

Vision

By making quality a global priority, an organizational imperative, and a personal ethic, ASQ becomes the community of choice for everyone who seeks quality technology, concepts, or tools to improve themselves and their world.

ASQ is...

- More than 90,000 individuals and 700 companies in more than 100 countries

- The world's largest organization dedicated to promoting quality

- A community of professionals striving to bring quality to their work and their lives

- The administrator of the Malcolm Baldrige National Quality Award

- A supporter of quality in all sectors including manufacturing, service, healthcare, government, and education

- YOU

Visit www.asq.org for more information.

TRAINING   CERTIFICATION   CONFERENCES   MEMBERSHIP   **PUBLICATIONS**

ASQ Membership

Research shows that people who join associations experience increased job satisfaction, earn more, and are generally happier*. ASQ membership can help you achieve this while providing the tools you need to be successful in your industry and to distinguish yourself from your competition. So why wouldn't you want to be a part of ASQ?

Networking

Have the opportunity to meet, communicate, and collaborate with your peers within the quality community through conferences and local ASQ section meetings, ASQ forums or divisions, ASQ Communities of Quality discussion boards, and more.

Professional Development

Access a wide variety of professional development tools such as books, training, and certifications at a discounted price. Also, ASQ certifications and the ASQ Career Center help enhance your quality knowledge and take your career to the next level.

Solutions

Find answers to all your quality problems, big and small, with ASQ's Knowledge Center, mentoring program, various e-newsletters, *Quality Progress* magazine, and industry-specific products.

Access to Information

Learn classic and current quality principles and theories in ASQ's Quality Information Center (QIC), *ASQ Weekly* e-newsletter, and product offerings.

Advocacy Programs

ASQ helps create a better community, government, and world through initiatives that include social responsibility, Washington advocacy, and Community Good Works.

Visit www.asq.org/membership for more information on ASQ membership.

*2008, The William E. Smith Institute for Association Research

TRAINING   CERTIFICATION   CONFERENCES   **MEMBERSHIP**   PUBLICATIONS

ASQ
The Global Voice of Quality™